Adobe®
Photoshop® 5.0

Studio

TECHNIQUES

Ben Willmore

ADOBE PRESS
201 West 103rd Street
Indianapolis, Indiana 46290

Official Adobe Photoshop 5.0 Studio Techniques

International Standard Book Number: 1-56830-474-9

Library of Congress Catalog Card Number: 98-86257

Printed in the United States of America

00 99 4

Trademarks

Warning and Disclaimer

Credits

Executive Editor	Chris Nelson
Development Editor	Jennifer Eberhardt
Managing Editor	Sarah Kearns
Project Editor	Mike La Bonne
Copy Editor	Bonnie Lawler
Indexer	Tina Trettin
Technical Editor	Robert Reinhardt
Software Development Specialist	Craig Atkins
Book Designer	Michael J. Nolan
Cover Designer	Aren Howell
Front Cover Artwork	Alicia Buelow
Back Cover Artwork	Howard Berman
	Derek Brigham
	Robert Bowen Studio
	Sony Electronics, Inc.
	Gordon Studer
Graphic Conversion	Wil Cruz
	Benjamin Hart
Production	Daniela Raderstorf
	Tina Trettin

Contents at a Glance

Contents

About the Author

Ben Willmore is the founder of Digital Mastery, a Boulder, Colorado-based training and consulting firm that specializes in electronic publishing. Ben has always been known to be a little nutty about all things technical, even as a child. Not long after he traded in his tricycle for training wheels, he started building cameras out of do-it-yourself kits. In 1981, at the tender age of 14, he made his official debut into computer nerd-dom when he attended CompuCamp. That's where he discovered his first two loves, computers and graphic design, and where he learned how to use a graphics tablet to produce art on an Apple][computer—three full years before the Macintosh said its first "Hello."

Not surprisingly, he went on to become a graphic designer. In those days that meant knowing all about such primitive things as typesetting, keylining, and stat cameras, which he picked up while still in high school. When the first tools of electronic publishing started showing up, Ben began his trend as an aggressive "early adopter" of new technologies. While most people in the business were holding back in a wait-and-see atttitude, Ben was charging ahead and embracing the new tools like long-lost friends. His first serious push into the new arena was when he converted his college's daily newspaper from traditional techniques to electronic tools in the late '80s.

Ben became known as someone who likes to push his tools to the limit, causing many printing companies and service bureaus to ask "How'd you do that?" His obsession with the nuts and bolts of electronic publishing turned him into an unwitting one-man customer support center for all his friends and coworkers. It was this, he discovered, that was his third love—helping others truly understand graphics software. And so he decided to go out on his own and teach his favorite program (Photoshop) full time. In 1994, he founded Digital Mastery (known back then as Willmore & Associates) and created what has become the hugely successful seminar "Master Photoshop in 3 Days." Since then he has taught more than 5,000 Photoshop users, and now travels to more than 25 cities each year presenting his seminars and speaking at events such as the Photoshop Conference. He is also a regular contributor to numerous magazines. Ben can be reached at Willmore@digitalmastery.com.

Author's Acknowledgments

Even though my name appears on the cover of this book, as with all collaborative efforts, this book would not have been possible without the help of the following people:

Regina "GNR's" Cleveland, the "Queen of Logistics" here at Digital Mastery who (as usual) went way beyond the call of duty to get this book out the door. She often stayed cooped up in her office into the wee hours of the morning (Saturdays and Sundays, too) to keep me in line and ensure that the huge jumble of words came out making sense and didn't drive readers crazy. Without her, I would never have been able to finish the book.

Susan Walton, at Adobe Press, for putting her trust in this first-time author, and allowing me to write this book the same way I teach—with no unnecessary techno-drivel, and complete candor.

Jennifer Eberhardt, development editor, for her gracious prodding, insight, and sometimes annoying questions, all of which have made this book much, much better than it would have been without her relentless input. She and her team of helpers have really made this book come a long way.

Mark Hamburg, principal scientist and architect of Photoshop, who allowed the Photoshop 6 release date to slip by a day or two by graciously answering all my pesky questions, even when he was busy welcoming his son Max into the world.

And finally, I thank all the people who have attended my seminars over the past four years. You've given me much inspiration and feedback and have allowed me to follow my passion for knowledge and understanding.

Publisher's Acknowledgments

Adobe Press and Macmillan Publishing especially thank the following people for all of their hard work and efforts:

Sau Tam, product support engineer at Adobe Systems, Inc., for her valuable technical reviews and Photoshop insights.

Tom Walton, who provided many great comments about the manuscript by looking at it through the eyes of a "new user."

Everyone who contributed artwork for the cover, parts pages, chapter openings, and chapter closings. Your artwork will inspire readers for a long time to come, and we thank you for allowing us to share it:

Don Barnett	David Plunkert
Betty Bates	Albert Sanchez
Howard Berman	Jeff Schewe
David Bishop	Michael Slack
Robert Bowen	Bronson Smith
Derek Brigham	Russell Sparkman
Robert Brünz	Gordon Studer
Alicia Buelow	Anna Ullrich
Jimmy Chen	Rick Valicenti
Ani DiFranco	William Valicenti
Steve Doppelt	Nik Willmore
Louis Fishauf	Adam Woolfitt
Andy Katz	Gary Fisher Bicycle Corp.
Chris Klimek	Lowe & Partners
Maria Kostyk-Petro	Schieffen & Somerset
Eric Meola	Sony Electronics, Inc.
Cliff Nielsen	Thirst Advertising
Brian Peterson	World West Communications

Books Crafted for Our Users

Our goal at Adobe Press is to publish the highest quality books possible. Your opinions and comments play a vital role in achieving that goal. You can fax, email, or write us directly.

When you write, please include this book's title and ISBN, as well as your name and phone or fax number. We'll review your comments with the same sincere effort you put forth to prepare them, and we'll share them with the author(s) and editors who worked on the book.

Fax:
317-581-4663

Email:
adobe_press@mcp.com

Mail:
Executive Editor
Macmillan Computer Publishing
201 West 103rd Street
Indianapolis, IN 46290 USA

Foreword

Learning to use Adobe Photoshop is similar to learning to play an electric guitar; with a little instruction and a little practice, you can create some very pleasant art. Or, if you're really motivated, you can lock yourself in a closet with it for 12 years and emerge playing some amazing "chops." Most of us fall somewhere inbetween, and all of us have more to learn.

But the thing is, while few people are frightened by a guitar, many people find Photoshop very intimidating. That's what is so great about Ben Willmore, the author of this book: he takes away your fear.

For the past several years, Ben has traveled across the United States, presenting his unique Photoshop seminar. Unique, because it focuses on real-world jobs done every day by Photoshop users, and unique because Ben explains concepts and techniques in a way that everyone in the room can understand. Ben's examples are based on his professional production experience, so everything he teaches helps you create images that successfully reproduce on paper or the Web.

Ben has a unique perspective on what people want to learn, because he addresses gatherings of professional Photoshop users one out of every four days of the year, all year long. The handbook that people take home from his seminar has been updated every month. Over four years, this natural progression of "seminar-feedback-rewrite" has led to the book you hold in your hands.

I attended his seminar and was especially impressed by his ability to avoid technical jargon, and by his uncanny knack for answering questions before they're asked. Ben is a rare teacher; even advanced users are satisfied, and rank beginners never feel lost. Like all great teachers, Ben uses metaphors, relating new ideas to concepts you're already comfortable with. In the pages of this book, you'll see Photoshop's most esoteric concepts clearly explained, while its major features are masterfully positioned into a framework of "how do I accomplish the task at hand?"

We each have different uses for Photoshop, and we each have different ways of learning. Fortunately for our increasingly overtaxed brains, less than half of Photoshop's features are used to accomplish most real-world tasks. And more fortunately for us, Ben Willmore has written this book.

Enjoy the time you share with Ben and Photoshop. I'm sure you'll find it a rare pleasure.

Jay J. Nelson
Editor
Design Tools Monthly
www.design-tools.com

Introduction

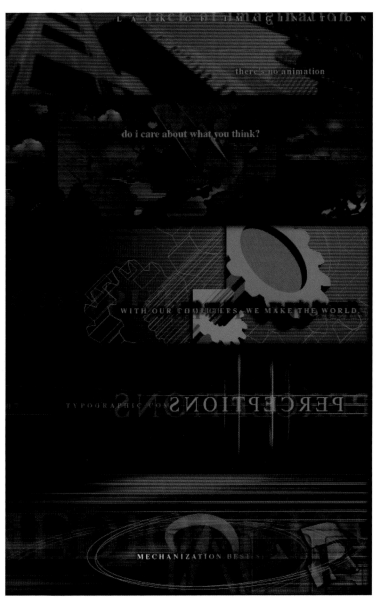

Does the world really need another Photoshop book?

Courtesy of Jimmy Chen, www.typographic.com.

Does the World Really Need Another Photoshop Book?

I asked myself that very question when the folks from Adobe Press asked me to write this one. In search of an answer, I took a field trip to Barnes & Noble and stood in front of the computer section. I stood gaping at what looked like a virtual shrine devoted to Photoshop—four shelves jam-packed with every imaginable title. Wow! I had to think about this. What was missing from those shelves? What could I contribute that would really be useful to all those Photoshop users who are reaching out for help?

The answer was easy. What's missing from these bookshelves is a particular kind of perspective. The kind of perspective that comes from five years of helping people, just like you, learn how to master the wonderful and terrifying program we call Photoshop. Last year alone I held my seminar (Master Photoshop in 3 Days) in 30 cities and saw more than 2,200 people. I spent 704 hours walking, talking, breathing, and teaching Photoshop. All of my three-day seminars are intense and in-depth, and I usually end up losing my voice after the last day.

But I don't just talk. I do a lot of listening, too. I've worked with just about every kind of Photoshop user under the stars: graphic designers, printers, color-specialists, production artists, photographers, architects, high-school teachers, medical imaging technicians, and some very interesting people from the FBI and the military intelligence community. I've done an enormous amount of hand-holding and working in the trenches side-by-side with people (just like you), and it's given me one heck of a perspective from the user's point of view. The seminar I present today is the result of five years of questions, feedback, debate and research, followed by more questions and more research.

So, I may not have written a thousand award-winning books, and I'm not a famous graphic designer, but there's one thing you can count on. Hands down, I know what it's like to look at Photoshop from your point of view, and I believe that I can help you get to where you want to go with Photoshop. In a roundabout way I guess you could say that this book was written as much by my students, as it was by me; it's the result of all my teaching (and learning) experiences with literally thousands of Photoshop users.

What's in This Book?

Well, first I'll tell you what's *not* in it. It's not a special effects cookbook that delivers page upon page of bizarre and exotic tricks and effects (although there are a few juicy ones in the "Creative Explorations" section), nor does it tackle the artistic aesthetics of digital design. There's a truckload of excellent books on those subjects, which will most likely be sitting right next to this one at the bookstore.

My mission is to help you graduate from "I'm just going through the motions." to "At last, I *really* understand Photoshop." Once you've made that leap, you will experience an incredible ripple effect. Your efficiency level will skyrocket. Your costs will go down. Your creative genius will come out of the closet like gangbusters, and your clients will be thrilled. Really! I've seen it happen more times than I can remember. And I still get a thrill whenever I see one of my students go through what I've come to think of as "the transformation."

No Technical Mumbo Jumbo!

First and foremost, I hate technical mumbo jumbo! If words like gamma, bitmapped, clipping paths, algorithms, dither, posterize, nonlinear, and anti-aliasing drive you crazy, you better believe that they drive me even crazier. So, you'll find that I'm very big on stories and metaphors. I'll do whatever it takes to communicate the concept to you, without relying on 10-syllable words or terms that sound like they came from the inside of an engineer's head. And for those of you who can't live without the technical terms, you can find all those icky words and their full definitions in "Ben's Techno-Babble Decoder Ring," at the end of most chapters.

Something for Everyone

There's a good deal of emphasis on preparing images for print media, but by no means are the multimedia folks left in the dust. In fact, if you're working primarily with images that will be seen on computer monitors or television screens, when you read about my approach to working with color images, you should be delighted. In terms of skill level, this book is written in such a way that users who are generally comfortable with their computer, should be able to fully comprehend the information, no matter how advanced the topic. I've made the assumption that you've either installed Photoshop, or that you're using the Photoshop User Guide to do that. (There's no reason to duplicate that kind of information here). And if you're an advanced user, don't worry. Just because the book is very understandable doesn't mean we won't get into the real meat of Photoshop.

Notes and Warnings and Lots-O-Shortcuts

Everyone wants to work fast, efficient and smart. So to help you transform yourself into a super Photoshop pilot, I've put special bits of information into their own little boxes. You'll find warnings to keep you out of trouble, and notes for important—but not essential—information and tips to speed up your work. And if you have a thing for keyboard shortcuts, I'll give you so many that you'll forget that you ever needed a mouse.

Adobe Speaks!

If you're anything like me when you glance through most books about Photoshop, you're probably still left with a mixed bag of unanswered questions. Odds and ends that only Adobe can answer. I'm very big on getting answers to absolutely everything, so I compiled a list of the most frequently asked questions that I've received from my students over the years, and gave them right to the source— Mark Hamburg, principal scientist and architect of Photoshop. He very graciously accepted my huge list of questions, and responded to each one with candor and detail. So, for those of you who would like detailed technical explanations from the ultimate Adobe authority, you can go to the "Ask Adobe" section at the end of each chapter. You'll also get the "insider" answer to all sorts of juicy questions like this one:

Q. Why is Adobe called Adobe? I don't see you guys building any little clay huts?

A. Named for the Adobe Creek, which flows behind the houses of the two founders of the company.

Mac and PC: One Big Happy Universe

Adobe folks have worked long and hard to make Photoshop virtually identical for both platforms. They've done such a good job that there was no need to write two versions of this book. However, because there is only one version of the book, I decided to choose a platform and run with it. I chose Mac for the simple reason that at most of my seminars, I find that there are more Mac users showing up than PC users. So, for that reason (and also because I wanted you to get a "clean" look at the program without hundreds of redundant keyboard commands cluttering up the page), I opted to use the Mac version when it came to providing examples of dialog boxes, menus, and palettes. I used the same line of reasoning for keyboard commands and shortcuts. But if you're using a PC you don't have to worry. All you need to know is that the keyboards are slightly different. In Windows, the Control key is the same as the Command key on a Mac, and Alt is the same as Option; your right mouse button does the same thing as the Control key on a Mac; and the Return key on a Mac does the same thing as the PC's Enter key. If you remember those four, you'll have no problem translating from Mac to PC.

Get Inspiration From Other's Perspiration!

Even though I claim that this is not a special effects cookbook, I've made sure that there's enough artistic inspiration in this book to help rev your creative engine. At the beginning and end of most chapters, you can feast your eyes on some samples from many of my favorite artists. They come from a wide range of talents and disciplines, and I hope you enjoy their work as much as I do.

Stuff in the CD at the Back of the Book

Because it's not possible to include everything on the pages within this book, I've also included a CD-ROM. On the CD, you'll find supplements for many of the chapters—covering such topics as working with CMYK color modes, understanding levels, and working with clipping paths—as well as an entire supplemental chapter devoted to web graphics. Each of these supplements is included as a PDF document, and Adobe's Acrobat Reader has been included so that you can easily view all of these PDF files.

In addition to Acrobat Reader, you'll be able to demo a version of Photoshop 5 (in the event you don't already own a copy!) and try out several third-party demo filters from AlienSkin, Extensis, ImageXpress, and many other leading software companies. And for when you're feeling like you've really mastered Photoshop, you might want to test yourself by trying out the questions on the sample Adobe Certification Exam.

And, to make it as easy as possible for you to follow along with my examples, we've provided many of the example images on the CD-ROM. You can find these in folder called Sample Images.

And the Beat Goes On...

Whenever a program like Photoshop weathers the throes of a new release, it's like a bunch of seedlings have been planted in a field, and it takes awhile before you can harvest the crop. The more I use the new version of Photoshop, the more I think of new angles and techniques. And as I start my seminar tour again, I'll be talking to countless Photoshoppers who are also figuring out interesting ways to squeeze more neat stuff out of Photoshop 5. So, everytime I think of a new technique or learn about a good one from someone else, I'll post it to my website (**www.digitalmastery.com**) so you can get it too. That way, the book doesn't have to stop here, and if you check out my website every few months, you'll get a bunch of new goodies.

Unveiling the New Goodies in Version 5.0

Adobe did a fine job of delivering the goods with 5.0 and it's clear that Adobe has been listening to its users. They delivered the four most-requested capabilities that topped designer wish lists in survey after survey—multiple levels of undo, editable text, tighter color management controls, and built-in support of spot color. There's also a bunch of new workflow and automation tools that should do a lot to make your life easier. We'll look at all of the new features and find out why they're worth getting excited about.

So, enough blabbing, let's get on with the "transformation." I'll make it as easy on you as I possibly can, but just remember the words of my favorite character, Miracle Max, from the movie "The Princess Bride": You rush a miracle man, you get rotten miracles.

Part I **Working Foundations**

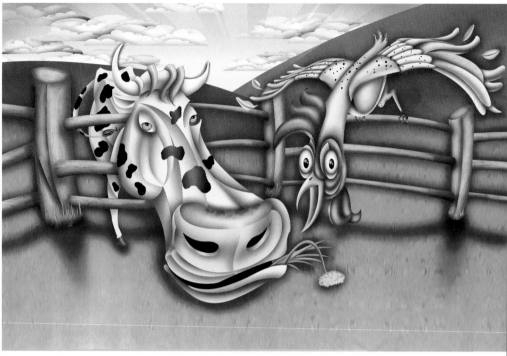

1 Tool and Palette Primer

Out of clutter,
find simplicity.
—Albert Einstein

Courtesy of Don Barnett, www.donbarnett.com.

Opening up Photoshop for the first time and seeing all the tools and palettes competing for space on your screen can be a dizzying experience. You might find yourself thinking "that's great, but they forgot to leave room in there for me to work!" Some of the more fortunate Photoshoppers get to have a second monitor, just to hold all their palettes. The rest of us make do and find ways to keep our screens neat and tidy. You'll discover that finding places to put your tools and palettes is almost as important as knowing how to use them. This chapter is all about effectively managing your workspace and getting acquainted with the oodles of gadgets and gizmos found in the tools and palettes.

Preparing Your Workspace

Before we get into functionality, we'll talk about how to control that prodigious profusion of palettes. But first, a word of advice: No matter how many times you feel like nuking a palette when it's in your way, no matter how many times your screen turns into a blinding jumble of annoying little boxes, just remember that you can organize the clutter into an elegant arrangement in just a few seconds.

Controlling Those Palettes

The first order of business is to get you enough space to work effectively with your image. We'll accomplish this by organizing the palettes so that they don't obstruct your view of your document. I don't think you'll like the default position of the palettes—that is, unless you use a 36" screen. The palettes take up too much valuable screen real estate (see Figure 1.1).

Collapsing the Palettes

One way to quickly maximize your workspace is to collapse the palettes when you're not using them and move them to the bottom of your screen. To collapse a palette, double-click any of the name tabs at the top of the palette. To reposition a palette, click the little gray bar at the top of the palette and then drag it toward the bottom of your screen. When you move a palette close to the bottom of the screen, it should snap in place (see Figure 1.2).

NOTE

To force a palette to snap to the edge of your screen, press the Shift key as you reposition the palette.

Figure 1.1
Photoshop's palettes take up the majority of the screen.

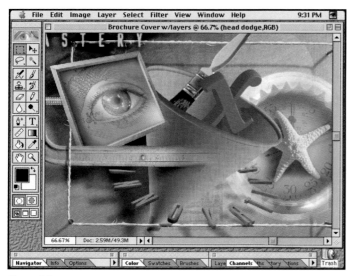

Figure 1.2
Stowing palettes at the bottom of the screen. (Image courtesy of Chris Klimek)

One thing you need to make sure of when repositioning your palettes is to not place any palettes too close to the right edge of your screen. This right edge of the screen, affectionately known as *palette alley*, can cause you great pains when zooming in on your images (see Figure 1.3). Here's why: If you have a palette too close to the right edge of your screen and you press Command-+ (plus sign), Photoshop can't resize the document window to the width of your screen. Instead, it leaves palette alley open and doesn't allow the document window to intrude into this space. This means your efforts to reposition the palettes in order to save space were futile.

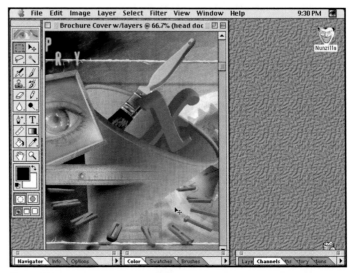

Figure 1.3
Palette alley stays clear whenever a palatte is close to the right edge of your screen.

If you need access to any of these palettes, double-click the palette's name tab and the palette will instantly pop open (see Figure 1.4). When you're done using the palette, just double-click its name tab to collapse it again.

Regrouping the Palettes

Another way to maximize your screen real estate is to change the way your palettes are grouped. For example, if your most frequently used palettes are the Color and

History palettes, you can put them in one group so that you have one palette open at any given time instead of two. To regroup the palettes, drag the name tab of the palette you want to move (in this case, Color) on top of the palette grouping you want to move the palette into (History in this case). You can then remove any palettes you don't want in this grouping by dragging the name tab of a palette onto an open area of the screen (see Figure 1.5).

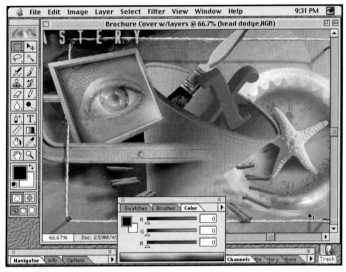

Figure 1.4
To collapse or expand a palette, double-click the name tab.

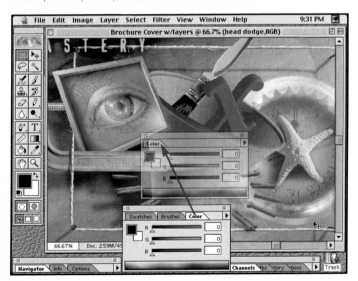

Figure 1.5
To separate a palette from a grouping, drag the name tab to an open area of your screen.

NOTE

If you really mess things up and your screen gets to looking like an Escher print, you can easily set all the palettes back to their default locations. To do this choose **File>Preferences>General** and click that huge button called Reset Palette Locations to Default.

If you turn off the Save Palette Locations check box in the same dialog box, each time you launch Photoshop, the palettes will be at their default locations.

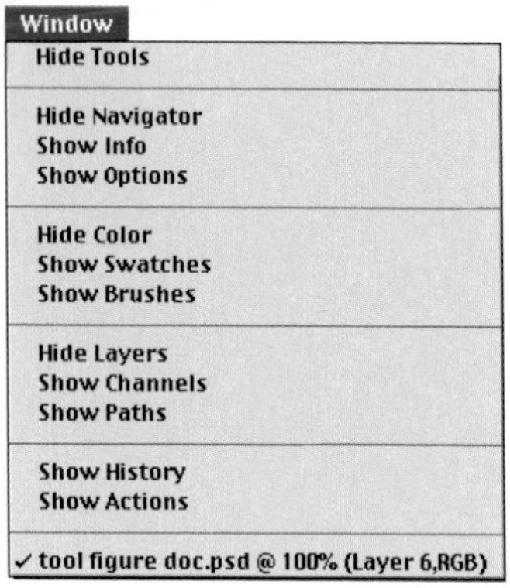

Window

Hide Tools

Hide Navigator
Show Info
Show Options

Hide Color
Show Swatches
Show Brushes

Hide Layers
Show Channels
Show Paths

Show History
Show Actions

✓ tool figure doc.psd @ 100% (Layer 6,RGB)

Figure 1.6
The Window menu lists all the
palettes available in Photoshop.

NOTE

If a gray surround isn't your taste, just
change the foreground color and then
grab the Paint Bucket tool and Shift-click
in the gray area to change it. Not too
many people know about this, so you can
use it to mess with your coworkers minds.
Just set the color to an irritating color such
as fluorescent green.

If, after moving and regrouping your palettes, you find
that a palette appears to be missing, don't panic. You can
always find it in the Window menu. This menu lists all the
palettes that are available (see Figure 1.6).

Working with Screen Modes

Even with the palettes conveniently stowed at the bottom
of your screen, your image still only uses a fraction of the
screen space available. You can use the three screen mode
icons at the bottom of the toolbox to easily solve this
problem.

Standard Screen Mode

The first icon, Standard Screen Mode, is the default
screen mode (see Figure 1.7). You're probably used to
working with this one. In this mode, the name of your
document is at the top of the document window, and the
scroll bars are on each side.

Full Screen Mode with Menu Bar

The second icon, Full Screen Mode with Menu Bar, lets
the image flow all the way across your screen and slip
right under the palettes (see Figure 1.8). If you click this
icon, the scroll bars will disappear, so you'll have to use
the Hand tool to navigate around your document. But
that's okay, because you can hold down the Spacebar at
any time to temporarily use the Hand tool. If you zoom
out of a document so that it doesn't take up the entire
screen, Photoshop will fill the area around the image
with gray.

Full Screen Mode

The third screen mode icon, Full Screen Mode, is my
favorite. In this mode, Photoshop even turns off the
menu bar! Now your image can take over the entire
screen (see Figure 1.9). You can still use many of the
menu commands as long as you use their keyboard equiv-
alents. If you zoom out while in this mode, Photoshop will
fill the area around your image with black (I don't know

how to change that one). I use this mode whenever I show images to clients. If you don't let them know you're in Photoshop, they might think you are in a cheap little slide-show program and won't ask you to make changes on the spot.) However, you won't be able to fool anyone if all those palettes are still on your screen. Just press Tab and they'll all disappear (see Figure 1.10). Don't worry, you can get them back just as fast by pressing Tab again.

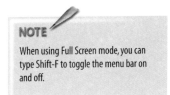

NOTE

When using Full Screen mode, you can type Shift-F to toggle the menu bar on and off.

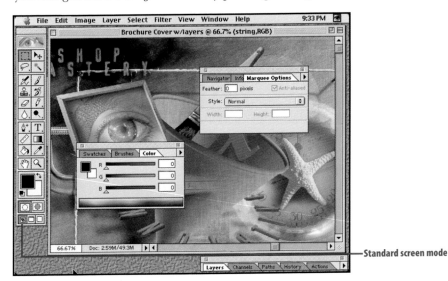

Standard screen mode

Figure 1.7
The first screen mode is Photoshop's default.

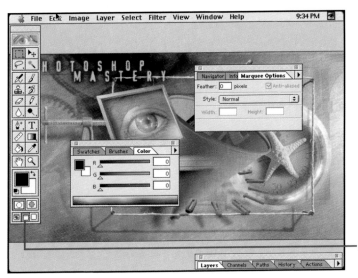

Full screen mode with menu bar

Figure 1.8.
The second screen mode allows you to use the entire screen.

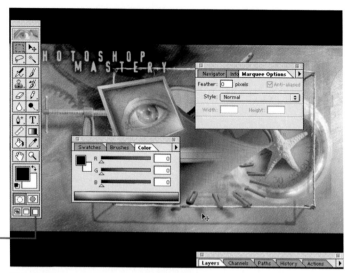

Full screen mode

Figure 1.9
The third screen mode uses the full screen and removes the menu bar.

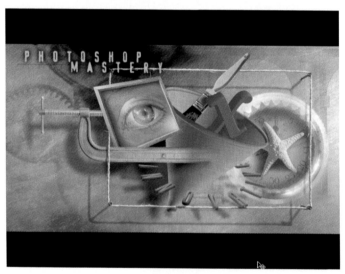

Figure 1.10
Press Tab to hide or show the palettes.

Screen Mode Shortcuts

I use the different screen modes every single day, but it's not very often that I actually click those three little tool-box icons. Instead, I use keyboard commands. Just press the F key on your keyboard to cycle through the different screen modes. You can even type F-F-Tab while an image is opening; then when it's done loading, Photoshop will switch to the third screen mode and rid your screen of all the palettes!

Now that you have your screen under control, we can start to explore some of the tools and palettes.

A Quick Tour of the Tools

There are more than 40 tools available in the Tool palette. Describing all of them in detail would take up a huge chunk of this chapter (which you probably don't have the patience for), so for now we'll take a look at the ones that you absolutely can't live without. Don't worry about missing out on anything—as you work your way through the book, you'll be introduced to the rest of the tools. In the meantime, I'll introduce you to some tool names so that when I mention one, you'll know what to look for (see Figures 1.11 and 1.12).

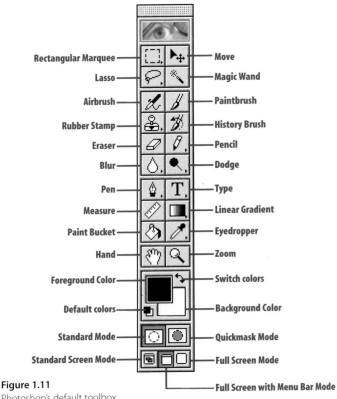

Figure 1.11
Photoshop's default toolbox.

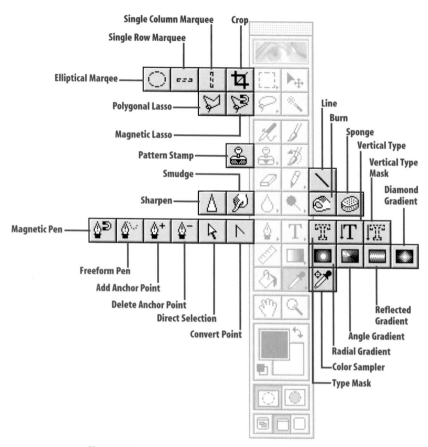

Figure 1.12
Photoshop's arsenal of tools.

NOTE

For information about keyboard shortcuts for each of the tools, look for the "Keyboard Shortcuts" sections at the end of most chapters.

The Tool Options Palette

Most of the tools have settings associated with them. To access these settings, double-click the tool you want to use (or select the tool and press the Return key). This will open the Tool Options palette.

You'll be able to change the various settings more quickly if you know exactly how to navigate the various Options palettes. For example, all the painting and retouching tools have a percentage setting in the upper-right corner of their respective Options palettes. There are quite a few ways to change this number. One way is to highlight the number and then type in a new one. You can also click the number and then use the Up Arrow and Down Arrow keys on your keyboard (add the Shift key to change the number by increments of 10). Finally, you can click the arrow to the right of the number and drag across the slider that appears.

If there's more than one setting that lets you enter a number, press Return to highlight the first one, then tab your way through the others. Once a number is highlighted, you can change it by pressing the Up Arrow and Down Arrow keys or by typing a new number.

Navigating Your Document

Most of us struggle with monitors that are not large enough to view an entire document (except, of course, the more privileged Photoshoppers who have monitors that are practically as large as drive-in movie screens). To deal with this ever-present limitation, you must train yourself to be a quick and nimble navigator. Photoshop offers you a huge array of choices, and, as usual, you'll need to weed through them to find your favorite method. In this section, we'll cover the palettes and tools you need to maximize the speed with which you get around your document.

The Navigator Palette

If you do a lot of detail work where you need to zoom in on your image as if you're wearing glasses as thick as Coke bottles, you should love the Navigator palette (see Figure 1.13). The Navigator palette floats above your document and allows you to quickly move around and zoom in and out of your image. A little red box indicates which area of the image you're currently viewing. By dragging this box around the miniature image of your document that appears in the Navigator palette, you can change which area you're viewing in the main image window. You can also just click outside the red box and the box will center itself on your cursor.

There are a number of ways to zoom in on your document by using this palette. Use the mountain icons to zoom in or out at preset increments (50%, 66.67%, 100%, 200%, and so on), or you can grab the slider between

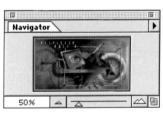

Figure 1.13
The Navigator palette.

NOTE

If you don't like the color of the little red box or if there's so much red in the image that the box becomes difficult to see, you can change the box color by choosing Palette Options from the side menu of the palette.

NOTE

To temporarily use the Zoom tool—that is, to use the Zoom tool without deselecting the active tool—hold down the Command and Spacebar keys.

them to zoom to any level. You can change the number in the lower-left corner of the palette to zoom to an exact percentage. However, my favorite method is to drag across the image while holding down the Command key to zoom into a specific area.

Hand Tool

The Hand tool is definitely the most basic tool in Photoshop. By clicking and dragging with the Hand tool, you can scroll around the image. This tool is—excuse the pun—*handy* for scrolling around images that are too large to fit on your screen and for moving without the scroll bars.

Zoom Tool

Whenever you click on your image by using the Zoom tool, you zoom in on the image to a preset level (just like the mountain icons in the Navigator palette). I almost never use the tool in this way because it takes too long to get where I want to be. Instead, I usually click and drag across the area I want to enlarge and Photoshop immediately zooms me into that specific area.

In addition to zooming in, you also have options for quickly zooming out. Double-click the Zoom tool icon in the Tool palette to view your image at 100% magnification. You can also double-click the Hand tool icon to fit the entire image onscreen. Option-clicking with the Zoom tool zooms you out at a preset level.

Figure 1.14
100% magnification.
(© 1998 PhotoSpin)

Figure 1.15
500% magnification.
(© 1998 PhotoSpin)

View Menu

If you're going to be doing a bunch of detail work in which you need to zoom in really close on your image, you might want to create two views of the same document (see Figures 1.14 and 1.15). That way, you can have one of the views at 100% magnification to give you an overall view of your image, and you can set the second one to 500% magnification, for instance, to see all the fine details. To create a second view, choose **View>New View**. This will create a second window that looks like a separate document, but it's really just another view of the same document. You can make your edits in either window and both of them will show you the result of your manipulations.

From the View menu, you can also select from the Zoom In, Zoom Out, Fit On Screen, and Actual Pixels options. As you'll probably notice, each of these actions can also be accomplished by using the Zoom and Hand tools. The reason they're also listed under the View menu is to allow you to quickly use them with keyboard commands. Here are the View menu options:

Zoom In/Zoom Out—Same as clicking with the Zoom tool. Uses the easy-to-remember keyboard shortcut Command-+ (plus sign) to zoom in and Command-– (minus sign) to zoom out.

Fit On Screen—Same as double-clicking the Hand tool. Uses the shortcut Command-0.

Actual Pixels—Same as double-clicking the Zoom tool. Uses the shortcut Option-Command-0.

Print Size—Allows you to preview how large or small your image will appear when it is printed.

Just when you thought there couldn't possibly be any more ways to zoom in and out of your document, Adobe threw in just one more method for good measure. The percentage that appears in the lower-left corner of your document window can also be changed by clicking and dragging across it.

There are indeed many ways to zoom around in Photoshop. Now all you have to do is test out all the options, decide which one you prefer, and ignore the rest.

Picking Colors

My father's Webster's Dictionary—a 1940 model that's over half a foot thick from cover to cover—devoted four entire pages to describing one word: color. These pages are filled with lush descriptions of hue, tint, shade, saturation, vividness, brilliance, and much, much more. It's no wonder that choosing colors can be such a formidable task. Do you want Cobalt Blue or Persian Blue? Nile Green

NOTE

Another method for determining the actual size your image will be when printed is to choose **View>Show Rulers**. You can set the ruler measurement system (inches, points, picas, and so on) by choosing **File>Preferences>Units & Rules**. The keyboard command to show the rulers is Command-R; then to hide the rulers you press Command-R again.

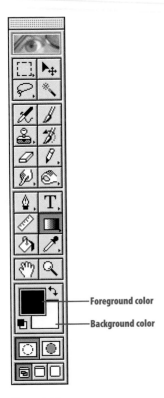

Foreground color

Background color

Figure 1.16
Foreground and background colors.

Figure 1.17
The warning triangle indicates a color that is not reproducible in CMYK mode.

or Emerald? Carmine or Vermilion? Fortunately, Photoshop has done an excellent job of providing the tools you need to find the colors you want. Of course, each tool has advantages and disadvantages. You just have to play around with them and decide which one you prefer.

Foreground and Background Colors

The two square boxes that appear toward the bottom of your toolbox are the foreground and background colors (see Figure 1.16). The top box is the foreground color; it determines which color will be used when using any of the painting tools. To change the foreground color, click it once (this will bring up a standard color picker). The bottom box is the background color; it's used when you're erasing the background image or when you increase the size of your document by using **Image>Canvas Size**. You can swap the foreground and background colors by clicking the small curved arrows next to them in the Tool palette. You can also reset the colors to their default settings by clicking the small squares in the lower-left corner of that same area.

Color Picker Dialog Box

The Color Picker dialog box is available in many areas of Photoshop. The easiest way to access it is to click your foreground or background color. There are many choices in this dialog box because there are many different ways to define a color. In this section, we'll cover all the various ways you can choose a color, and I'll start off by showing you how to preview the color you're selecting.

Previewing a Color

While you're choosing a color, you can glance at the two color swatches to the right of the vertical gradient to compare the color you've chosen (the top swatch) to the color you had previously (the bottom swatch).

Just be sure to watch for the out-of-gamut warning, which is indicated by a small triangle that appears next to these color swatches (see Figure 1.17). This triangle warns you that the color you have chosen is not reproducible in CMYK mode, which means that it cannot be printed.

Fortunately, Photoshop provides you with a preview of what the color would have to shift to in order to be printable. You can find this preview in the small color swatch that appears directly below the triangle icon, and you can select this printable color by clicking the color swatch.

Selecting with the Color Field

Usually, the simplest method for choosing a color is to eyeball it. In the Color Picker dialog box, you can click the general color you want to use in the vertical gradient. Then you click and drag around the large square area at the left to choose a shade of that color.

Selecting by Hue, Saturation, and Brightness

You can also change what appears in the vertical gradient by clicking any of the radio buttons on the right side of the dialog box (see Figures 1.18 to 1.20).

In this dialog box, H = Hue, S = Saturation, and B = Brightness. You can use the numbers at the right of the dialog box to describe the color you've chosen (this can be a big help when you're describing a color to someone on the phone). If you know the exact color you need, you can type in exact numbers into that area.

NOTE

CMYK colors are meant to be printed, which involves ink, whereas RGB colors, which involve light, are meant for multimedia. Due to impurities in CMYK inks, you can't accurately reproduce every color you see on your screen.

WARNING

If your method for picking white is to drag to the upper-left corner of the color field, be sure to drag beyond the edge of the square; otherwise, you might not end up with a true white. Instead, you'll get a muddy-looking white or a light shade of gray.

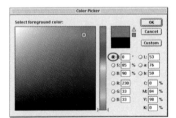

Figure 1.18
Hue.

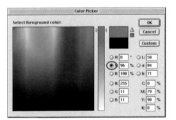

Figure 1.19
Saturation.

Figure 1.20
Brightness.

Selecting Custom Colors

If you want to pick your colors from one of those swatch books you can purchase at an art supply store (PANTONE, TruMatch, and so on), you click the Custom button. This will bring up the Custom Color Picker (see Figure 1.21). Choose the swatch book you want to use from the pop-up menu at the top of the dialog box; then scroll through the list to find the color you desire. You

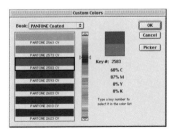

Figure 1.21
The Custom Color Picker.

WARNING

Although the Color Picker palette is great for users printing with CMYK inks, it's *not* for those who are using true spot colors (metallic, fluorescent, and other colors that cannot be reproduced using CMYK inks). If you're going to be by using true spot colors, see Chapter 9, "Channels."

can also type in numbers to select a specific color (I know, there isn't the usual text field to enter them in, but just start typing), but make sure you type really fast. I'm not sure why it works this way, but this part of Photoshop gets impatient with slow typists. For example, if you slowly type the number 356, Photoshop might jump to a color number starting with 3 and then go to one that starts with 5. It's sort of annoying but shouldn't pose a problem as long as you type the number quickly.

Color Palette

You can think of the Color palette as a simplified version of the Color Picker dialog box. Just like in the Color Picker, you can pick colors by typing in numbers. However, you first need to choose the type of numbers you want to use from the side menu (see Figure 1.22).

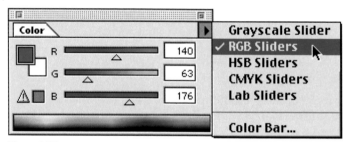

Figure 1.22
Choosing the slider type from the palette's menu.

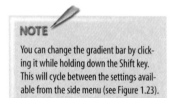

NOTE

You can change the gradient bar by clicking it while holding down the Shift key. This will cycle between the settings available from the side menu (see Figure 1.23).

Figure 1.23
Changing the color bar's setting.

You can also pick colors by clicking the color bar at the bottom of the palette (use Option-click to change your background color). You can change the appearance of the color bar by choosing Color Bar from the side menu of the palette. Here are the options:

RGB Spectrum—Displays all the colors that are usable in RGB mode. Use this setting for multimedia.

CMYK Spectrum—Shows you all the colors usable in CMYK mode. Use this setting for publishing.

Grayscale Ramp—Shows you shades of gray from black to white. Use this setting anytime you need shades of gray that do not contain a hint of color (also known as *neutral grays*).

Current Colors—Displays a gradient using your foreground and background colors.

Eyedropper Tool

In addition to using the Color Picker and Color palette to select colors, you can use the Eyedropper tool. One advantage to using the Eyedropper is that you can grab colors from any open Photoshop file. After selecting the Eyedropper, you can click any part of your image and bingo!—you've got a new foreground color. You can also Option-click to change your background color. You don't have to click within the document you're currently editing; you can click any open image.

You can also double-click the Eyedropper tool to choose how it looks at, or samples, the area you click (see Figures 1.24 to 1.27). Here are your options:

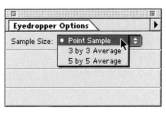

Figure 1.24
The Sample Size option determines the area the Eyedropper tool will average when you're choosing a color.

Point Sample—Picks up the exact color of the pixel you click.

3-by-3 Average—Averages the area around your cursor by looking at an area that's three pixels wide and three pixels tall.

5-by-5 Average—Works the same way as 3-by-3 Average, but it just uses a larger area.

In many cases, you'll find it helpful to use one of the latter settings. The 3-by-3 Average and 5-by-5 Average settings prevent you from accidentally picking up an odd-colored speck in the area from which you're grabbing, thereby preventing you from selecting a color that isn't representative of the area from which you're choosing.

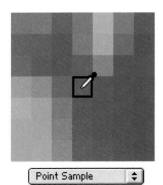

Firugre 1.25
Point sample.

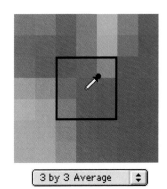

Figure 1.26
3-by-3 Average.

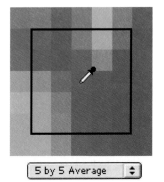

Figure 1.27
5-by-5 Average.

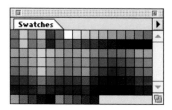

Figure 1.28
The Swatches palette.

Figure 1.29
The dialog box for saving swatches.

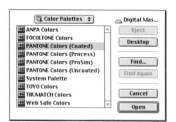

Figure 1.30
Choosing a PANTONE palette.

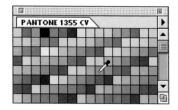

Figure 1.31
Choosing PANTONE colors.

Swatches Palette

The Swatches palette is designed to store colors that you'll need to use again and again (see Figure 1.28). To paint with one of the colors stored in the Swatches palette, move your cursor over a swatch and click the mouse button. Your foreground color will change to the color you clicked. To change your background color, press Option while clicking any swatch.

To store your current foreground color in the palette, just click in the open space below the swatches. If there is no open space, resize the palette by dragging its lower-right corner.

You can also remove a color from the palette by Command-clicking on the swatch. By Shift-clicking, you can change the color of an existing swatch to match your foreground color. To reset the swatches back to their default settings, choose Reset Swatches from the side menu of the palette.

After you've stored the colors you want, you can choose Save Swatches from the Swatches palette's side menu. This will bring up a standard Save dialog box to allow you to assign a name to your personal set of swatches (see Figure 1.29). After saving a set of swatches, you can reload them by choosing Replace Swatches from the side menu.

Photoshop comes with a bunch of swatch files you can load into the Swatches palette. These files are stored in the Goodies folder, which resides in your Photoshop folder (**Photoshop>Goodies>Color Palettes**). After loading one of these files, move your cursor over the swatches—the tab at the top of the palette will change to indicate the color that's directly below your cursor (see Figures 1.30 and 1.31).

Info Palette

Although you can't actually choose a color by using the Info palette, you'll find it helpful for measuring the colors that already reside in your document. The top part of the Info palette measures the color that appears below your cursor.

You can change the measurement method used by the Info palette by clicking the tiny Eyedropper icons within the palette (see Figure 1.32). RGB is usually used for multimedia purposes; CMYK for publishing. Total Ink adds together the C, M, Y, and K numbers to indicate how much ink coverage will be used to reproduce the area under your cursor.

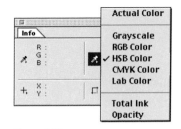

Figure 1.32
Changing how the Info palette measures color.

There are four areas of your image that you have to adjust when performing color correction (highlight, shadow, flesh tone, and neutral gray). You can set up the Info palette to keep track of these areas—or any area for that matter—so you can see what's happening when you make adjustments. You can do this by clicking your image using the Color Sampler tool. This will deposit a little crosshair on the area you click and will also add another readout to the Info palette (see Figure 1.33). You can add up to four of these "samples" to your image. To remove a sample, just drag it off the screen. Occasionally you may want to hide the sample points when you're working on your image; you can do this by choosing Hide Color Samples from the side menu of the Info palette. We'll use these samples when you read about color correction in Chapter 8, "Color Correction."

Figure 1.33
Color Samples and Info palette readouts.
(Original image © 1998 Adobe Systems, Inc.)

Basic Editing Tools

Like the majority of Photoshop features, you'll find that there's more than meets the eye with the editing tools. For now, we'll cover their most blatant applications, but as you make your way through the rest of the book, keep in mind that these deceivingly simple tools can perform some remarkable tricks. The painting and gradient tools can be used for more than just painting and adding color—they can also be used for making intricate selections, compositing photos, and creating cool fadeouts. You can use them to create an infinite number of dazzling effects.

Painting Tools

Although each of the painting tools gives you a slightly different end result, they all share the same basic settings. Only a few settings are unique to each tool. Before we dive into their options, let's look at the basic difference between the Pencil, Paintbrush, and Airbrush tools.

To begin with, the Paintbrush and Airbrush tools always have soft edges, whereas the Pencil tool always has a hard edge (see Figures 1.34 to 1.36).

You can change the softness of the Paintbrush and Airbrush tools by choosing different brushes from the Brushes palette.

Figure 1.34
Airbrush.

Figure 1.35
Paintbrush.

Figure 1.36
Pencil.

Opacity

If you lower the Opacity setting of the Paintbrush tool (called **Pressure** for the Airbrush), you can paint across the image without worrying about overlapping your paint strokes (see Figure 1.37). As long as you don't release the mouse button, the areas that you paint over multiple times will not become more opaque than the areas that you paint with a single stroke. Using the Airbrush tool is a different story. When you paint over an area multiple times, the Airbrush increases the opacity of the paint each time you drag the tool across the area (see Figure 1.38). The Pencil tool acts just like the Paintbrush when painting with a low opacity setting.

NOTE

All painting tools use the current foreground color when you're painting on the image, so before you begin painting, make sure the active foreground color is the one you want to paint with.

NOTE

To quickly change the Opacity setting of a painting tool, use the number keys on your keyboard (1 = 10%, 3 = 30%, 65 = 65%, and so on).

Figure 1.37
Paintbrush.

Figure 1.38
Airbrush.

If you're not familiar with the concept of opaque versus transparent, take a look at Figures 1.39 and 1.40.

Now let's take a look at the options available to you when using the painting tools. The majority of these options will be shared among all three painting tools.

Blending Mode

The pop-up menu in the upper-left corner of the Options palette is known as the *blending mode menu*. We'll be covering all the options under this menu in Chapter 12, "Enhancement," so right now I'll just explain a few basic uses (see Figures 1.41 to 1.43). If you would like to change the basic color of an object instead of completely covering it up, you can set the blending mode to Hue. If you're using a soft-edged brush, you can set the blending mode to Dissolve to force the edges of your brush to

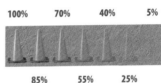

Figure 1.39
Opaque versus transparent. (© 1998 PhotoSpin)

Figure 1.40
Varying opacity. (© 1998 PhotoSpin)

dissolve out. That's all for now, we'll explore the rest of this menu in Chapter 12.

Fade

When the Fade option is checked, the painting tools will begin applying the foreground color but then will fade out to your background color or will become transparent (see Figures 1.44 and 1.45). The higher the fade number, the longer you have to paint before the paint fades all the way out. This number is not measured in pixels, inches, or any other measurement system you would recognize. In order to understand exactly how this setting is calculated, you must first understand how the brushes work, and we'll talk about that in the "Brushes Palette" section later in this chapter.

Figure 1.41
Normal. (© 1998 PhotoSpin)

Figure 1.42
Dissolve.

Figure 1.43
Hue.

Figure 1.44
Setting the Fade option to Transparent.

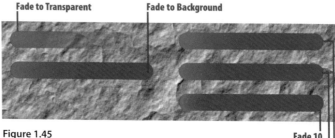

Fade to Transparent   **Fade to Background**

Fade 10
Fade 20
Fade 30

Figure 1.45
Various fade effects.

Wet Edges

The Wet Edges option will apply the full intensity of the paint only in the areas of your brush that are fading out.

The center of the brush will look as if you lowered the Opacity setting to 51%. This can simulate the look of water color paints or magic markers (see Figure 1.46).

Figure 1.46
The Wet Edges effect.

Stylus Options

The Stylus options will be grayed out on the majority of machines you use. The only time they become available is when you have a pressure-sensitive graphics tablet installed. These options allow you to control the size, opacity setting, and color of the paint while you're painting, without having to let go of the mouse button (see Figure 1.47).

Graphics Tablets

Ever try signing your name with a mouse? It looks like you wrote it with your arm in a plaster cast. I can't begin to tell you how much more control you'll have over your images if you use a graphics tablet. I think it's cruel and unusual punishment to force Photoshop users to use a mouse. Those pesky mice make it hard to do just about everything in Photoshop, and they can even make your wrists hurt. In contrast, tablets are designed for precision and control. Not only can you sign your name with a flourish, you can also trace the most intricate shapes and edges, even on magazines that are half an inch thick. Try doing that with a mouse. If you haven't already taken the plunge, you really should think about getting in the market for one. When you do, get a Wacom brand tablet, they are simply the best I've found (and no, they didn't pay me to say that). Get one about the size of your mouse pad.

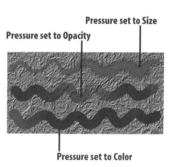

Figure 1.47
Various Stylus options.

NOTE

To draw straight lines, Shift-click in multiple areas of your image and Photoshop will connect the dots (see Figure 1.48). You can also hold down the Shift key when painting to constrain the angle to a 45% increment.

Figure 1.48
Shift-click to create straight lines.

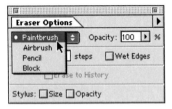

Figure 1.49
Choosing Eraser tool behavior.

NOTE

If you want a transparent background that will still be transparent in other programs (for instance, if you're preparing an image for use in PageMaker), be sure to refer to the file extras.pdf on the accompanying CD-ROM for supplemental information about clipping paths.

NOTE

If you want the size of your cursor to reflect the size of your brush, choose **File>Preferences>Displays & Cursors.** When you set the Painting Cursors setting to Brush Size, your cursor changes into a circle that reflects the exact size of the brush you have chosen.

You'll end up forking over less than $150 for the smallest one (4×5 inches) and around $300 for an average size tablet (6×9 inches).

Eraser Tool

If you use the Eraser tool while you're working on a background image (we'll talk about the background in Chapter 3, "Layer Primer"), it acts like one of the normal painting tools. In fact, it lets you choose which type of painting tool it should mimic by selecting an option from the pop-up menu in the upper-left corner of the Options palette (see Figure 1.49). When you're working on the background image, the only difference between the Eraser tool and the painting tools is that the Eraser tool will use the background color instead of the foreground color.

However, when you use the Eraser tool on a layer, it *really* erases the area. If you lower the opacity setting, it makes an area appear partially transparent. Bear in that mind that the same does *not* apply to the background image. You cannot "erase" the background.

Brushes Palette

All the painting and retouching tools available in the toolbox use the Brushes palette to determine their brush size (see Figure 1.50). Each individual tool remembers the last brush size that was used with it and will return to that same size when you select the tool. Therefore, if you're using the Paintbrush tool with a huge brush and then you decide to switch to the Airbrush tool, where you were previously using a tiny brush, you might end up using a radically different brush size. In other words, the brush size you choose does not stay consistent when you switch among the tools.

The currently active brush is shown with a bold border. You can change the active brush by clicking once on any brush that's available in the Brushes palette. If you create a brush that's larger than the squares in the palette, a small version will be displayed (just to show you if it has a hard or soft edge), and a number will appear beneath the preview indicating exactly how wide the brush is.

Now for even more fun, open the Brushes palette and then press the [or] key on your keyboard. You can use these keys to choose the brush you want to use. For those of you who love keyboard commands, try typing Shift-[and Shift-] and see what happens in the palette—no, I'm not going to tell you, you have to try it out for yourself. When you do, you'll know why I use these keyboard commands at least every ten minutes. Hint: Look at your cursor while you're typing the keyboard commands.

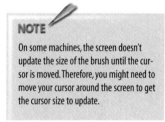

NOTE

On some machines, the screen doesn't update the size of the brush until the cursor is moved. Therefore, you might need to move your cursor around the screen to get the cursor size to update.

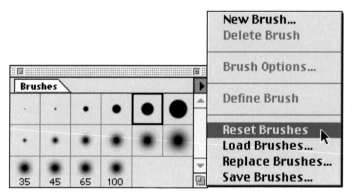

Figure 1.50
The Brushes palette and side menu.

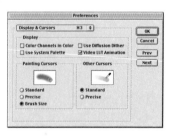

Figure 1.51
The File>Preferences>Display & Cursors dialog box.

Brush Options

To change the settings on any brush, double-click it in the Brushes palette. This brings up a dialog box that allows you to change the brush size, edge softness, and other settings (see Figure 1.52). Here's an explanation of the settings:

Diameter—Determines the size of the brush (see Figure 1.53).

Hardness—Determines how quickly the edge fades out. Default brushes are either 100% soft or 0% soft (see Figure 1.54).

Roundness—Determines whether the brush will be round or oval shaped (see Figure 1.55 and 1.56).

Angle—Rotates oval brushes but has no effect on round ones (see Figure 1.57).

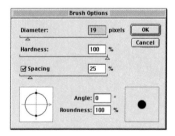

Figure 1.52
Double-click any brush to get the Brush Options dialog box.

Spacing—Determines how far you have to paint when using the Fade option (see Figure 1.58). For example, a Fade setting of 12 means the brush will be applied 12 times before it fades out.

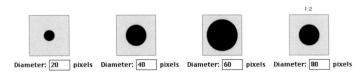

Diameter: 20 pixels   Diameter: 40 pixels   Diameter: 60 pixels   Diameter: 80 pixels

Figure 1.53
Diameter determines the size of the brush.

Softness: 0% —

Softness: 100% —

Figure 1.54
Hardness determines how quickly the edge fades out.

> **NOTE**
>
> Lower the Spacing setting when using large brushes to prevent rough edges.

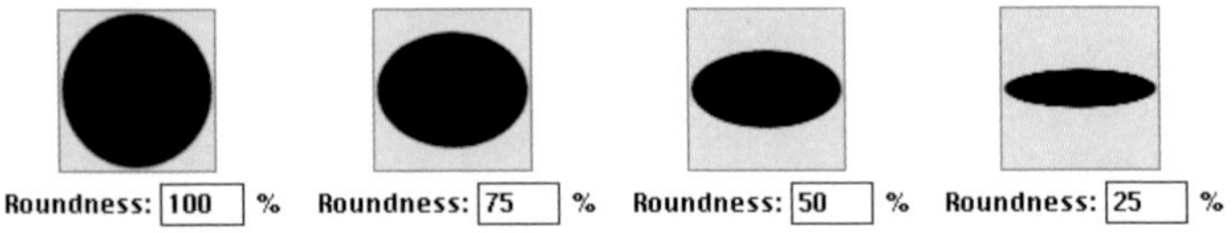

Roundness: 100 %   Roundness: 75 %   Roundness: 50 %   Roundness: 25 %

Figure 1.55
Roundness determines if the brush will be round or oval shaped.

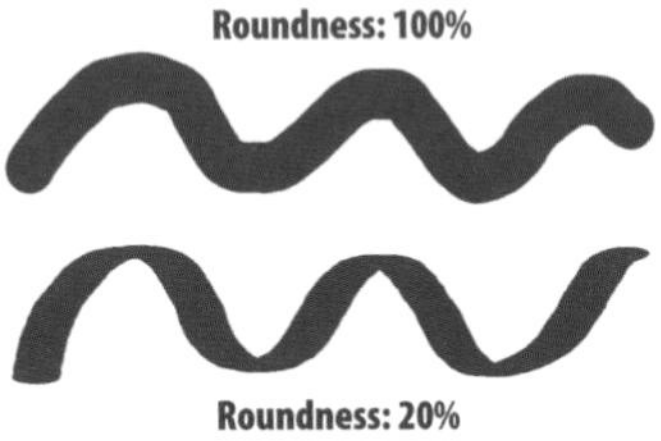

Roundness: 100%

Roundness: 20%

Figure 1.56
Effects of the Roundness setting.

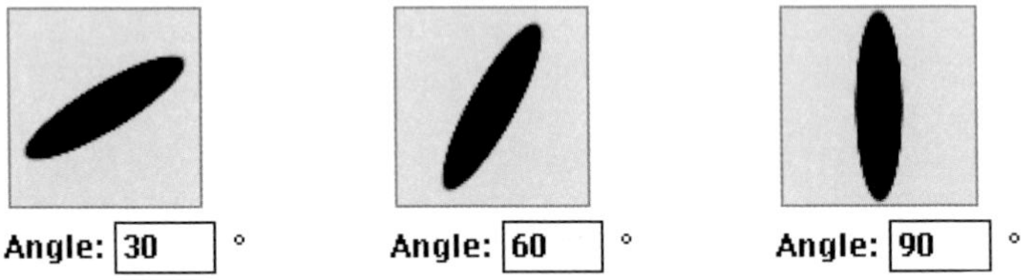

Angle: 30 °   Angle: 60 °   Angle: 90 °

Figure 1.57
Angle rotates oval brushes but has no effect on round ones.

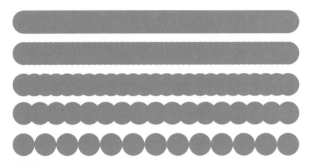

Figure 1.58
From top to bottom: Spacing 1%, Spacing 25%, Spacing 50%, Spacing 75%, Spacing 100%.

Saving Brushes

Once you have created a set of brushes you like, you can choose Save Brushes from the side menu of the palette to save the set in a little file. If you ever need to get back to a saved set of brushes, choose Replace Brushes from the same menu. You can also choose Reset Brushes to get the brushes back to the default settings.

Preset Brushes

Photoshop comes with a variety of preset brushes. You can access these sets by choosing Replace Brushes. They are hidden within your Photoshop folder inside another folder called Goodies. Inside Goodies, you should find the Brushes and Patterns folder. These preset brushes are not like the normal brushes found in the default Brushes palette. They were created by converting a picture into a brush and therefore do not offer the same options as normal brushes when you double-click them (see Figures 1.59 to 1.61).

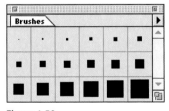

Figure 1.59
Square brushes.

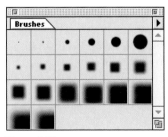

Figure 1.60
Drop shadow brushes.

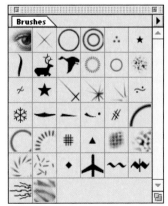

Figure 1.61
Assorted brushes.

Figure 1.62
Anti-aliased off.

Figure 1.63
Anti-aliased on.

If you double-click one of these preset brushes, you'll find only two options available: Spacing and Anti-Aliased. The Spacing setting works just like it does with normal brushes. The Anti-Aliased setting softens the edge of the brush by one pixel, allowing it to blend into the image and appear smoother (see Figures 1.62 and 1.63).

Custom Brushes

You can create your own custom brushes based on photographs by selecting any area (selections are covered in Chapter 2, "Selection Primer") and choosing Define Brush from the Brushes palette's menu (see Figure 1.64). This will copy the area that's selected, convert the copy to grayscale (if it was color to start with), then turn it into a custom brush.

Any shades of gray that appear in the brush will effectively lower the opacity of the brush when it's applied to the image (20% gray areas will look the same as painting with a normal brush set to 20% opacity). White areas will be ignored when creating custom brushes because that would lower the opacity of the brush to 0% in that area, so nothing would be applied when painting.

If the area you select is larger than the squares in the palette, only the upper-left corner of the brush will appear in the Brushes palette. You cannot create a multi-colored brush because brushes always use the current foreground color to paint with.

Custom brushes are great. For instance, you can plunk your company logo right in the Brushes palette so you always have it available. You can also create cool textured brushes by clicking once with a normal brush, applying filters to the image, and then turning the filtered image into a custom brush. These custom brushes become more useful when you increase the spacing to a setting above 100% (see Figure 1.65).

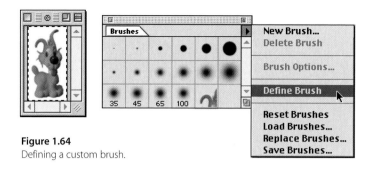

Figure 1.64
Defining a custom brush.

Spacing 25% (default)

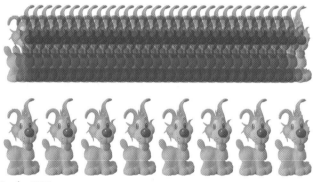

Spacing 100%

Figure 1.65
Painting with a custom brush. (© 1998 PhotoSpin)

Figure 1.66
Using a pressure-sensitive tablet with a custom brush.

Paint Bucket Tool

With the Paint Bucket tool, you can click an area and the color you're applying (foreground color) will spread out to fill any immediate areas that contain colors similar to the one you clicked. You can specify how sensitive the tool should be by changing its Tolerance setting (see Figures 1.67 to 1.69).

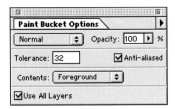

Figure 1.67
The Paint Bucket Options palette.

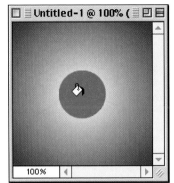

Figure 1.68
Tolerance: 32.

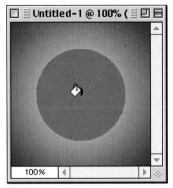

Figure 1.69
Tolerance: 75.

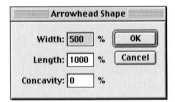

Figure 1.70
The Line Options palette.

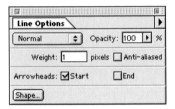

Figure 1.71
The Arrowhead Shape dialog box.

NOTE

To quickly change the Tolerance setting, press Return, type the setting you would like to use, and then press Return again.

Line Tool

The Line tool allows you to easily create straight lines. Its options are relatively straightforward. The items I think need your attention are the Arrowheads setting and the Shape button (see Figure 1.70 and 1.71). The Anti-Aliased setting works just like the one described in the Brushes section.

Within the Arrowhead Shape dialog box, you can set the Width, Length, and Concavity of your arrowheads:

Width—Determines how wide the back of the arrowhead will be (see Figure 1.72). This is measured as a percentage of the width of the line. Therefore, if the line width is set to 10 pixels and the arrowhead width is set to 200%, the width of the arrow head will be 20 pixels.

Length—Determines how much space there will be between the back of the arrowhead and its tip (see Figure 1.73). Again, this is measured as a percentage of the line width.

Concavity—Determines the shape of the back of the arrowhead (see Figure 1.74). A setting of zero produces a straight backed arrowhead. A setting of 50% produces a V-shaped back that ends 50 percent of the distance between the back and tip of the arrowhead.

Figure 1.72
Width: 200%, 500%, 1000%

Figure 1.73
Length: 250%, 500%, 1000%

Figure 1.74
Concavity: -50%, 0%, 50%

Measurement Tool

The Measurement tool allows you to measure the distance between two points or the angle of any area of the image, which can be helpful when you want to rotate or resize objects precisely. In order to see the angle and distance measurements, you must have the Info palette open. As you drag with the Measurement tool, the Info palette indicates the angle (A = Angle) and length (D = Distance) of the line you're creating (see Figure 1.75). You can change the measurement system used to measure the distance by clicking the small cross in the lower-left corner of the Info palette. After creating a line, you can click directly on the line and drag it around to different positions. You can also click and drag one end of the line to change the angle or distance.

If you want to resize an image so that it perfectly fits between two objects, you can measure the distance between them with this tool and then choose **Image>Image Size** to scale the image to that exact width.

You can also use the Measurement tool to determine the angle between two straight lines. If you Option-click the end of the line, you can pull out a second line and move it to any angle you desire. Now the angle (A) number in the Info palette displays the angle between those two lines.

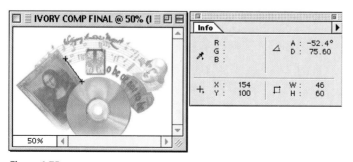

Figure 1.75
The Info palette indicates the angle of the Measurement tool.
(Courtesy of Derek Brigham)

NOTE

To straighten a crooked document, first use the Measurement tool to drag across the area you want to straighten; then choose **Image>Rotate>Arbitrary** and click the OK button. Photoshop calculates the exact angle needed to rotate the image.

Gradient Tool

At first, you might not be able to find any great reasons to get excited about using the Gradient tool. However, after we cover the Layers palette in Chapter 3, the Channels palette in Chapter 9, and compositing techniques in Chapter 11, you should find that the Gradient tool is not only worth getting excited about, it's downright indispensable. I want to make sure you know how to edit and apply gradients before we get to those chapters, so let's give it a shot.

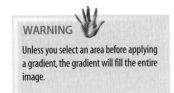

WARNING

Unless you select an area before applying a gradient, the gradient will fill the entire image.

First let's look at how to apply gradients to an image. To apply a gradient, simply click and drag across an image using the appropriate Gradient tool. You'll get different results depending on which type of gradient you're applying (see Figure 1.76).

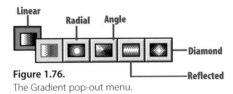

Figure 1.76.
The Gradient pop-out menu.

Here's an explanation of the gradient settings (see Figures 1.77 to 1.81):

Linear—Applies the gradient across the length of the line you make. If the line does not extend all the way across the image, Photoshop fills the rest of the image with solid colors—the colors you started and ended the gradient with.

Radial—Creates a gradient that starts in the center of a circle and radiates to the outer edge. Where you first click determines the center of the circle; where you let go of the mouse button determines the outer edge of the circle. All areas outside this circle will be filled with a solid color—the color that the gradient ends with.

Angle—Sweeps around a circle like a radar. Your first click determines the center of the sweep; then you drag to determine the starting angle.

Reflected—Creates an effect similar to applying a linear gradient twice, back to back.

Diamond—Similar to a radial gradient except it radiates out from the center of a square.

Figure 1.77
Linear gradient.

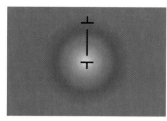

Figure 1.78
Radial gradient.

Figure 1.79
Angle gradient.

Figure 1.80
Reflected gradient

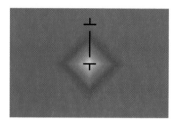

Figure 1.81
Diamond gradient.

Gradient Colors

You can change the color of the gradient by choosing one of the presets from the Gradient menu in the palette (see Figure 1.82). You can also reverse the direction of the gradient by turning on the Reverse check box. Then, if you have a gradient that usually starts with blue and ends with red, it would instead start with red and end in blue (see Figures 1.83 and 1.84). Some of the preset gradients will contain transparent areas. To apply one of those gradients and prevent areas from becoming transparent, turn off the Transparency check box.

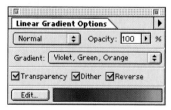

Figure 1.82
The Linear Gradient Options palette.

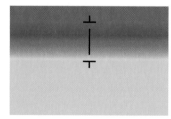

Figure 1.83
Reverse "off."

Figure 1.84
Reverse "on."

Dithered Gradients

When you print an image that contains a gradient, you'll sometimes notice banding across the gradient (also known as *stair-stepping* or *posterization*). To minimize this, be sure to turn on the Dither check box. This will add noise to the gradient in an attempt to prevent banding. You won't be able to see the effect of the Dither check box onscreen, it just makes the gradient look better when it's printed (see Figures 1.85 and 1.86).

Figure 1.85
Dither "off."

Figure 1.86
Dither "on."

Custom Gradients

The Gradient pop-up menu might not always contain the exact type of gradient you need. When that's the case, click the Edit button to create your own custom gradient. The dialog box that appears has so many options that it can sometimes feel overwhelming, but if you take it one step at a time, you shouldn't run into any problems (see Figure 1.87).

Figure 1.87
Editing the color of a gradient.

The scrolling list at the top of the dialog box shows you all the gradients that usually appear in the Gradient Options palette. Click any one of them, and you'll be able to pre-view what it looks like at the bottom of the dialog box. You can change the name, delete, duplicate, or add a new choice to the list by using the buttons on the right side of the dialog box. Once you have chosen the gradient you want to edit, you can modify it by changing the gradient bar that appears in the middle of the dialog box. To add additional colors (up to a maximum of 32), click just below any part of the bar. This adds a color swatch to the bar and changes the colors that appear in the gradient.

You have three choices of what to put in these swatches. You'll find these choices just below and to the left of the gradient bar. "F" stands for the foreground color and "B" is for your background color. The option on the left is for any other color. The "F" and "B" choices don't just grab your foreground and background colors at the time you create the gradient. Instead, they look at the foreground and background color when you *apply* the gradient. Therefore, each time you apply the gradient, you can get a different result by changing the foreground and background colors. When you use the leftmost choice, you'll need to click the color sample to the right of that area to choose a color.

After you have added a swatch of color to the gradient bar, you can reposition it by dragging it from left to right, or by changing the number in the Location area. I like to click the Location number and then use the Up Arrow and Down Arrow keys on my keyboard to slide the color swatch around. A little diamond shape, known as the *midpoint*, will appear between each of the color swatches; it indicates where the two colors will be mixed equally.

Transparent Gradients

You can also make areas of a gradient partially transparent by clicking the Transparency radio button in the Gradient Editor (see Figure 1.88). In this area, you cannot change the color of a gradient; you can only make the gradient more or less transparent. The shades of gray in this dialog box represent how transparent the gradient will become (for example, 10% gray = 10% opaque). You can add and move the swatches just like you do

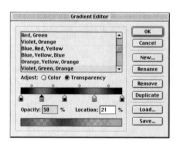

Figure 1.88
Editing the transparency of a gradient.

NOTE

You can remove a color swatch by simply dragging it away from the gradient bar.

when editing the colors of a gradient. The gradient shown at the bottom of the dialog box gives you a preview of the gradient you're creating. Transparent areas are represented by the checkerboard pattern.

Closing Thoughts

If you've made it through this entire chapter, you've just passed through Photoshop's welcoming committee of tools and palettes. By now your screen should look neat and tidy; you should be able to zoom in and out and scroll around your image with ease. You should also be on a nodding acquaintance with most of the tools and palettes— at least familiar enough to know which ones you want to get more friendly with later.

Don't panic if some of it still seems like a blur. It will all begin to take shape once you spend some more time with the program. After a few intense Photoshop sessions, the things you learned in this chapter will become second nature to you. But if any of the tools are *completely* new to you, you should probably play around with them before you move on to the next chapter.

But for now, let's get into the first installment of Ask Adobe and Ben's Techno-Babble Decoder Ring. And just for the fun of it, I'll throw in some keyboard commands that can really speed up your work.

Ask Adobe

Q: When zooming into an image, does 100% mean 100% of the print size? And if not, what does it mean?

A: Unlike layout programs, 100% means that you are seeing the pixels in the image in a one-to-one relationship to the pixels on the screen. Since this relationship does not depend on the image resolution, it bears no relationship to the print size. You can access a view at an estimate of print size (using the same mostly invalid assumption as most other programs use—that the monitor is at 72 ppi) by using the Print Size command in the View menu.

Q: When creating a brush, what was the idea behind the "spacing" setting?

A: The spacing setting allows you to control how tightly spaced the brush tip applications will be. More widely spaced brush tip applications will result in faster painting because there will be fewer applications; but the more widely spaced tip applications may also be more visible as distinct tips rather than as a continuous stroke.

Q: Why are RGB colors measured with the 0-255 numbering system and Grayscale and CMYK colors are measured with percentages?

A: They are both stored as 0-255 internally. Historically, RGB has been mapped to computer monitors and they generally use 8-bit values over which people want full control. Hence, the full 8-bit range of 0-255 is available. CMYK values are generally used for press work, and people in that industry generally speak in terms of ink percentages.

Ben's Techno-Babble Decoder Ring

Anti-aliased—Smoothing the edge of an otherwise hard-edged object by adding partially transparent pixels. These transparent pixels help to blend the edge of the object into the surrounding image, making it harder to see the edge of the pixels.

Posterization—The process of breaking up a smooth gradient into visible steps of solid color. Often called stair-stepping, or banding, when referring to a gradient.

Dither—Simulating color by using a pattern of two solid colors (example: adding a pattern of red dots to a yellow area to create orange). It also refers to adding a pattern of noise to a sharp transition to make the edge less noticeable.

RGB—A model for creating color using Red, Green, and Blue (RGB) light. You are able to see color because your eye contains light cones in its retina that are sensitive to red, green, and blue. Scanners capture information by measuring how much RGB light is reflected off the original image. Computer monitors display information by shining RGB light into your eyes. All the colors you have ever seen with your eyes have been made from a combination of red, green, and blue light. It really is an RGB world out there.

CMYK—A model for reproducing RGB colors using Cyan, Magenta, Yellow, and black (abbreviated "K" for Key) inks. Any time you print an image you will be using CMYK inks. Ideally, Cyan ink would absorb only Red light, Magenta ink would absorb only Green light, and Yellow ink would absorb only Blue light; and you could therefore reproduce an RGB image by absorbing the light falling on a sheet of paper instead of creating the light directly. But due to impurities in these inks, CMYK inks (also known as process color) cannot reproduce all the colors that can be created using RGB light.

HSB—A method of manipulating RGB or CMYK colors by separating the color into components of Hue, Saturation, and Brightness. Hue is the pure form of the color (Red is the pure form of pink, maroon, and candy-apple red). Saturation is the intensity or vibrancy of the color (pink is a not very saturated Red, candy-apple red is a very saturated Red). Brightness is how bright or dark a color appears (pink is a bright, just not vibrant, tint of Red, maroon is a dark shade of Red). So, when talking about the Hue of a color, you are not describing how bright and vibrant (saturated) the color appears. When talking about Saturation of a color, you do not reveal its basic color (Hue), or how bright or dark it appears (Brightness). When talking about the Brightness of a color, you are not describing the basic color (Hue) or how vibrant it appears (Saturation).

Lab—A scientific method of describing colors by separating them into three components called Lightness, A, and B. The Lightness component describes how bright or dark a color appears. The "A" component describes colors ranging from red to green. The "B" component describes colors ranging from blue to yellow. Lab color is the internal color model used in Photoshop for converting between different color modes (RGB to CMYK, etc.).

Keyboard Shortcuts

Zoom in	Command-+ (plus sign)
Zoom out	Command-- (minus sign)
Fit in window	Command-0
Temporarily use Zoom tool	Command-Spacebar
Show/Hide palettes	Tab
Toggle between screen modes	F
Temporarily use Hand tool	Spacebar
Show/Hide rulers	Command-R
Select previous brush	[
Select next brush	]
Select first brush	Shift-[
Select last brush	Shift-]
Hand tool	H
Paintbrush tool	B
Eraser tool	E
Airbrush tool	J
Pencil tool	N
Reset Foreground/Background Colors	D
Exchange Foreground/Background Colors	X

Courtesy of Don Barnett, www.donbarnett.com.

This image and the image on the first page of this chapter were created by using primarily the Brush tool in Photoshop. The Brush tool is my favorite tool in the tool palette because of its flexibility. Combined with a pressure-sensitive tablet, it is an excellent combination. I usually paint at about 30% opacity to build up a layered look and to lay in highlights and shadows. An opaque silhouette form can be created on a layer, then when the Preserve Transparency button is clicked, I can add all the transparent highlights and shadows I wish without disrupting the form. A perfectly even glaze can be achieved until you raise the pressure off the pen and tablet. (Be sure that pressure sensitive transparency is off). This method is very fast when you consider any traditional paint form of layering and glazing effects; even with acrylic paint and a hair dryer (like we used to do) the speed factor is increased and the surface quality can be just as luminous if not more.
–Don Barnett

Courtesy of Betty Bates, bettybates@hotmail.com.

Courtesy of Betty Bates, bettybates@hotmail.com.

Because I come from a back-ground of traditional print-making, I have found that my imagery translates well into digital media. My method is fairly simple. Using a Wacom tablet, I draw most of my images directly into the com-puter. I use the Lasso selec-tion tool to define a shape and the Airbrush tool to add layers of color. I usually paint with light transparent colors on a dark background.
–Betty Bates

2 Selection Primer

Courtesy of Jeff Schewe.

"I choose a block of marble and chop off whatever I don't need."
—François-Auguste Rodin, when asked how he managed to make his remarkable statues.

You've got to love the selection tools. I like to think of them as the chisels of Photoshop. With names such as Lasso, Magic Wand, Feather, and Transform, you get a sense that these aren't just everyday tools—they're the fine instruments of a digital sculptor. Selection tools can do so much more than just draw outlines: They can help you dig down into the guts of an image and perform wondrous transformations. What's more, you don't have to be a wizard to know how to use them. Selection tools take a little getting used to, but once you're familiar with them, they can help you tremendously.

Whatever you do, don't skip this chapter, because the selection tools are central to your success in Photoshop. They allow you to isolate areas of your image and define precisely where a filter, painting tool, or adjustment will change the image. Also, a selection is not specific to a particular layer (we'll talk about layers in Chapter 3, "Layer Primer"). Instead, it's attached to the entire document. That means you can freely switch among the different layers without losing a selection. After you've mastered the basics, you'll be ready to jump into more advanced selections in Chapter 9, "Channels."

What Is a Selection?

Before you can edit an image, you must first *select* the area with which you want to work. People who paint cars for a living make "selections" very much like the ones used in Photoshop. If you've ever seen a car being painted, you know that painters carefully place masking tape and paper over the areas they don't want to paint (such as the windows, tires, door handles, and so on). That way, they can freely spray paint the entire car knowing that the taped areas are protected from "overspray." At its most basic level, a selection in Photoshop works much the same way. Actually, it works much better, because with one selection, you have a choice—you can paint the car and leave the masked areas untouched, or you can paint the masked areas and leave the car untouched.

When you select an area by using one of Photoshop's selection tools (Marquee, Lasso, Magic Wand, and so on), the border of the selection looks a lot like marching ants. Once you've made a selection, you can move, copy, paint, or apply numerous special effects to the selected area (see Figures 2.1 and 2.2).

Figure 2.1
When no selection is present, you can edit the entire image. (© 1998 PhotoDisc)

Figure 2.2
When a selection is present, you can only change the selected area.

There are two types of selections in Photoshop: a normal selection and a feathered selection (see Figures 2.3 and 2.4). A *normal selection* has a hard edge. That is, when you paint or apply a filter to an image, you can easily see where the effect stops and starts. On the other hand, *feathered selections* slowly fade out at their edges. This allows filters to seamlessly blend into an image without producing noticeable edges. An accurate selection makes all the difference when you're enhancing an image in Photoshop. To see just how important it can be, take a look at Figures 2.5 to 2.7.

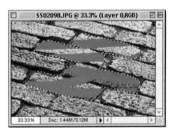

Figure 2.3
Normal selections have hard edges. (© 1998 PhotoDisc)

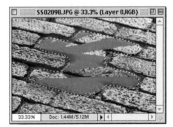

Figure 2.4
Feathered selections have soft edges.

Figure 2.5
The original image. (© 1998 PhotoDisc)

Figure 2.6
An unprofessional selection.

Figure 2.7
A professional selection.

Basic Selection Tools

The Marquee, Lasso, Magic Wand, and Type Mask tools are the essential ingredients in your selection toolkit, and they're the ones you'll be using the most in your everyday work. It's a good indication that you've come to master these tools when you find yourself trying to use them in other software programs where they don't exist. When using other programs, I sometimes find myself muttering, "Why can't I just lasso this thing?"

The Marquee tool is the most basic of all the selection tools, and we'll cover it first. However, don't let this tool's simplicity fool you—it can perform a surprising number of tasks, so there's quite a bit to learn about it. If you hold your mouse button down while your cursor is over the Marquee tool icon, you'll get a variety of choices in a pop-up menu. We'll cover these choices one at a time, and I'll throw in some tricks along the way.

Rectangular Marquee Tool

The Rectangular Marquee tool is the first choice listed in the Marquee pop-up menu. It can select only rectangular shapes. With it, you can create a rectangle by clicking and dragging across your document. The first click creates one corner, and the area where you release the mouse button creates the opposite corner (see Figure 2.8). To start in the center and drag to an outer edge (instead of going corner to corner), press Option after you have started to drag (see Figure 2.9). If you want to create a square, just hold down the Shift key after you start to drag. You can even combine the Option and Shift keys to create a square selection by dragging from the center to an outer edge.

WARNING

If you press any combination of the Option and Shift keys before you begin a selection, they might not perform as you expect, because these keys are also used to manipulate existing selections.

If you hold down the Spacebar and drag around your screen while you're making a selection, you'll move the selection instead of changing its shape. This can be a real lifesaver. If you botch up the start of a selection, this enables you to reposition it without having to start over with a new selection. After you have moved the selection into the correct position, just let go of the Spacebar to continue editing the selection. After you've finished making the selection, you no longer need to hold the Spacebar to move it. To move a selection after it's created, select the Marquee tool and then click and drag from within the selection outline. (See Figures 2.10 and 2.11).

NOTE

To discard the areas that appear outside the selection border, use the Rectangular Marquee tool and then choose **Image>Crop**.

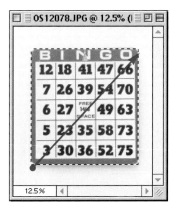

Figure 2.8
A corner-to-corner selection. (© 1998 PhotoDisc)

Figure 2.9
A center-to-edge selection.

Figure 2.10
Original selection is misaligned. (© 1998 PhotoSpin)

Figure 2.11
Use the Spacebar to reposition a selection while creating it.

Figure 2.12
The Elliptical Marquee tool in action (from center to edge). (©1998 PhotoDisc)

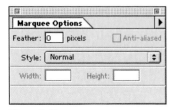

Figure 2.13
The Marquee Options palette.

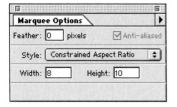

Figure 2.14
The Constrained Aspect Ratio option.

Elliptical Marquee Tool

The second choice under the Marquee pop-up menu is the Elliptical Marquee tool. This tool works in the same way as the rectangular version, except it creates an ellipsis (see Figure 2.12). The only problem is that you can't just grab an edge of the shape to resize it. Instead, you have to work from the "corner" of the ellipse. (I know, I know, an ellipse doesn't really have a corner. What were they thinking when they came up with this idea?) Actually, I find it much easier to choose **View>Show Rulers** and then drag out a few guides (you can get them by dragging from the rulers) and let the "corners" snap to them.

Now let's look at the choices in the Marquee Options palette (see Figure 2.13). Double-click the Marquee tool (or just press Return when using it) to open the Marquee Options palette. The following list describes the options you'll find in this palette:

Feather—Allows you to fade out the edge between selected and unselected areas. I usually leave this option turned off, because I don't often have the Marquee Options palette open, and I might forget that a feather setting had been typed in previously. This one little setting might mess up an otherwise great selection. Instead, I find it much easier to make a selection and then press Option-Command-D (or choose **Select>Feather**).

Anti-Aliased—This check box determines whether the pixel on the edge of a selection will blend with the image surrounding it. This provides nice, smooth transitions, and it helps prevent areas from looking jagged (see Figures 1.62 and 1.63 in the preceding chapter for examples). I recommend that you leave this check box on at all times, unless, of course, you have a great need for jaggies (sometimes they're preferred for multimedia applications).

Style menu— Controls the shape and size of the next selection made. When the Style pop-up menu is set to Normal, your selections are not restricted in size or shape (other than they have to be rectangles or ellipses). After changing this menu to Constrained Aspect Ratio, you'll be confronted with Width and Height settings (see Figure 2.14). By changing the numbers in these areas, you can constrain the shape of the next selection to the ratio between the Width and Height settings. For example, if you change Width to 2 and leave Height at 1, your selections will always be twice as wide as they are tall. This can be useful when you need to find out how much of an image needs to be cropped when printing it as an 8×10, for example.

However, I use the Fixed Size option much more often than the Constrained Aspect Ratio option. Fixed Size lets you type in an exact width and height; that way, anytime you click using either the Rectangular or Elliptical Marquee tool, you'll get a selection exactly that size. What's more, if you didn't get it in exactly the right spot, you can just drag the selection around the screen before releasing the mouse button. For instance, Macintosh desktop icons are always 32 pixels wide and 32 pixels tall, so I use these numbers when selecting something I want to use as an icon. The only problem with the Fixed Size option is that the Width and Height settings are always measured in pixels (you don't have the option for inches, picas, etc.). In the next section, I'll show you how to quickly convert from the measurement system you want to use to pixels (the measurement system required in this palette).

Converting Units of Measurement

To convert between pixels and another measurement system, first choose **File>New** (as if you were going to create a new document). The New dialog box will appear (see Figure 2.15). The resolution setting must be the same as the one in the document in which you're going to use the selection. You can do this quickly by choosing the name of the document from the Window menu and this will change the Width, Height, and Resolution settings to match the document you choose. Next, change the Width and Height pop-up menus to the measurement system you desire; then enter the Width and Height numbers you want. Finally, click in the Document Name area (just so Photoshop knows you're done changing the Width and Height settings) and then change the Width and Height pop-up menus back to pixels. The numbers should change, indicating exactly how many pixels will be needed to produce the width and height you originally typed in. Now you can click Cancel and type these numbers into the Marquee Options palette (see Figure 2.16). This technique might seem lengthy, but after a few tries, you'll find that it really is fast and easy.

Figure 2.15
The New dialog box.

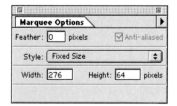

Figure 2.16
The Fixed Size options.

Single Row and Single Column Marquee Tools

The third and fourth choices under the Marquee tool pop-up menu are the Single Row and Single Column Marquee tools. These tools are limited in that they only select a one-pixel-wide row or one-pixel-tall column. To be honest, I hardly ever use them (maybe once or twice a year). However, they have gotten me out of few tight spots, such as when I had to clean up a few stray pixels from in between palettes when taking screen shots for this book.

Crop Tool

The fifth and final tool available under the Marquee tool pop-up menu is the Crop tool. Using this tool, you can crop an image as well as resize and rotate it at the same time. (See Figures 2.17 and 2.18)

What's more, if you double-click this tool, you get a different set of options than what's available with the normal Marquee tools (see Figure 2.19).

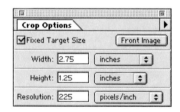

Figure 2.17
The original image. (© 1998 PhotoDisc)

Figure 2.18
The original image cropped and rotated.

Figure 2.19
The Crop Options palette.

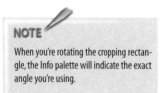

NOTE

When you're rotating the cropping rectangle, the Info palette will indicate the exact angle you're using.

When you click and drag over an image with the Crop tool selected, a dashed rectangle appears (see Figure 2.20). Anything beyond the edge of the rectangle is discarded when the image is cropped. You can drag any one of the hollow squares on the edge of the rectangle to change its size. Also, you can hold down Shift while dragging a corner to constrain the rectangle's shape.

Figure 2.20
The cropping rectangle. (© 1998 PhotoDisc)

NOTE
If you don't want to resize the image when you crop it, be sure the Fixed Target Size check box is turned off. More on this option in just a bit.

NOTE
If the cropping rectangle extends beyond the edge of your screen, the extended areas will be filled with the current foreground color.

If you need to rotate the image, you can move your cursor just beyond one of the corner points and drag (look for an icon that looks like a curve with arrows on each end). You can also drag the crosshair in the center of the rectangle to change the point from which the rectangle will be rotated. To complete the cropping, press Return (or double-click within the cropping rectangle). Press Esc to cancel.

Occasionally, you'll need to crop and resize an image at the same time. Maybe you need three images to be the exact same size, or perhaps you need your image to be a specific width. You can do this by turning on the Fixed Target Size check box (this refers to the size you're shooting for). After turning on the check box, you can specify the exact Width, Height, and Resolution settings you desire. By typing in both a Width and a Height setting, you constrain the shape of the rectangle that you draw. I occasionally leave one of these values empty so that I can still create any rectangle shape.

NOTE
If you want to match the size of another open document, click that document to make it active for editing and then click the Front Image button in the Crop Options palette. This will enter the Width, Height, and Resolution settings of that document into the palette. Now you can use the Crop tool on any open document and the result will match the size of the original document.

Lasso Tool

The Lasso tool is the most versatile of the basic selection tools. By holding down the mouse button, you can use the Lasso to trace around the edge of an irregularly shaped object (see Figure 2.21). When you release the button, the area will be selected. Be sure to create a closed shape by finishing the selection exactly where you started it; otherwise, Photoshop will complete the selection for you by adding a straight line between the beginning and end of the selection.

Figure 2.21
The Lasso tool in action. (© 1998 PhotoSpin)

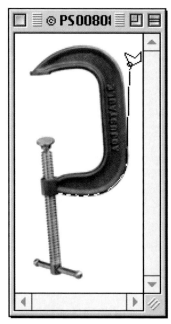

Figure 2.22
Using the Option key while clicking to create straight-line segments. (© 1998 PhotoSpin)

Sometimes you'll need to add a few straight segments in the middle of a freeform shape. You can do this by holding down the Option key and then releasing the mouse button (but not the Option key). Now, each time you click your mouse, Photoshop will connect the clicks with straight lines (see Figure 2.22). To go back to creating a freeform shape, just start dragging and then release the Option key.

Polygonal Lasso Tool

You can use the Polygonal Lasso tool whenever you need to make a selection that consists mainly of straight lines. Using this tool, you just click multiple areas of the image, and Photoshop connects the dots for you (see Figure 2.23). If you need to create a freeform selection, hold down the Option key and drag. To finish a selection, you can either click where the selection began or double-click when you add the final point.

NOTE

You can scroll around your screen when you're in the middle of a selection by holding down the Spacebar. As long as this key is held down, the Hand tool is used. This can be a great help when you're really zoomed in on your image and the pixels are as big as ice cubes.

Figure 2.23
The Polygonal Lasso tool in action. (© 1998 PhotoSpin)

Magnetic Lasso Tool

Whereas the Lasso and Polygonal Lasso tools are relatively straightforward, the Magnetic Lasso tool has a bunch of neat tricks up its sleeve. This tool can be a huge timesaver in that it allows you to trace around the edge of an object without having to be overly precise. You don't have to break a sweat making all of those tiny, painstaking movements with your mouse. Instead, you can make big sloppy selections, and the Magnetic Lasso will do the fine-tuning for you. What's more, if it doesn't do a great job in certain areas, you can hold down the Option key to use the

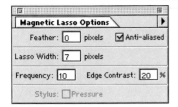

Figure 2.24
The Magnetic Lasso Options palette.

Freeform Lasso tool. However, before using the Magnetic Lasso tool, you'll want to double-click its icon and change the settings in the Magnetic Lasso Options palette (see Figure 2.24). Let's take a look at these settings:

Feather and Anti-Aliased—These options work just as they would with any selection or painting tool.

Lasso Width— Determines how far away from your cursor Photoshop will look for the edge of an object (just like a paint-brush, it uses a circular area surrounding your cursor). You can see this area by pressing the Caps Lock key or by choosing **File>Preferences>Displays & Cursors** and setting the Other Tools option to Precise. You can quickly change the Lasso Width setting by typing [to increase the setting in increments of 1 or] to decrease the setting. If you're like me and really like keyboard commands, you can also press Shift-[to change this setting to the lowest possible value (1) or Shift-] for the highest possible value (40). You can even use these keyboard commands while you're dragging around the edge of an image.

Frequency— Determines how often Photoshop will add anchor points (higher settings add more points). The complexity of the object you're tracing usually determines the proper Frequency setting; that is, as objects get more complex, you should use a higher setting (see Figures 2.25 and 2.26).

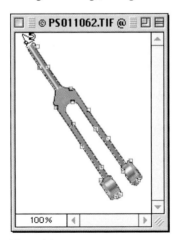

Figure 2.25
A Frequency setting of 10. (© 1998 PhotoSpin)

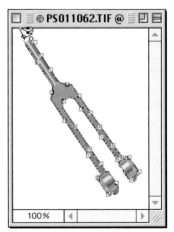

Figure 2.26
A Frequency setting of 50.

Edge Contrast—I think this setting is the most important of the bunch. It determines how much contrast there must be between the object and the background in order for Photoshop to select the object. If the object you're attempting to select has well-defined edges, you should use a high setting (see Figure 2.27). You can also use a large Lasso tool width. On the other hand, if the edges are not well defined, you should use a low setting and try to be very precise when dragging (see Figure 2.28).

Figure 2.27
High edge contrast (20%). (© 1998 PhotoDisc)

If the Magnetic Lasso tool is not behaving itself, you can temporarily switch to the freeform Lasso tool by holding down the Option key as you drag. You can also periodically click to manually add anchor points to the selection edge. If you want to use the Polygonal Lasso tool, hold down the Option key and click in multiple areas of the image (instead of dragging). If you don't like the shape of the selection, you can press the Delete key to remove the last anchor point. Pressing Delete multiple times deletes multiple points. Once you have a satisfactory shape, finish the selection by pressing the Return key or double-clicking. Remember, if you don't create a closed shape, Photoshop will finish it for you with a straight-line segment.

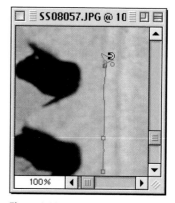

Figure 2.28
Low edge contrast (7%). (© 1998 PhotoDisc)

If you really get used to the features available with the Magnetic Lasso tool, you'll be able to create most of your basic selections with just this tool alone. This will take some time, and you must supplement its use by holding down the Option key to access the Lasso and Polygonal Lasso tools for areas the tool has trouble selecting.

Magic Wand Tool

The Magic Wand tool is great for selecting solid (or almost solid) colored areas, because it selects areas based on color—or shades of gray in grayscale mode—as shown in Figure 2.29. This is helpful when you want to change the color of an area or remove a simple background.

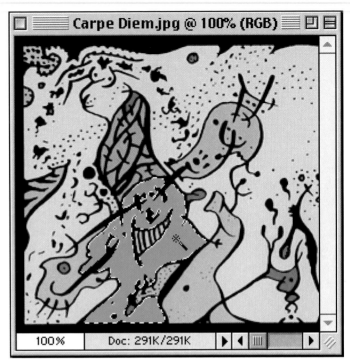

Figure 2.29
A simple click of the Magic Wand tool can select a solid area of color with ease.
(Courtesy of Nik Willmore)

Figure 2.30
Tolerance: 10.

Figure 2.31
Tolerance: 20.

Figure 2.32
Tolerance: 30.

You'll probably find it easier to understand how this works if you think about grayscale images, because they're less complex than color images. Grayscale images can contain up to 256 shades of gray. When you click one of these shades with the Magic Wand tool, it will select any shades that are within the tolerance specified in the Options palette. For instance, if you click shade 128 (Photoshop numbers the shades from 0 to 255) and the tolerance is set to 10, you'll get a selection of shades that are 10 shades darker and 10 shades brighter than the one you clicked (see Figures 2.30 to 2.32). The only shades that will be selected are those within an area that touches the spot you clicked—Photoshop cannot jump across areas that are not within the tolerance.

Because Photoshop uses the 0 to 255 numbering system, you might need a conversion table to figure out how many shades of gray will be selected using different tolerance settings. Otherwise, you can make this conversion by multiplying any percentage by 2.55 (1% in the 0 to 255 numbering system). Remember, the Magic Wand tool will select twice as much as the number you type in.

Color images are a little more complex. They're made from three components: red, green and blue (that is, when you're working in RGB mode). The Magic Wand tool will analyze all the components (known as channels) in your file to determine which areas to select. For example, if you click a color made up of the components 32 red, 120 green, 212 blue (these numbers can be found in the Info palette) and use a tolerance setting of 10, Photoshop will look for colors between 22 and 42 in the red channel, 110 and 130 in the green channel, and 202 and 222 in the blue channel. The only colors that will be selected are ones that fall between all three ranges. Doesn't that sound complicated? Well, I have to confess, I don't usually think about the numbers, because they're something of a pain. Instead, I just experiment with the setting until I get a good result. Now, doesn't that sound a lot easier than dealing with all those numbers? If you really want to understand all about the color channels, take a look at Chapter 9, "Channels."

Type Mask Tool

The Type Mask tool allows you to create a selection in the shape of text. We'll cover the options of this tool in Chapter 14, "Type and Background Effects." The only difference between the Type Mask tool and the normal Text tool is that the Type Mask tool does not fill in the shape of the text (see Figure 2.33).

Refining a Selection

Selecting complex objects in Photoshop usually requires using multiple selection tools. In order to combine these selection tools, you'll need to learn about a few keyboard commands that will allow you to add, subtract, or intersect a selection.

Percentage Conversions

Percentage	Tolerance Setting
0	0
10	26
20	51
30	77
40	102
50	128
60	153
70	179
80	204
90	230
100	255

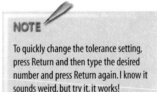

NOTE

To quickly change the tolerance setting, press Return and then type the desired number and press Return again. I know it sounds weird, but try it, it works!

Figure 2.33
Result of using the Type Mask tool.
(© 1998 PhotoDisc)

Adding to a Selection

To add to an existing selection, hold down the Shift key when you start making the new selection. You must press the key as you start the selection; then you can release it as soon as you've clicked the mouse button (see Figures 2.34 to 2.36). If you press it too late, the original selection will be lost. If, for example, you would like to select multiple round objects, you can use the Elliptical Marquee tool multiple times while holding down the Shift key.

Figure 2.34
The original selection. (© 1998 PhotoDisc)

Figure 2.35
Adding to the selection.

Figure 2.36
The end result.

Removing Part of a Selection

To remove areas from an existing selection, hold down the Option key when you begin making the selection. If, for example, you want to create a half circle, you could start with an Elliptical Marquee tool selection and then switch over to the Rectangular Marquee tool and drag while holding down the Option key to remove half of the circle (see Figures 2.37 to 2.39).

Figure 2.37
The original selection. (© 1998 PhotoDisc)

Figure 2.38
Subtracting a second selection.

Figure 2.39
The end result.

Clicking while holding down the Option key is particularly helpful when you're using the Magic Wand tool to remove areas of a selection (see Figures 2.40 and 2.41). With each click of the Magic Wand tool, you can use a different Tolerance setting.

Intersecting a Selection

If you hold down both the Shift and Option keys when editing an existing selection, you end up with the areas where the two selections overlap. Sometimes I use the Magic Wand tool to select the background of an image and then choose **Select>Inverse** to get the object (or objects) of the selected image (see Figure 2.42). However, if there are multiple objects in the image, I often have to restrict the selection to a specific area by dragging with the Lasso tool while holding down the Shift and Option keys (see Figures 2.43 and 2.44).

Figure 2.40
The original selection.

Figure 2.41
Option-clicking with the Magic Wand tool.

Figure 2.42
Applying the Magic Wand tool to the background and then choosing **Select>Inverse**. (© 1998 PhotoSpin)

Figure 2.43
Dragging with Lasso tool while holding down the Shift and Option keys.

Figure 2.44
The end result.

The Select Menu

The Select menu offers you many choices that supplement the basic selection tools. Learning these features is well worth your time, because they'll help you save heaps of it in your everyday work. We'll look at these features in the same order they appear in the menu.

Select All

Select>All selects the entire document. This can be useful when you need to trim off any "big data," or the part of an image that extends beyond the edge of the document (see Figure 2.45). You can crop big data by choosing **Select>All** and then **Image>Crop** (see Figure 2.46). Also, if you need to copy an entire image, you'll need to select everything, because without a selection, the Copy command will be grayed out.

Figure 2.46
Layers repositioned after the image has been cropped.

Figure 2.45
An example of "big data" (these areas are not usually visible). (Original image © 1998 PhotoDisc)

Deselect/Reselect

If you're done using a selection and would like to work on the entire image, choose **Select>Deselect**. If you don't have a selection, you can work on the entire image. Now if you need to use the last active selection (and there isn't a selection on your screen), you can choose **Select>Reselect**. This is great when you need to use the same selection over and over again. I use these two commands all the time. However, I usually opt for the keyboard commands Command-D (for Deselect) and Shift-Command-D (for Reselect).

Inverse

As you might expect, the Inverse command selects the exact opposite of what you originally selected. If, for example, you have the background of an image selected, after choosing **Select>Inverse**, you'll have the object of the image selected instead (see Figures 2.47 and 2.48). I use this command constantly, especially when using the Magic Wand tool. Sometimes it's just easier to select the areas that you don't want and then choose **Select>Inverse** to select what you really want to isolate. Sound backwards? It is, but it works great.

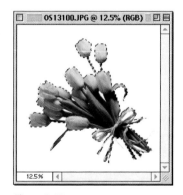

Figure 2.47
A Magic Wand tool selection. (© 1998 PhotoDisc)

Figure 2.48
The selection after the **Select>Inverse** command is used.

Color Range

You can think of the **Select>Color Range** command as the Magic Wand tool on steroids. With Color Range, you can click multiple areas and then change the Fuzziness setting (how's that for a technical term?) to increase or reduce the range of colors that will be selected (see Figure 2.49 and 2.50).

Figure 2.49
The original figure. (© 1998 PhotoDisc)

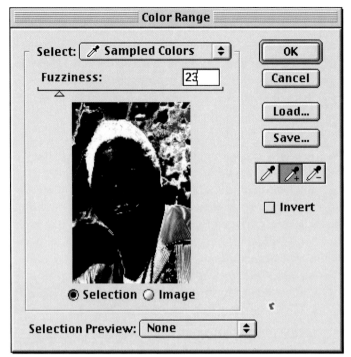

Figure 2.50
The same figure in the Color Range dialog box.

As you click and play with the Fuzziness control, you'll see a preview of the selection in the middle of the Color Range dialog box. Areas that appear white are the areas that will be selected. The Selection and Image radio buttons allow you to switch between the selection preview and the main image. (I never actually use these two controls because I find it easier to switch to the image view at any time by holding down the Command key.) You can also see a preview of the selection within the main image window by changing the Selection Preview pop-up menu to Grayscale, Black or White Matte, or Quick Mask (see Figures 2.51 to 20.53).

The Eyedropper tool on the right side of the dialog box allows you to add and subtract colors from the selection. Using the Eyedropper with the plus symbol next to it is really helpful, because it allows you to click the image multiple times. With each click, you tell Photoshop which colors you want it to search for. A low Fuzziness setting with many clicks usually produces the best results (see Figures 2.54 and 2.55).

Figure 2.51
Choosing Grayscale will display the same preview that appears in the Color Range dialog box.

Figure 2.52
Choosing Black Matte or White Matte will fill the unselected areas with black or white.

Figure 2.53
Choosing Quick Mask places these settings in the Quick Mask dialog box.

The selections you get from the Color Range command are not ordinary selections in that they usually contain areas that are not completely selected. For instance, if you're trying to select the red areas in an image and there happens be a flesh tone in the same image, the flesh will most likely become partially selected. If you then adjust the image, the red will be completely adjusted and the flesh tones will only shift a little bit.

If a selection is already present when you choose **Select>Color Range**, the command will only analyze the colors within the selected area. This means you can run the command multiple times to isolate smaller and smaller areas. If you want to have the Color Range command add to the current selection, be sure to hold down the Shift key when choosing **Select>Color Range**.

Feather

Unlike the Feather option in the selection tools, this version only affects the selection that's currently active and has no effect on future selections. You can't reduce the amount of feathering with this command. Therefore, if you apply it once with a setting of 10 and then try it again

Figure 2.54
An example of a single click with a high Fuzziness setting.

Figure 2.55
An example of five clicks with a low Fuzziness setting.

on the same selection using a setting of 5, it will simply increase the amount again. It's just like blurring an image, each time you blur the image, it becomes more and more blurry.

I prefer using this command instead of entering Feather settings directly into the Tool Options palette. If you enter these values directly, you might not remember the setting is turned on days later when you have to spend hours trying to select an intricate object. By leaving the tools set at 0, you can quickly press Option-Command-D (to bring up the Feather dialog box) and enter a number to feather the selection. Because this only affects the current selection, it can't mess up any future ones. (See Figures 2.56 and 2.57.)

Figure 2.56
A watch pasted with a normal selection.
(© 1998 PhotoDisc)

Figure 2.57
A watch pasted with a feathered selection.

Modify

The features in this menu have helped get me out of many sticky situations. At first glance, it might not be obvious why you would ever use these features, but I guarantee you that they'll come in very handy as you continue through the book. Here's a list of the commands found under the **Select>Modify** menu as well as descriptions of what they do:

Border—Selects a border of pixels centered on the current selection. If you use a setting of 10, the selection will be five pixels inside the selection and five pixels outside the selection. You can use this to remove pesky halos that appear when you copy an object from a light background and paste it onto a darker background. (See Figures 2.58 and 2.59)

Smooth—Attempts to round off any sharp corners in a selection (see Figure 2.60). This can be especially useful when you want to create a rounded-corner rectangle. This can also produce an interesting effect after you've used the Type Mask tool (see Figures 2.61 and 2.62).

Figure 2.58
The original selection. (© 1998 PhotoDisc)

Figure 2.59
A 10-pixel border.

Figure 2.60
Smooth 16 pixels.

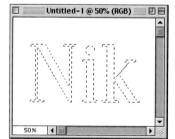

Figure 2.61
The original selection.

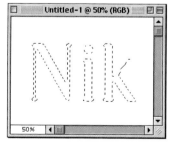

Figure 2.62
After applying a Smooth setting of 6.

Expand—Enlarges the current selection while attempting to maintain its shape (see Figure 2.63). This command works well with smooth, freeform selections, but it's not my first choice for straight-edged selections because it usually slices off the corners.

Contract—Reduces the size of the current selection while attempting to maintain its shape (see Figure 2.64). The highest setting available is 16. If you need to use a higher setting, just use the command twice.

Figure 2.63
Expand 12 pixels.

Figure 2.64
Contract 12 pixels.

Grow

The **Select>Grow** command will search for colors that are similar to an area that has already been selected (see Figures 2.65 and 2.66). In effect, it will *spread* your selection in every direction, but only into areas that are similar in color. It cannot jump across areas that are not similar to the ones selected. The Grow command uses the Tolerance setting that's specified in the Magic Wand Options palette to determine the range of colors it will look for.

Similar

The **Select>Similar** command works just like the Grow command except that it looks over the entire document for similar colors (see Figures 2.67 and 2.68). Unlike, the Grow command, the colors Similar selects do not have to touch the previous selection. This can be very useful when you've selected one object out of a group of the same colored objects. For example, if you have a herd of gray elephants standing in front of a lush green jungle, you can select the first elephant and then use **Select>Similar** to get the rest of the herd (provided, of course, that they're all a similar shade of gray). The same works for a field of flowers, and so on.

Figure 2.65
The original selection. (© 1998 PhotoSpin)

Figure 2.66
The selection after **Select>Grow** is used.

Figure 2.67
The original selection.

Transform Selection

After making a selection, you can scale, rotate, or distort it by choosing **Select>Transform Selection**. This command places handles around the image. By pulling on the handles and using a series of keyboard commands, you can distort the selection as much as you like. Let's take a look at the neat stuff you can do with Transform Selection:

Figure 2.68
The selection after **Select>Similar** is used.

Scale—You can scale a selection by pulling on any of the handles. Pulling on a corner handle will change both the width and height at the same time. Hold the Shift key to retain the proportions of the original selection. Pulling on the side handles will change the width of the selection without modifying its height. This can be a great help when working with elliptical selections, because it lets you pull on the edges of the selection instead of its so-called "corners" (see Figures 2.69 to 2.71).

Rotate—If you move your cursor a little bit beyond one of the corner points, the cursor should change into an arc with arrows on each end. This indicates that you can rotate the image by dragging from this location. You can control where the center point of the rotation will be by moving the crosshair that appears in the center of the selection. (See Figures 2.72 to 2.74.)

Figure 2.69
The original selection. (© 1998 PhotoSpin)

Figure 2.70
After choosing **Select>Transform** to scale the selection.

Figure 2.71
The end result.

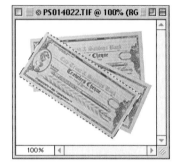

Figure 2.72
The original selection. (© 1998 PhotoSpin)

Figure 2.73
Rotating and scaling the selection.

Figure 2.74
The end result.

Distort— To distort the shape of the selection, hold down the Command key then drag one of the corner points. Using this technique, you can pull each corner independently. (See Figures 2.75 to 2.77.)

Also, you can distort a selection so that it resembles the shape of a road vanishing into the distance. You do this by dragging one of the corners while holding down the Shift-Command-Option keys. (See Figures 2.78 to 2.80.)

To move two diagonal corners at the same time, hold down Command-Option while dragging one of the corner handles. (See Figures 2.81 and 2.82.)

You can finalize your distortions by pressing Return (or by double-clicking inside the selection). You cancel them by pressing Esc.

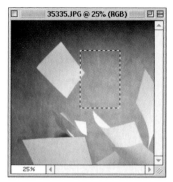

Figure 2.75
The original selection. (© 1998 PhotoDisc)

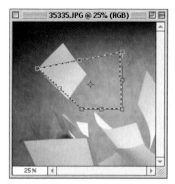

Figure 2.76
Dragging a corner while holding down the Command key.

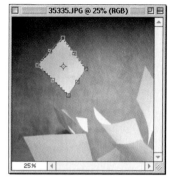

Figure 2.77
The selection after all four corners have been dragged.

Figure 2.78
The original selection. (© 1998 PhotoDisc)

Figure 2.79
Dragging a corner while holding down the Shift-Command-Option keys.

Figure 2.80
The end result.

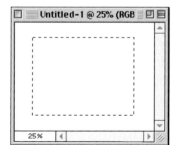

Figure 2.81
The original selection.

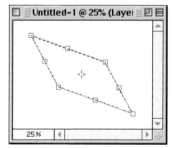

Figure 2.82
Dragging a corner handle while holding down the Command-Option keys.

NOTE

If you forget the keyboard commands that are required to distort a selection, you can instead choose **Select>Transform Selection** and then Control-click to choose the type of distortion you want to perform (see Figure 2.83).

Load Selection and Save Selection

If you've spent hours perfecting a selection and think you might need to use it again in the future, you can apply the **Select>Save Selection** command (see Figure 2.84). This stores the selection as an *alpha channel* (you can think of channels as *stored selections*). Don't worry, you don't need to know anything about channels to use these commands—all you have to do is supply a name for the selection. If you want to find out more about channels, you can check out Chapter 9.

When you want to retrieve the saved selection, choose **Select>Load Selection** and pick the name of the selection from the Channel pop-up menu (see Figure 2.85). This gives you the exact same selection you had when you chose **Select>Save Selection**. When you use this command, it's just like re-creating the selection with the original selection tool you used.

These saved selections remain in your document until you manually remove them using the Channels palette (see Chapter 9 to find out how to delete a channel). If you want to save these selections within your document, be sure to save the file using the Photoshop or TIFF file formats.

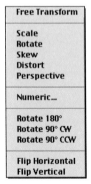

Figure 2.83
The menu that appears as a result of Control-clicking while you're transforming a selection.

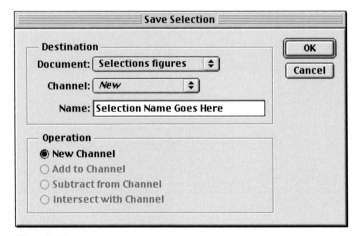

Figure 2.84
The Save Selection dialog box.

Load Selection

Source

Document: Selections figures ▲▼

Channel: Selection Name Goes Here ▲▼

☐ Invert

OK

Cancel

Operation

⦿ New Selection
◯ Add to Selection
◯ Subtract from Selection
◯ Intersect with Selection

Figure 2.85
The Load Selection dialog box.

Closing Thoughts

After a few practice rounds with the various tools we covered in this chapter, you should be selecting like a pro. We'll go over more advanced methods of creating selections in Chapter 9, "Channels." But until then, it really is worth your while to build up your selection skills because you will be using them every day in Photoshop. And now it's time for another dose of Ask Adobe and Ben's Techno-Babble Decoder Ring.

Ask Adobe

Q: What inspired the Magnetic Lasso tool?

A: Cf. Eric N. Mortensen and William A. Barrett (Brigham Young University), "Intelligent Scissors for Image Composition," SIGGRAPH 1995 Conference Proceedings. Adobe has made a large number of alterations and improvements to this technology since then.

Q: How do selections and layers relate? Is a selection attached to the layer or the document itself?

A: A selection is independent of any layers. Think of it as cutting through the entire layer stack. Hence, the target for any changes is determined by the combination of the selection, the target layer, and the target channels.

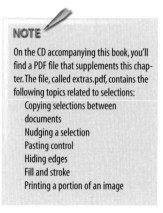

NOTE

On the CD accompanying this book, you'll find a PDF file that supplements this chapter. The file, called extras.pdf, contains the following topics related to selections:

Copying selections between documents
Nudging a selection
Pasting control
Hiding edges
Fill and stroke
Printing a portion of an image

Ben's Techno-Babble Decoder Ring

Feather—The process of converting a hard-edged selection into one that blends into the underlying image as you move closer to its edge.

Marching Ants—Term used to describe the edge of a selection. Used because the edges appear as very small moving specks (similar to ants).

Marquee—Like the rectangular marquees (signs) used at movie theaters to display the movies that are currently showing. In Photoshop, the Marquee tool is used to create rectangular (or elliptical) selections, and the resulting marching ants even resemble the flashing lights that used to be found surrounding movie marquees.

Big Data—Any area of a layer that extends outside of the physical dimensions of the document.

Crop—The process of reducing the dimensions of an image by removing unneeded space from the edge of the document. Also used to remove Big Data.

Keyboard Shortcuts

Select All	Command-A
Select None	Command-N
Reselect	Command-Shift-D
Select Inverse	Command-Shift-I
Feather	Option-Command-D
Marquee Tool	M
Lasso Tool	L
Fill Selection	Shift-Delete
Magic Wand Tool	W
Fill with Foreground	Option-Delete
Fill with Background	Command-Delete

Courtesy of Louis Fishauf, www.magic.ca/~fishauf/.

Courtesy of Louis Fishauf, www.magic.ca/~fishauf/.

3 Layer Primer

The first rule to tinkering is to save all the parts.
—Paul Erlich

Courtesy of Gordon Studer.

Our capacity to take things for granted seems to have no bounds. How often do you sit back and think, "Wow, life has really changed since the days when Smith Corona ruled and an Apple was just something you ate for lunch"? Probably not that much. However, if you really think about it, you'll realize that colossal changes have taken place. We attained a unique kind of digital freedom when we evolved from the primordial ooze of manual typewriters, stat cameras, and typesetters. For graphic artists, this change has been nothing short of revolutionary.

In its own way, Photoshop's introduction of the Layers palette has had an equally profound impact on the graphic arts community. Before the Layers palette, we were forced to be very precise and final in our thoughts, because having to redo the work was incredibly time consuming. The Layers palette released us from the shackles of single-layer images and gave us the ability to really let loose and explore our creative ideas.

How Do Layers Work?

At first glance, layers might seem complex, but the idea behind them is rather simple. You isolate different parts of your image onto independent layers (see Figure 3.1). These layers act as if they were separate documents stacked one on top of the other. By putting each image on its own layer, you can freely change the look and layout of your document without committing to the changes. If you paint, apply a filter, or make an adjustment, it will only affect the layer on which you're working. If you get into a snarl over a particularly troublesome layer, you can throw it away and start over again. The rest of your document will remain untouched.

You can make the layers relate to each other in interesting ways, such as by poking holes in them to reveal the underlying image. I'll show you some great techniques using this concept in Chapter 12, "Enhancement."

Figure 3.1
Layers isolate different parts of the image.

But first, you need to pick up on the basics, or I guess I should say the foundations, of layers. If you've used layers for awhile, you might find some of this chapter to be a bit too basic. On the other hand, you might want to glance through it anyway—you might find some juicy tidbits that you're not aware of.

Meeting the Layers

Before we jump in and start creating a bunch of layers, you should get familiar with their place of residence—the Layers palette (see Figure 3.2). You're going to be spending a lot of time with this palette, so you should take a moment now to get on friendly terms with it. It's not a terribly complicated palette, and after you've used it a few times, you should know it like the back of your hand.

As you make your way through this chapter, you'll learn more about the Layers palette as well as the fundamental tasks associated with it. Also, I'll throw in a few layer effects just for the heck of it. Now, assuming that you've done your part and introduced yourself to the Layers palette, let's get on with the business of creating and manipulating layers in Photoshop.

Creating Layers

Photoshop will automatically create the majority of layers for you. A new layer is added anytime you copy and paste an image or drag a layer between documents (we'll talk about this later in the chapter). If you're starting from scratch, however, you can click the New Layer icon at the bottom of the Layers palette to create a new, empty layer.

Give it a try: Open a new document and then use the Layers palette to create a new layer (see Figure 3.3). Pick a bright color to paint with and then use any painting tool to draw a big circle. Now create another layer and draw a square on it, using a different color (see Figure 3.4). Finally, create a third layer and draw a triangle on it (see Figure 3.5). You can use this simple document you've just created in the following sections that describe the features of the Layers palette (see Figure 3.6).

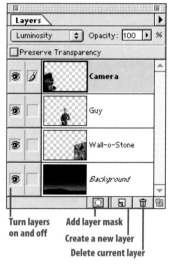

Turn layers on and off
Add layer mask
Create a new layer
Delete current layer

Figure 3.2
The Layers palette.

NOTE

I often create a new layer before using any of the painting tools or the Gradient tool, because these tools apply changes directly to the active layer; consequently, the changes are difficult to modify once they've been applied. I like working with a safety net, so I usually create a new layer before using these tools; then I can easily edit the changes without disturbing the underlying image.

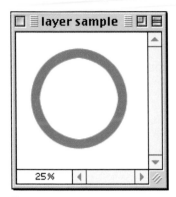

Figure 3.3
A new layer.

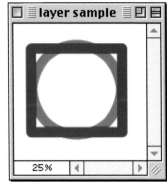

Figure 3.4
The second layer.

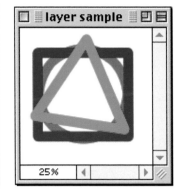

Figure 3.5
The third layer.

Figure 3.6
The Layers palette view.

Active Layer

You can only edit one layer at a time. Remember, Photoshop thinks of the layers as if they were separate documents. The layer you're currently working on is highlighted in the Layers palette. You should also see a little paintbrush icon next to it—that's just another indication that the layer is active for editing. To change the active layer, just click the name of another layer. Only one layer can be active at a time.

Stacking Order

You can change the stacking order of the layers by dragging the name of one layer above or below the name of another layer. The topmost layers can often obstruct your view of the underlying images. You can change this by reordering the layers so that small images are near the top of the stack and the larger ones are near the bottom. (See Figures 3.7 to 3.10.)

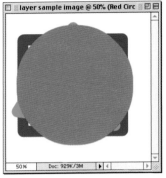

Figure 3.7
The original image.

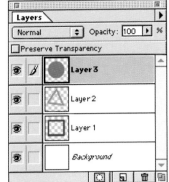

Figure 3.8
The original Layers palette.

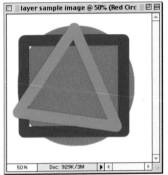

Figure 3.9
The changed stacking order.

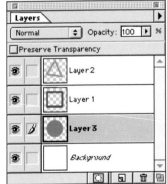

Figure 3.10
The revised Layers palette.

Background Image

Photoshop will not permit you to drag a layer below the background, because it doesn't think of the background as a layer. If you liken the layers to the individual pages in a pad of tracing paper, you could think of the cardboard back as the background layer. The background is always opaque and cannot be moved. In some circumstances, though, you might want to delete the background. For example, when you output images to videotape, they can't be overlaid onto video if the background layer is present. However, most of the time, it's a personal preference. You don't have to have a background in your document. If

NOTE

If your document doesn't have a background (because you accidentally deleted or renamed the background), you can create one by choosing **Layer>New> Background**. Just changing it's name back to "Background" will not do the job.

you want to convert the background into a normal layer, just change its name (the background image must be named "Background," otherwise it becomes a normal layer). To change the name of a layer, double-click its name in the Layers palette.

The Eyeballs: What They See Is What You Get

The eyeballs in the Layers palette aren't just cute, they determine which layers will be visible in your document as well as which ones will print. Clicking the eyeballs gives you a toggle effect: Now you see them, now you don't.

If you turn off all the eyeballs in the Layers palette, Photoshop will fill your screen with a checkerboard. This checkerboard indicates that there's nothing visible in the document (if Photoshop filled your screen with white instead, you might assume that there's a layer visible that's filled with white). You can think of the checkerboard as the areas of the document that are transparent. When you view a single layer, the checkerboard indicates the transparent areas of that layer. As you turn on the other layers in the document, the checkerboard will be replaced with the information on the other layers. When multiple layers are visible, the checkerboard indicates where the underlying image will not be obstructed by the elements on the visible layers. (See Figures 3.11 to 3.14.)

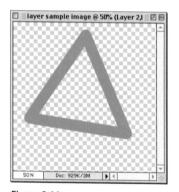

Figure 3.11
The checkerboard indicates a transparent area.

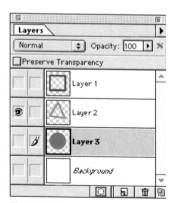

Figure 3.12
The Layers palette view.

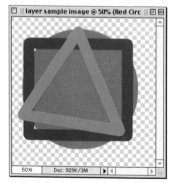

Figure 3.13
As more layers become visible, the transparent areas become smaller.

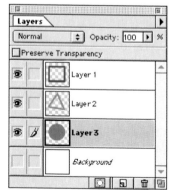

Figure 3.14
The Layers palette view.

Opacity

The Opacity setting at the top of the Layers palette controls the opacity of the active layer. By lowering this setting, the entire layer will become partially transparent (transparent is the exact opposite of opaque). Instead of lowering the opacity on an entire layer, you can lower the opacity of the Eraser tool and then brush across the area of the layer you want to become more transparent—that is, unless the background is active. If you use the Eraser tool on the background, it will simply paint with your background color instead of truly deleting areas (remember, the background is always opaque).

Try this: Open the document you created earlier in this chapter. Create a new layer and then use any painting tool to brush across the layer. Now lower the opacity setting in the Layers palette to 70%. (See Figures 3.15 to 3.17.)

NOTE

To quickly turn off all the eyeballs in the Layers palette and view only the layer you're interested in, simply Option-click one of the eyeball icons. You can turn all the eyeball icons back on by Option-clicking the same eyeball a second time.

NOTE

To quickly change the opacity of a layer, switch to the Move tool and then use the number keys on your keyboard (1 = 10%, 3 = 30%, 56 = 56%, and so on).

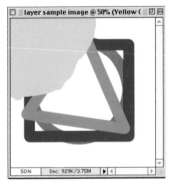

Figure 3.15
Layer at 100% opacity.

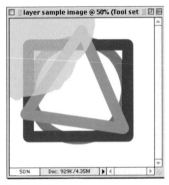

Figure 3.16
Layer at 70% opacity.

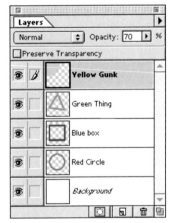

Figure 3.17
Lowering the opacity of a layer affects the entire layer.

Now let's compare this effect to what happens when you lower the Opacity setting of one of the painting tools. Create another new layer; however, this time, leave the Opacity setting of the layer at 100%. Now choose a painting tool, change the Opacity setting of the tool to 70% (use the Options palette), and then brush across the layer. The paint should look exactly the same as the paint that appears in the other layer. (See Figures 3.18 and 3.19.) Finally, create one more new layer and paint across it with the tool's Opacity setting at 100%. Now brush across an area with the Eraser tool using an Opacity setting of 30%. (See Figures 3.20 and 3.21.)

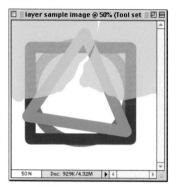

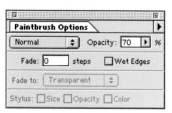

Figure 3.19
The Paintbrush Options view.

Figure 3.18
Painting with a low opacity setting.

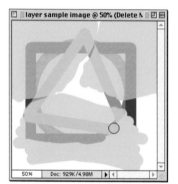

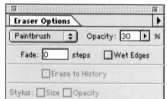

Figure 3.21
The Eraser Options view.

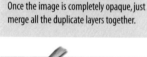

NOTE

If you've made a portion of a layer partially transparent with the Eraser or Paint tool set to a low opacity, you can attempt to bring a layer back to 100% opacity by duplicating it multiple times. Keep in mind that it might take quite a few duplicates to get the layer back to full opacity. Once the image is completely opaque, just merge all the duplicate layers together.

NOTE

When I need to precisely position a layer, I usually lower the Opacity setting just enough so I can see the underlying layers. You can do this quickly by using the number keys on your keyboard (0 to 9) when using the Move tool. After positioning the layer, just press 0 to bring the layer back to 100% opacity.

Figure 3.20
Using the Eraser tool with a low Opacity setting will also make areas of a layer transparent.

All of these options do the same thing to your image. You just have to think a bit: Do you want to apply the Opacity setting to the entire layer? If so, use the Layer palette's Opacity setting. Do you want to apply the Opacity setting to only part of the layer? If so, use the Opacity setting in the tool's Options palette. Do you want to change the opacity of an area you've already painted across? If so, use the Eraser tool with an Opacity setting.

Photoshop always (well, almost always) offers you more than one way of doing things. It reminds me of my favorite hardware store: McGuckins. It's the kind of place that takes your breath away. It has everything! If you just want a screwdriver, you'll probably find an entire aisle full of screwdrivers, each one designed for a specific use. Photoshop has the same approach; you just have to play around with it to figure out which tool best suits your needs.

Moving Layers

If you want to move everything that's on a particular layer, first make that layer active by clicking its name; then use the Move tool to drag it around the screen (see Figure 3.22). If you drag it onto another document window, Photoshop will copy the layer into that document. If you want to move just a small area of the layer, you can make a selection before using the Move tool.

Trimming the Fat

If you use the Move tool to reposition a layer and a portion of the layer starts to extend beyond the edge of your document, Photoshop will remember the information beyond the edge (see Figure 3.23). Therefore, if you move the layer away from the edge, Photoshop is able to bring back the information that was not visible. You can save a bunch of memory by getting Photoshop to clip off all the information beyond the edge of the document (see Figure 3.24). Here's a little trick for trimming off that fat (or big data as Adobe calls it). Just choose **Select>All** and then **Image>Crop**—no more wasted memory.

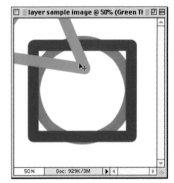

Figure 3.22
Using the Move tool to reposition a layer.

NOTE
You'll be using the Move tool a lot. Because of this, Adobe has provided a quick way to temporarily switch to the Move tool—just hold down the Command key. As long as that key is held down, you're using the Move tool (even though it isn't highlighted in the Tool palette).

NOTE
You can use the arrow keys (Up Arrow, Down Arrow, and so on) to nudge a layer one pixel at a time. Use Shift with the arrow keys to nudge a layer 10 pixels at a time.

Figure 3.23
The original image. (© 1998 PhotoDisc)

Figure 3.24
After the image is cropped.

WARNING
Only use the "trim the fat" technique if you're absolutely sure you'll not need the information beyond the edge of the document, because you cannot get it back once you've cropped it (that is, without resorting to the History palette).

NOTE

When dragging between documents, you can hold down the Shift key to center the image in the other document.

Copying Between Documents

When you use the Move tool, you can do more than just drag a layer around the document on which you're working. You can also drag a layer on top of another document (see Figure 3.25). This copies the entire layer into the second document. This layer will be positioned directly above the active layer. This is similar to copying and pasting, but it takes up a lot less memory because Photoshop doesn't store the image on the Clipboard. You can achieve the same result by dragging the name of a layer from the Layers palette onto another document window.

When you drag layers between documents, occasionally it appears as if an image has not only been copied, but also scaled at the same time. That's not what's really happening. Instead, you're viewing the two images at different magnifications (see Figure 3.26). Look at the top of the documents; if the percentages do not match, it will appear as if the image size changes when you drag it between the documents. If you view both images with the same magnification, this won't happen. It doesn't change how large the image is; it simply gives you a preview of how large it will look. It's just like putting your hand under a magnifying glass. Your hand looks larger, but when you pull your hand out, it looks normal again.

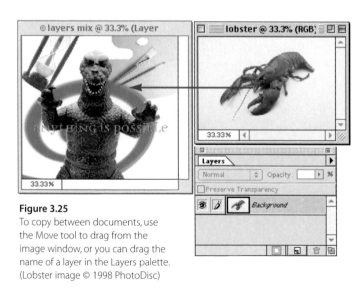

Figure 3.25
To copy between documents, use the Move tool to drag from the image window, or you can drag the name of a layer in the Layers palette. (Lobster image © 1998 PhotoDisc)

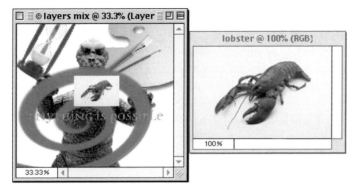

Figure 3.26
Images viewed at different magnifications.

Duplicating Layers

If you have a picture of Elvis, and you want to make Elvis twins, just drag the name of the layer onto the New Layer icon at the bottom of the Layers palette. This icon has two purposes: It will duplicate a layer if you drag one on top if it, or it will create a new empty layer if you just click it.

Deleting Layers

If you've created a document that looks a little cluttered, you can delete a layer by dragging its name onto the Trash icon at the bottom of the Layers palette. However, this icon does not work like the Trash Can on a Mac or the Recycling Bin in Windows (Bill Gates is such an environmentalist). Once you put something in it, you can't get it back (that is, without resorting to the History palette).

Leapin' Layers! More Tools and Toys

Photoshop packs a large array of layer manipulation controls. These controls allow you to go way beyond just creating, duplicating, and deleting layers. You'll be able to distort, adjust, and add wild effects after you wade through all these options.

Figure 3.27
The Layers palette view.

Figure 3.28
Transforming a layer.

Figure 3.29
The chain icon indicates linked layers.

Transforming Layers

To rotate, scale, or distort a layer, choose one of the options in the **Edit>Transform** menu; then pull the handles to distort the image. This will distort the current layer as well as any other layers linked to it (see Figures 3.27 and 3.28). If you want to know more about the transformation controls, see Chapter 2, "Selection Primer."

Linking Layers

If you need to move or transform more than one layer at a time, just click to the left of one of the preview icons in the Layers palette. When you do, a link (chain) symbol will appear (see Figure 3.29). This indicates that the active layer is now linked to all the layers that have the link symbol next to them. When you use the Move tool or choose **Edit>Transform**, the current layer and all the layers linked to it will change. This feature doesn't allow you to do anything other than move or transform layers (for example, you can't run a filter). When layers are linked, you can choose one of the options from the **Layer>Align Linked** menu to change their position relative to each other. For example, you can align the top edges of the linked layers, or you can center them horizontally.

Preserve Transparency

The Preserve Transparency checkbox at the top of the Layers palette gets in my way the most (because I forget it's turned on). Preserve Transparency prevents you from changing the transparency of areas. Each layer has its own Preserve Transparency setting. Therefore, if you turn on the Preserve Transparency checkbox for one layer and then switch to another layer, the Layers palette will display the setting for the second layer, which might be different than the first one.

Try using the Eraser tool when Preserve Transparency is turned on—it will mess with your mind! Because the Eraser tool usually makes areas transparent (by completely deleting them), it will start painting instead when Preserve Transparency is turned on. It will fill any areas you drag over with the current background color. However, if you paint across an area that's transparent, it doesn't change the image at all (because the transparent areas are being preserved). You can see how it can get in your way if you forget you turned it on.

Try this: Open a photo and delete areas around it using the Eraser tool. To accomplish this, you'll have to change the name of the background first (you can't poke a hole in the background, but you can on a layer); then make sure Preserve Transparency is turned off. Otherwise, you can't make areas transparent. Now choose **Filter>Blur> Gaussian Blur** and use a really high setting. You'll notice that the edge of the image fades out and blends with the transparent areas surrounding it (see Figure 3.30). Now, choose **Edit>Undo** and try doing the same thing with the Preserve Transparency option turned on (see Figure 3.31). Notice that the edge cannot fade out because Photoshop will not change the transparency with this option turned on.

NOTE

When dragging linked layers between documents, be sure to drag from the image window instead of the Layers palette; otherwise, only one layer will be moved.

Figure 3.30
Preserve Transparency off.

Figure 3.31
Preserve Transparency on.

Here is another example: Create a new layer and scribble across it with any painting tool, making sure the Preserve Transparency option is turned off (see Figure 3.32). Next, drag across the image with the Gradient tool (the gradient should fill the entire screen). Now, choose **Edit>Undo** and try doing the same thing with the Preserve Transparency option turned on (see Figure 3.33). Because Photoshop can't change the transparency of the layer, it cannot fill the transparent areas, that makes them opaque.

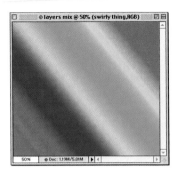

Figure 3.32
Preserve Transparency off.

Figure 3.33
Preserve Transparency on.

When you're trying to use any of the techniques in this book, be sure to keep an eye on that little Preserve Transparency checkbox. If it's turned on when you don't want it to be, it might screw up the entire effect you're trying to achieve. Therefore, unless I specifically tell you to turn it on, you should assume it should be left off (that's the default setting). If I ever tell you to turn it on, I'll let you know when to turn it back off again so that you don't get messed up when trying to reproduce a technique from this book. Now, turn off that pesky (but useful) checkbox and let's continue exploring Photoshop.

Layer Effects

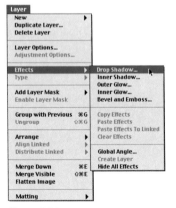

Figure 3.34
The Layer>Effects menu.

A bunch of really neat options are available under the **Layer>Effects** menu (see Figure 3.34). To experiment with these options, first create a new, empty layer and paint on it with any of the painting tools. Then apply one of the effects found in the **Layer>Effects** menu: Drop Shadow, Inner Shadow, Inner or Outer Glow, Bevel, or Emboss (see Figures 3.35 to 3.37). You can use the default settings for now. After applying an effect, use the Eraser tool to remove some of the paint on that layer. Did you notice that the layer effect updates to reflect the changes you make to the layer? Layer effects create in one simple step the same results that would usually require multiple layers and a lot of memory. In fact, you can choose **Layer>Effects>Create Layer** to have Photoshop create the layers that would usually be needed to create the effect. One reason you might want to choose Create Layers is when you're going to give your file to someone who is using an older version of Photoshop (previous versions don't support layer effects).

Let's take a look at what different layer effects do to your image. (See Figures 3.39 to 3.41.)

Figure 3.35
The original image.

Figure 3.36
Drop Shadow effect shown in the upper-right corner of the document.

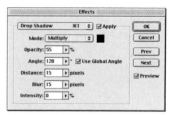

Figure 3.37
The Effects dialog box view.

Figure 3.38
Inner Shadow effect shown in the upper-right corner of the document.

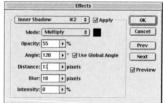

Figure 3.39
The Effects dialog box view.

Figure 3.41
The Effects dialog box view.

Figure 3.40
Outer Glow effect shown in the upper-right corner of the document.

Adjustment Layers

When you choose an option available in the **Image>Adjust** menu, it only affects the layer that's currently active (remember, Photoshop treats each layer as if it were a separate document). However, there's a special type of layer that will allow you to apply these adjustments to multiple layers. This is known as an *adjustment layer*.

To create an adjustment layer, choose **Layer>New> Adjustment Layer**. After choosing which type of adjustment you want to use (we'll discuss adjustment settings in Chapters 5, "Line Art Scanning," 6, "Optimizing Grayscale Images," and 8, "Color Correction") and specifying the desired adjustment settings, the changes will modify all the layers that are underneath the adjustment layer. You can move the adjustment layer up or down in the layers stack to affect more or fewer layers. These changes are not permanent; at any time you can simply turn off the eyeball icon on the adjustment layer and the image will return to normal. You can also lessen the effect of the adjustment layer by lowering its Opacity setting. To change the adjustment settings, simply double-click the name of the adjustment layer. (See Figures 3.42 to 3.46.)

The Blending Mode Menu

The Blending Mode menu at the top of the Layers palette is immensely useful. It allows the information on one layer to blend with the underlying image in very interesting and useful ways. Using this menu, you can quickly change the color of objects, colorize grayscale images, add reflections to metallic objects, and much, much more. This is an advanced feature, so you'll have to wait until you get to Chapter 12 to find out more about it.

Figure 3.42
New Adjustment Layer dialog box.

Figure 3.43
The Hue/Saturation adjustment layer at top of Layers palette.

Figure 3.44
Hue/Saturation affects all layers.

Figure 3.45
Re-ording Hue/Saturation adjustment layer.

Figure 3.46
The adjustment layer applies to all layers below it but not to the layers above it.

Automatic Selections

To select everything on a particular layer, just click the name of the layer while holding down the Command key. You can add the Shift key to add to a selection that already exists or use the Option key to take away from the current selection. (See Figures 3.47 to 3.50.)

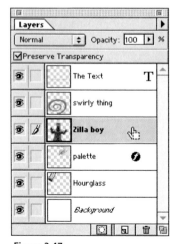

Figure 3.47
Command-click a layer to select all the objects on that layer.

Figure 3.48
The result of Command-clicking.

Figure 3.49
Refining the selection with the Lasso tool (while holding down Option to take away from the selection).

Figure 3.50
After part of the swirl layer has been deleted.

Via Copy

The Layers menu offers you a wide variety of options for copying, merging, and manipulating layers. Let's look at one of these choices. If you select an area of your image and then choose **Layer>New>Via Copy**, the area you've selected will be copied from the layer you were working on and moved to a brand new layer in the same position (see Figure 3.51). Where this is particularly handy is when you want to move just a portion of a layer so that you can place it on top of another layer.

Use All Layers

When you're editing on a layer, some of the editing tools might not work the way you expect them to. This happens because most of the tools act as if each layer is a separate document—they ignore all layers except the active one. That is, unless the tool has the Use All Layers checkbox turned on in the Options palette of the tool you're using. This checkbox allows the tools to act as if all the layers were combined together into one layer. (See Figures 3.52 to 3.54.)

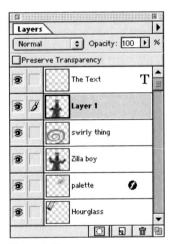

Figure 3.51
A layer after **Layer>New>Via Copy** has been applied.

Figure 3.52
Without Use All Layers.

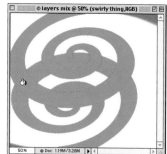

Figure 3.53
Use All Layers turned on.

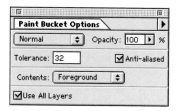

Figure 3.54
The Use All Layers checkbox in the Paint Bucket Options palette.

Shortcuts

You'll be doing a lot of switching between layers, and this can get a wee bit tedious. Therefore, I'll show you some quick shortcuts. First, you can Command-click anywhere in the image window when using the Move tool to activate the layer directly below your cursor. Then you can find out which layer you're working on by glancing at the Layers palette. You won't always need the layer below your cursor, so instead of Command-clicking, try Control-clicking. This will bring up a menu of all the layers directly below your cursor; you just choose the name of the layer you want to work on and Photoshop will switch to that layer. Remember that you can get to the Move tool temporarily at any time by holding down the Command key. Therefore, if you hold down Command and Control at the same time, no matter what tool you are using, Photoshop will present you with the pop-up menu.

Merging Layers

When you create a complicated image that contains dozens of layers, your project can start hogging memory, which, in turn, makes it difficult to manage all the layers. Whenever possible, I try to simplify my image by merging layers together. Every time you create a new layer and add something to it, more memory is gobbled up, because Photoshop not only has to think about what's on that layer, but it also has to remember what appears below the layer (even if that information is completely covered by the information on the layers above). To reduce memory requirements and simplify your image, you can merge multiple layers together. This combines the layers into a single layer and thus saves memory (because Photoshop no longer has to remember the parts of those layers that were previously being covered). The side menu on the Layers palette gives you several ways to do this:

WARNING

Once you've merged two layers, it's awfully hard to get them apart—the only way is to use the History palette. However, even with the History palette, you might lose all the changes you've made since you merged the layers.

Merge Down—Merges the active layer into the layer directly below it.

Merge Visible—Merges all the layers that are currently visible in the main image window.

Merge Linked—Merges all the layers that have the link symbols next to them along with the active layer.

Flatten Image—Merges all visible layers into the background and discards any hidden layers.

Note that if you want to know how much extra memory these layers take up as you're modifying your image, just look at the numbers in the lower-left corner of your document (see Figure 3.55). The number on the left should stay relatively consistent (unless you scale or crop the image); it indicates how much memory your image would use if all the layers were merged together. The number on the right indicates how much memory the image is using with all the layers included. This number changes as you add and modify your layers. Keep an eye on it so that you can see how memory intensive the different layers are. The number on the right might get huge if you're using a lot of layers; however, keep in mind that you'll know exactly how large the image will be when you're all done by glancing at the left number.

Figure 3.55
Memory usage indicator.

Done Playing Around?

You've spent hours toiling away on your image, and now you're ready to save your file so it can go on to its next stop (which might a printing company or one of your clients, or perhaps it's going to be posted to the Web). Then again, maybe its not going anywhere—perhaps you just want to rest your eyes, take a break, and work on it later. Wherever the image ends up, you need to make sure you save it in a format you can work with in Photoshop (complete with layers, paths, channels, and so on). Then you can save it in another format that's appropriate for its destination. It would be wonderful if all software programs could work with the same format, but, alas, they can't. Therefore, it's worth your while to get familiar with the various file formats available in Photoshop.

Saving Layered Files

If you're not too familiar with file formats, you might wonder why there are so many options in the Save dialog box. It's like anything else with Photoshop, you just have to think about the end use. If you're going to use the file in Photoshop and keep the layers, you'll want to save it in the Photoshop file format (also known as a PSD file). The Photoshop file format is the only format that recognizes layers—that's why the other choices in the Save dialog box are grayed out when you're using layers. Unfortunately, most other programs cannot open files saved in the Photoshop file format, so it's a good habit to save the original image in Photoshop's native PSD format and then make a copy of the image without layers and save it in another format—JPEG or TIFF, for example.

NOTE

I usually choose **File>Save A Copy** when I need to save a layered file. This allows me to choose file formats that do not support layers; Photoshop flattens a copy of the image for me and leaves the original layered file unchanged onscreen.

Formats other than Photoshop's native PSD format (TIFF, EPS, JPEG, and so on) can't handle multiple layers, so you'll have to merge all the layers into the background of your image. You can do this quickly by choosing Flatten Image from the side menu of the Layers palette. Flatten Image combines all your layers, and any areas that were transparent are filled with white. The transparent areas are filled in because the other file formats don't know what to do with them. I usually save two versions of my files—one in the Photoshop file format (so I can get back to the layers) and one in TIFF or EPS format (to use in my page layout program).

Closing Thoughts

Layers play such a huge role in Photoshop that to deny yourself any crucial information about them is asking for trouble. With every new release, Adobe likes to pack more and more functions into the Layers palette. So as time goes on, it will become even more crucial to understand them. This is definitely a chapter you should feel comfortable with before you move on to the more advanced areas of Photoshop.

Ask Adobe

Q: What's the difference between the background image and a normal layer, and what was the thinking behind the concept?

A: A normal layer has a transparency component and can extend beyond the bounds of the canvas. A background image has no transparency and is exactly the size of the canvas. Many of the raster file formats in existence have no notion of transparency or image data beyond the image bounds. Hence, these formats essentially require that the image consist of only a background image.

Q: Why does Photoshop always ask if I want to flatten my image when converting between modes? Should I? And if so, why?

A: Unless you are using only Dissolve mode, changing image modes will change the way colors blend. This applies even to Normal mode. Hence, if you like the particular compositing effects you have achieved, you will be better able to preserve them if you flatten before performing a mode change.

Q: How did Preserve Transparency come about?

A: Simple answer: It seemed useful.

More specifically, there are times when you create a shape in a layer and then you're interested only in modifying the color values within the layer rather than the overall shape defined by the transparency. Loading the transparency data for a layer as a selection is a very, very bad way to achieve this effect for two reasons: First, because it doesn't work. If the layer has soft, anti-aliased edges, the mask at those edges will be soft but it will allow paint or other operations to make at least limited changes to the layer. Hence, every editing operation that could affect transparency will have at least some effect. So, if anyone ever tells you to load the transparency of a layer as a selection before performing edits on that layer, it's a good sign that you should stop listening to that person. There are good reasons to load the transparency for a layer as a selection, but protecting the existing shape of the layer isn't one of them.

If you want to protect the existing shape of the layer, you want the editing operations to not affect the transparency channel. That's precisely what the Preserve Transparency control does.

Ben's Techno-Babble Decoder Ring

Preserve Transparency: A function in Photoshop that temporarily "freezes" the transparency of a layer. While Preserve Transparency is in effect, you cannot increase or decrease how transparent an area will appear.

Opacity: The Opacity setting determines how opaque (the opposite of transparent) the information on a layer will appear. An Opacity setting of 100% will not allow you to see the underlying image. A setting below 100% will blend the information on the current layer with the underlying image.

Keyboard Shortcuts

Show/Hide Layers Palette	F7
New Layer	Shift-Command-N
New Layer Via Copy	Command-J
New Layer Via Cut	Shift-Command-J
Toggle Preserve Transparency	/
Make Top Layer Active	Shift-Option-]
Make Next Layer Active	Option-]
Make Previous Layer Active	Option-[
Make Bottom Layer Active	Shift-Option-[
Move Layer Up	Command-Option-]
Move Layer Down	Command-Option-[
Merge Down	Command-E
Merge Visible	Shift-Command-E

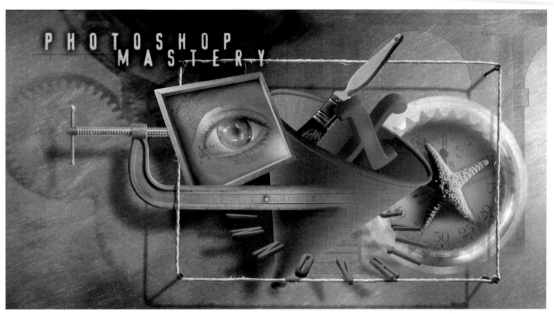

Courtesy of Chris Klimek.

This image started from a pencil sketch of the character. I scanned an image of the human digestive tract to the background layer. This layer was then copied two more times saturating one layer and darkening and adjusting the color balance of the other. I then scanned the original pencil sketch on top. A path was created around the character's outline, and I deleted the selected area from all the layers, exposing the background. After flattening the layers, I then added all the other little goodies, eyes, hands, feet, etc.
–Michael Slack

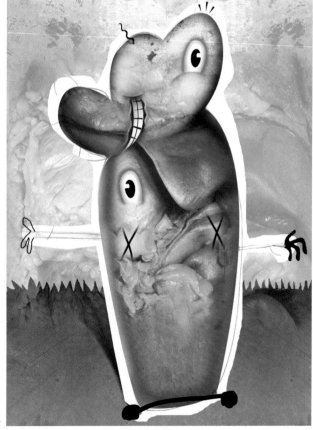

Courtesy of Michael Slack, www.slackart.com.

Courtesy of Gordon Studer.

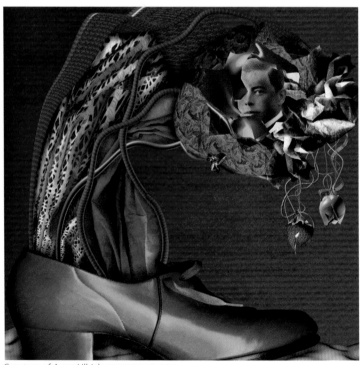

Courtesy of Anna Ullrich, www.annau.com.

Part II **Production Essentials**

Courtesy of Robert Bowen Studio. Photography by Eric Meola. Art Director Bronson Smith, Schieffelin & Somerset.

4 Scanning Settings

The difference between failure and success is doing a thing nearly right, and doing it exactly right.
—Edward C. Simmons

© 1997 Adam Woolfitt, adampix@dircon.co.uk.

I could talk about the finer points of resolution and scanning settings until I'm blue in the face. But I've found that most people just want to know what it takes to achieve the best possible image. So, consider this chapter your own personal set of crib notes taken from a class called "Resolution Solutions."

There's a bunch of misconceptions out there about resolution and how it translates among the various devices through which your image travels. So when you're thinking about resolution, you need to ask yourself: Are you talking about the resolution of your monitor, your scanner, or your printer? We'll make those distinctions in this chapter.

But regardless of how you approach it, it all boils down to one thing: The key to getting high-quality output is to use the correct resolution setting when scanning or manipulating your images. The resolution setting determines how large the pixels of your image will be when they are printed. Since all images in Photoshop are made out of pixels, image resolution is measured in pixels per inch (ppi).

The DPI Dilemma

Most inexpensive scanners mislabel the ppi setting as dpi (dots per inch) to be consistent with book authors who regularly misuse the term dpi. DPI should be used only when describing the output of a *printer*. If you are not talking about a printer, you shouldn't use the term dpi—it's that simple. All images in Photoshop are made out of pixels, and are therefore measured in pixels per inch (ppi). The next time you read a book or article that instructs you to change the dpi setting of an image within Photoshop, I challenge you to find anything in Photoshop that lets you change a setting called dpi—it's not there!

I'm sorry, but this really bugs me. It's like calling a hat a shoe; you can wear both of them, but you put one on your foot and the other on your head. If everybody interchanged those terms, you'd either start wearing shoes on your head or you'd just get awfully confused. With resolution, most people choose to just get confused, and I don't blame them when the majority of authors use the wrong term to describe image resolution. Just go and flip through the Photoshop manual and try to find dpi mentioned. If you find it, it will be referring to a printer, *not* your image. Because the misuse of the term dpi is so widespread, I usually don't even use a term when describing the resolution of an image. Instead, I just say: "The resolution of this image is 300." That way the person I'm talking to can insert the correct(ppi) or incorrect (dpi) term without getting confused. The main thing is that you will never catch me calling the resolution of an image "dpi"—it's simply not correct. So throughout this book, you'll find that I usually use the term resolution instead of ppi or dpi.

A quick recap: Scanning and image resolution are measured in ppi. *Only printer resolution is measured in dpi.*

Optimal Scanning Settings

The type of printer you use for your final output will determine the correct resolution setting to use when scanning an image. I'll give you the correct resolution settings for all the different types of output devices I can think of. You can use settings that are lower than the ones listed below; but if you do, you will be sacrificing quality for the convenience of a smaller file size. I suggest you glance over this section and just read the information below the headings that apply to you. If you never print to an ink jet printer, there would be no reason to read the section on ink jets.

Halftones

Most popular printer types (laser printers, imagesetters, printing presses, thermal wax printers, etc.) cannot truly reproduce shades of gray. They either leave the paper white or turn it pure black. To simulate shades of gray (or shades of color), they use something called a halftone. Halftones fool your eyes into thinking they see grays when they're really looking at pure black and pure white. The halftone does this by substituting small black circles for the shades of gray, using large circles for dark shades of gray and small ones for the light shades (see Figure 4.1).

Figure 4.1
Halftones use different-sized circles to simulate shades of gray or tints of color.
(© 1998 PhotoSpin)

There is a setting called lines per inch, or simply lpi, that determines the spacing of the circles used to simulate shades of gray. As the circles get packed closer together (higher lpi settings), the amount of detail your printer is capable of reproducing also increases (see Figures 4.2 to 4.4). High lpi settings can cause problems when printing images on a printing press (the smallest circles start to disappear); therefore, the printing process usually dictates the highest lpi setting that can be used. The following table will show you the most common settings used and the defaults that are built into your laser printer. The default settings are used whenever you print from a program that is not designed for publishing (spreadsheets, databases, etc.).

Figure 4.2
53 lpi.

Figure 4.3
85 lpi.

Figure 4.4
150 lpi.

Common LPI Settings

LPI	General Use
85	Newspaper Advertisements
100	Newspaper Editorial Section
133	Magazines and Brochures
150	High-end Magazines & High Quality Brochures
175	Annual Reports & High-end Brochures
53	300 dpi Laser Printers
106	600 dpi laser printers
212	1200 dpi Laser Printers

Whenever you scan an image that will be printed with a halftone, you'll need to know the lpi setting (see previous table) before you scan the image because it dictates how much detail you're going to get out of your printer. Once you know the lpi setting, multiply it by 1.5 if you would like your image to appear as sharp as possible, or multiply it by 2 if your want it to look a little soft. Use the soft setting for portraits (unless you really don't like the person); otherwise, every pore on their face might show up.

Ink Jet

Most ink jet printers do not use halftones to simulate shades of gray, instead they use what appear to be random dots. To simulate grays, they pack these same-sized dots close together for dark shades or space them apart for bright shades (see Figure 4.5). That's why if you look really close at the output from an ink jet, it might look noisy.

To find out the scanning setting needed for images that will be output on an ink jet printer, just divide the resolution of the printer by 3. Example: ink jet printer resolution=720 dpi, 720 x .33=238 ppi.

Line Art

Images than contain only pure black and pure white—no grays—are known as line art (see Figure 4.6). The most common types of line art are logos and text.

NOTE

The ink jet settings shown here are what the ink jet printer manufacturers recommend. I find you can usually get away with lower settings as long as your image does not contain high contrast straight lines. So if you have an image of a sailboat (the mast is a high contrast line), then use the settings above; otherwise, experiment with lower settings.

Figure 4.5
Ink jet printers use same-sized dots to simulate shades of gray or tints of color.

Figure 4.6
Line art images contain only pure black and pure white.

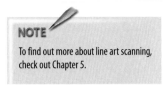

NOTE

To find out more about line art scanning, check out Chapter 5.

Figure 4.7
Dye-sub printers can truly reproduce the shades of gray or color that appear in your images.

Figure 4.8
For multimedia, think of the width and height in pixels instead of the resolution setting.

To get the highest-quality line art (regardless of what type of printer you are using), you'll need the pixels in your image to be the same size as the dots your printer uses. To accomplish that, find out the resolution of your printer (measured in dpi) and type that number into your scanning software where it asks for a resolution setting. The highest setting you should ever need is 1200. Settings above 1200 create overly large file sizes without noticeable improvements in quality.

Dye-Sub Printers

Unlike lasers and ink jets, dye-sub printers are capable of reproducing 256 shades of gray and/or 16.7 million colors. The output from a dye-sub printer looks just like a real photo (see Figure 4.7). To get the highest quality from a dye-sub printer, you need the pixels in your image to be the same size as the dots the printer uses. To accomplish this, find out the resolution of the printer (measured in dpi) and use that number for the resolution setting in your scanning software.

Multimedia

If your image is going to end up being displayed on a computer monitor and not printed, I'd call that multimedia (see Figure 4.8). For multimedia, you don't need to get the size of the pixels (resolution) to be just right; instead, you want to end up with the exact number of pixels that would fill the monitor on which you are displaying the image. The table that follows indicates how much information can be displayed on most common monitors. If you create an image that contains more information than the monitor can display at one time, the edges of the image will be clipped off. To view the entire image, you would need to scroll. Or, if your image doesn't contain enough information to fill the monitor, there would be extra black space around the image.

If your image has already been scanned, choose **Image> Image Size**, turn on the Resample Image checkbox, then change the width of the image in pixels to the exact amount of information the monitor can display (see the following table).

Monitor Sizes and Pixel Dimensions

Monitor	Width and Height in Pixels
13 Inch	640 x 480
15 Inch	832 x 624
20 Inch	1024 x 768
21 Inch	1152 x 870
VGA	640 x 480
SuperVGA	800 x 600
Video	640 x 480

NOTE

When preparing images for the Web, you need to always be thinking about two things: the size of the smallest monitor that might be used to view your site (typically, a 13-inch monitor) and the browser interface that you'll have to leave room for. The browser interface usually leaves 590W x 325H of space for your site. For more information about preparing graphics for the Web, be sure to check out the file WGraphics.pdf on the accompanying CD.

The physical dimensions of VGA, SuperVGA, and Video monitors can vary and therefore are not listed as a specific size.

To find out the scanning settings needed to produce an image that will fill a specific monitor, divide the width of the monitor, measured in pixels (see previous table), by the width of the original image, measured in inches. The result is the exact scanning resolution needed to capture enough information to fill that specific monitor size.

35mm Slides

When you send an image to be output to a 35mm slide (see Figure 4.9), the output device is called a film recorder. The type of slide recorder used determines the amount of information needed in your image. The resolution of a slide recorder is measured in "K" (usually 2K or 4K). The letter K stands for 1,024 and indicates how many pixels can be reproduced in the width of a slide. So a 2K slide recorder can reproduce 2,048 pixels (2x1024) in the width of a slide. The ratio between width and height of a 35mm slide is 3:2.

Slide Recorder	Width & Height in Pixels
2K	2,048 x 1,365
4K	4,096 x 2,731

Figure 4.9

For slides, think of the width and height in pixels instead of the resolution setting. (© 1998 PhotoDisc)

NOTE

If you are using a digital camera, you can change the size of the pixels that make up your image by choosing **Image>Image Size**. If you don't want to change the total number of pixels in your image (you just want to change their size), turn off the Resample Image checkbox. If the camera is not capable of capturing enough information for your specific type of output device, turn on the Resample Image checkbox.

NOTE

You can access most scanners from the **File>Import** menu. If your scanner does not appear in this menu, then you must install the proper Import plug-in, which should be on the disks that came with your scanner.

Use the following technique to find out the scanning resolution needed to capture the exact amount of information needed for a 35mm slide. First, determine how many pixels your film recorder can reproduce in the width of a slide (see the table), then divide this number by the width of your original image measured in inches. The result is the exact scanning resolution needed to capture the proper amount of information.

Proper Scaling

If you need to reproduce an image larger or smaller than the original, you're going to need to scale it. To get the highest quality, you should scale the image at the time it's being scanned. This is the only time that you can actually capture more information from the original image.

The problem is, many scanners don't have a scale setting (I think it's really dumb of them not to include one). But if your scanner doesn't have a scale setting, all you have to do is multiply the resolution you need by the amount you are going to scale the image. So, if you need a resolution of 150 and need it to be twice as large as the original (200%), you'd multiply 150 by 2 and end up with 300. That's the setting you would use to scan the image. Then, after the image is scanned and is open in Photoshop, choose **Image>Image Size**, and turn off the Resample Image checkbox. Then change the resolution setting to what you wanted it to be in the first place. The reason you have to go through all this is just because some propeller-head at the company that made your scanner decided not to include a scale setting. Make sure to write a comment on your registration card the next time you buy a scanner.

Post Scan Adjustments

If you don't know the final output size ahead of time, you can use Photoshop to change the resolution of an image or to enlarge or reduce it. You can do this by choosing **Image>Image Size** (see Figure 4.10). What happens to your image is dependent on the Resample Image checkbox at the bottom of the dialog box.

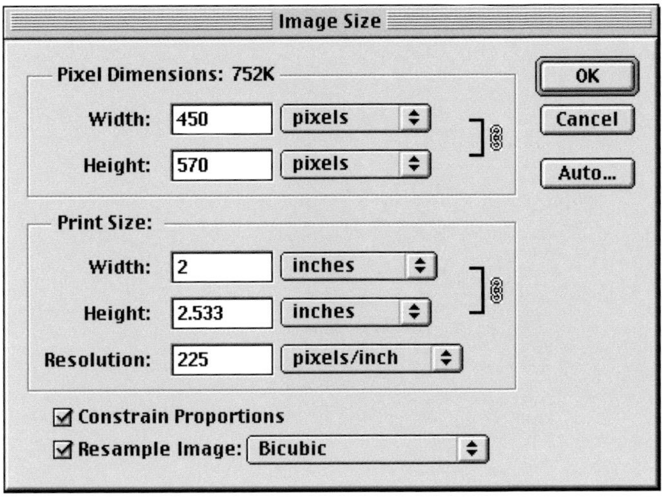

Figure 4.10
The Image Size dialog box.

Resample Off

When the Resample Image checkbox is turned off, Photoshop will not be able to change the amount of information in the file (see Figure 4.11); it will only be able to change how large the pixels are when the image is printed (that's called resolution). If you make the pixels larger, by lowering the resolution setting, the width and height of the image (in inches) will also have to become larger, which is why a link symbol appears between the dimensions and the resolution setting.

I turn off the Resample Image checkbox any time someone gives me a scan that doesn't have the resolution settings I need. Then I just change the resolution setting to what I really need, and then I can see exactly how large the image can be used at that resolution.

Resample On

When the Resample checkbox is turned on, Photoshop will be able to add or throw away information (pixels). This is known as resampling or interpolation. With resample turned on, you can change the resolution setting (size of the pixels), and the width and height of the image will not change. That's because Photoshop is either adding or throwing away pixels in the image. (See Figures 4.12 and 4.13.)

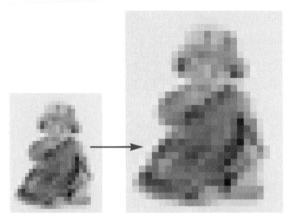

Figure 4.11
Resample off. Only the size of the pixels changes.

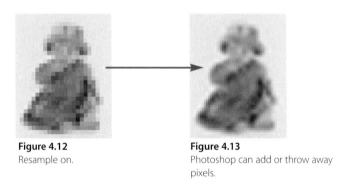

Figure 4.12
Resample on.

Figure 4.13
Photoshop can add or throw away pixels.

I turn on the Resample Image checkbox anytime I have an image that has the proper resolution setting, but is too large or small. By turning off that checkbox, I can change the width and height of the image without messing with how large the pixels are (resolution). It doesn't harm the image much when you make an image smaller, but any time you enlarge an image using resampling, it always looks slightly blurry. That's why it's better to scale an image when it is being scanned.

Scaling Images in Other Programs

When you scale an image in a page layout or illustration program, you are effectively changing the resolution of the image. Unlike Photoshop, these programs cannot change the number of pixels in an image and therefore can only change how large the pixels are. (Remember, pixel size is also called resolution and is measured in pixels per inch (ppi).) Scaling an image to 50% of its original size in a page layout program effectively doubles its resolution.

If you are not sure how large your image will need to be, then scan the image for the largest possible size you think you might need. After you have scaled the image in your page layout program, write down the final size from the measurements palette. Then, to ensure the highest quality, open the image in Photoshop and use the Image Size dialog box to scale the image to its final size. Finally, reload the image into the page layout program at 100% scale.

Closing Thoughts

There are so many misconceptions about resolution that it's very easy to get mixed signals about how to deal with it. Many people just scan their images with a generic resolution setting of 300 ppi and wonder why the results are so often disappointing. But by finding out the exact setting that is needed for the specific type of output you will be using, you'll be able to have smaller files that actually look better when printed. I hope that this chapter shed some light on the subject for you. I suggest you use it as a reference whenever you are dealing with an unfamiliar output device. The key is to get resolution to work for you rather than against you.

Ask Adobe

Q: Why does Photoshop complain when I'm trying to print an image that has an overly high resolution (that is, over 2.5 times the line screen)?

A: Because when you print at a resolution significantly higher than your line screen, you are taking time for the computer to send, the network to transfer, and the printer to receive and process information that won't be of use in the actual halftoning process.

Q: Why is the resolution setting in my scanning software called dpi, but the same setting in Photoshop is called ppi? Which one is correct?

A: Both terms get used interchangeably, perhaps a bit overly freely. When people want to make a distinction, dpi generally refers to actual dots that are either colored or not; that is, they can only have two states. PPI in contrast refers to how dense the pixel values are, and each pixel value can represent a range of colors.

Q: If the resolution of my printer is measured in dpi, and the resolution setting in my scanning software is also measured in dpi, then should I type the resolution of my printer into my scanning software? And if not, why not?

A: It depends on what your scanning software will do with the information. If it will use it to directly control the sampling of the image, then you probably don't want to do this for a variety of reasons. The printer's dots, for example, will be used to form larger halftone cells (or to do diffusion dithering for stochastic screens); and hence the actual pixel resolution that can be viably reproduced on the printer will generally be much lower than the number of dots per inch supported by the printer.

Ben's Techno-Babble Decoder Ring

Samples Per Inch (SPI)—Determines how small of an area a scanner will measure to determine the color of a single pixel. The samples per inch setting can be determined by multiplying the desired image resolution (ppi) and the amount the image will be scaled. Example: desired resolution 300 ppi, scale 200%; 300x200%=600 spi.

Pixels Per Inch (PPI)—Determines how small the pixels in an image will appear when printed. 150 ppi means that pixels will be 1/150th of an inch when printed. The higher the setting, the smaller the pixels become.

Dots Per Inch (DPI)—Determines how small the dots an output device will use when printing an image. A 300 dpi laser printer uses black dots that are 1/300th of an inch in size. This term is often used incorrectly to describe the resolution of an image (which should be measured in ppi).

Lines Per Inch (LPI)—Determines the spacing of halftone dots and therefore their maximum size. The higher the lpi setting, the more apparent detail you can reproduce.

Imagesetter—A type of high-end output device that is used to output images onto photographic paper or film. Imagesetters are capable of outputting only pure black and pure white dots. The minimum resolution of an imagesetter is 2540 dpi.

Thermal Wax—A type of CMYK output device that bonds a waxy substance to a special type of paper. If you scratch the output of a thermal wax printer with your fingernail, you will usually be able to scratch off some of the waxy substance.

Ink Jet—A type of output device that sprays CMYK inks onto special paper. Upon close inspection, the output of an ink jet printer typically appears noisy because it uses a diffusion dither pattern to simulate shades of gray.

Dye Sub—A type of output device that produces a continuous tone result by heating CMY dyes until they turn into a gas (without first becoming a liquid). The output of a dye-sub printer has a continuous-tone glossy look that resembles a photographic print.

5 Line Art Scanning

*Only those who have the
patience to do simple
things perfectly will
acquire the skill to do
difficult things easily.
—Johann Schiller*

Courtesy of Nik Willmore.

Scanning line art is a wonderful opportunity to learn how to do a relatively simple thing, perfectly. Line art images are fundamental: black lines on a white background. It should be easy, shouldn't it? Scanning and printing line art is easy, but first you have to know how to control your scanner, as well as how to enhance the scanned image after it's loaded into Photoshop.

Almost all scanners have a scanning mode called *line art mode* that gives you a pure black and pure white end result. However, don't be fooled by your scanner. Images scanned in line art mode don't contain anywhere near the amount of detail found in the original image.

If you scan an image in line art mode, it will automatically end up in bitmap mode after it's loaded into Photoshop. As a result, Photoshop is rendered practically useless because it's not able to enhance images that are in bitmap mode (for example, you can't use most of the editing tools, rotate the image in precise increments, or apply filters). This is why so many people end up with line art reproductions that have jagged edges, broken lines, and dense areas that are all clogged up.

But that's not going to happen to you. You're going to ignore your scanner's advice and scan in *grayscale mode* instead of line art mode. After the image is scanned in grayscale mode, you can take full advantage of Photoshop's enhancement controls. With very little practice and a handful of tricks you learn in this chapter, you'll be able to create beautiful line art reproductions as they were intended to be—with crisp edges and sharp detail.

When you're all done producing your line art and are pleased with the result, you should convert your image into bitmap mode. This will keep your file size small and prevent you from accidentally adding shades of gray to the image. After all, true line art contains only pure black and pure white, and no shades of gray. By converting your image to bitmap mode in the end, you'll guarantee that it won't be contaminated with grays.

Avoiding the Jaggies

The most common complaint I hear about line art is that it has jagged edges. This happens when the pixels in the image are so large that you can easily see them when the image is printed. Thankfully, avoiding the "jaggies" is the easiest part of dealing with line art.

Resolution Is the Key

Photoshop gives users the ability to try a lot of wild things with images; however, the one thing all users have in common is the desire to get the highest quality possible. If your end result is pure black and pure white line art, you'll want each pixel in your image to be the exact same size as the smallest dot your printer can reproduce.

The size of the pixels in your document is determined by the resolution setting of your file—this is known as pixels per inch, or PPI. The resolution of your printer dictates the smallest dot it can reproduce—this is known as dots per inch, or DPI. You'll want to find out the resolution of your printer and use that setting when scanning your image. This makes your pixels the same size as the smallest dot your printer can reproduce, thus giving you the best possible result.

Unfortunately, most people think higher settings produce better results, but that's not the case. If your printer has a resolution of 300 dots per inch and you feed it an image with 350 pixels per inch, it must distill the image and discard the extra information—and that's when your image will suffer. You're much better off using the correct resolution setting in the first place.

Printing companies and service bureaus have expensive output devices that offer resolutions of at least 2,540 dots per inch. After experimenting, I've found that it doesn't really help to use resolution settings above 1,200 for line art. Files with resolutions above 1,200 don't seem to produce better detail, they just give you huge file sizes and therefore slow down your computer. Figures 5.1 through 5.6 show the effect of resolution on file size and quality.

NOTE

When scanning a line art image for display onscreen (for multimedia, the Web, and so on), it will usually look better if it includes shades of gray. I know, I know, that really isn't true line art, but it will look better on screen. This happens because the pixels that make up your screen are quite large (72 PPI on most Macs and 96 PPI on most Windows machines), so it's easy to see the jagged edges of the pixels that make up your image. By including shades of gray, the edges of the image will fade out and have a softer look. When scanning for onscreen use, use a resolution setting of 72 for the Mac and 96 for Windows.

Figure 5.1
Resolution: 150 PPI. File size: 38K.

Figure 5.2
Resolution: 300 PPI. File size: 153K.

Figure 5.3
Resolution: 600 PPI. File size: 230K.

Figure 5.4
Resolution: 800 PPI. File Size: 306K.

Figure 5.5
Resolution: 1,200 PPI. File size: 459K.

Figure 5.6
Resolution: 2,400 PPI. File size: 1.4MB.

Photoshop Can Fake It

If your scanner is not capable of using a resolution setting as high as you need, you can have Photoshop add the additional information by scanning with the highest resolution setting available and then choosing **Image>Image Size**. When you select the Resample Image checkbox, Photoshop will be able to increase the resolution of the image and add the extra information that your scanner could not deliver. Therefore, select the Resample Image checkbox, set the pop-up menu to Bicubic (that's the kind of math Photoshop will use to add information to your image), type in the resolution of your printer in the Resolution field, and then click OK. Remember, your image must be in grayscale mode; otherwise, this step will not improve image quality.

Straightening the Image

If the image you've scanned needs to be straightened, use the Measure tool to draw a line across an area that should be perfectly vertical or horizontal. If there's more than one area of the image that should be straightened, you can click the middle of the measurement line and drag it around your screen to make sure it matches all the areas that should be horizontal. If you need to adjust the angle of the measurement line, just drag one of its ends. When you're certain the line is at the proper angle, check to make sure the background color is set to White and then choose **Image>Rotate Canvas>Arbitrary**. Photoshop has a great feature that automatically calculates how much the image needs to be rotated, so all you have to do is click OK (see Figure 5.7). Once you're done, you can choose any tool other than the measurement tool to hide the measurement line

Also, you should straighten a scan while it's still in grayscale mode. If your image is in bitmap mode, it can only be rotated in 90 degree increments.

Improving Definition

When you convert an image to bitmap mode (which we'll do at the end of this chapter), any areas that are darker than 50 percent gray will become pure black. This usually causes detail in the darkest, most densely packed areas to disappear. You can prevent this from happening by sharpening the image. Sharpening will add more contrast to those densely packed areas and produce better detail. However, before you sharpen an image, you'll want to take a snapshot of the unsharpened image so you can use it later to enhance the result.

NOTE

When you scan grayscale images that have already been printed using a halftone screen, you'll often get an unwanted repetitive pattern. You can often get a better result by scanning the preprinted image as line art (even though it's a grayscale photo). This will try to capture the halftone look instead of converting the image into a grayscale file. Scanning grayscale images that were printed with a halftone screen of 85 lines per inch or below can be done using the line art technique described in this chapter. If an image was printed with a halftone screen above 85 lines per inch, the image should be scanned as a normal grayscale image instead of using the line art technique.

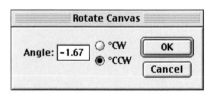

Figure 5.7
Photoshop automatically calculates the rotation amount needed.

NOTE

Whenever possible, you should avoid straightening scans in other software programs, such as your page layout program. If scans are straightened in other programs, the screen redraw will take longer and printing time will increase. Also, the quality of the art will suffer, and you'll not have a true preview of what the image will look like.

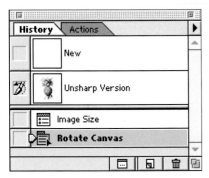

Figure 5.8
After creating a new snapshot, click to the left of the snapshot icon to set the History brush to that snapshot.

Taking a Snapshot

Before sharpening an image, you want to make sure you can get back to the unsharpened version if needed—this can help you fine-tune the detail in the end result. Choose New Snapshot from the side menu of the History palette to record what the image looks like before you sharpen it. Name the snapshot something like "Unsharp Version" so you can remember what it contains. The snapshot you create will appear near the top of the History palette (see Figure 5.8). Click the column just to the left of the snapshot thumbnail icon to tell Photoshop to use this version of the image when using the History brush.

Sharpening the Image

Now that you've created a snapshot version of the image, it's safe to proceed with the sharpening process. Double-click the Zoom tool to view the image at 100% magnification; otherwise, the onscreen preview of the sharpening filter will not be accurate. Choose **Filter>Sharpen>Unsharp Mask**; then set the amount to 500, the radius to 1.2, and the threshold to 2. This is usually a good starting point because it will make the detail in the dark, densely packed areas become more defined. You can increase the radius setting if needed to open up and display more shadow detail. Radius settings between 1 and 5 usually produce the best results (see Figure 5.9). A threshold setting of 0 will sharpen all shades in the image, including the lightest grays. I usually keep the threshold setting at 2, unless the paper texture starts to show up. Light gray areas are often texture picked up from the paper or dirt. A setting around 7 will usually suppress the paper texture. If the image contains very fine detail, you might need to use a lower threshold setting. High threshold settings will only sharpen the darker thick lines in the image.

Converting to Line Art

When you print an image that contains shades of gray, your printer uses a halftone screen, which prevents your grayscale image from having crisp edges. In order for you to get nice, crisp edges, the image must *only* contain pure black and pure white—that's true line art.

NOTE

The Unsharp Mask filter is used here because it's the only sharpening filter that gives you enough control over the end result. The other filters don't ask you for any settings.

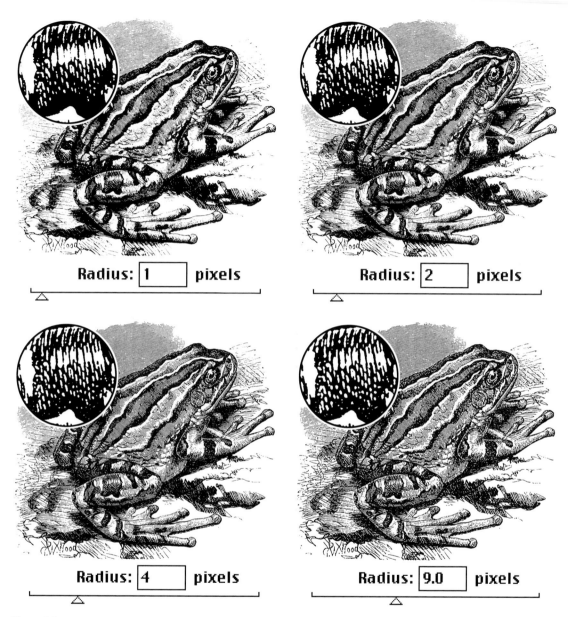

Figure 5.9
The radius setting controls how much shadow detail will appear.

Adding a Threshold Adjustment Layer

The Threshold command will rid the image of all shades of gray, leaving only pure black and pure white. By using an adjustment layer instead of applying Threshold directly to the image, you'll be able to easily make changes after the image is black and white. To achieve an accurate pre-view when using Threshold, you must view the image at 100% magnification. Double-click the Zoom tool in the Tool palette to quickly zoom to 100%. Create a new Threshold adjustment layer by choosing Adjustment Layer from the **Layer>New** menu and choosing Threshold from the pop-up menu. Adjust the slider until the lines in the image have the proper thickness and detail appears where it's most important in the image. You can compare the adjustment to the grayscale version of the image by turning the Preview option off and on (this enables you to toggle between the grayscale and black-and-white ver-sions of the image).

The Threshold dialog box forces anything *darker* than the threshold number to black, and anything *lighter* than the threshold number to white (see Figures 5.10 to 5.14). Refer to the table in Chapter 6, "Optimizing Grayscale Images," to see what the threshold numbers mean.

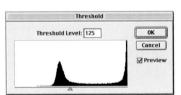

Figure 5.11
The threshold setting is too low.

Figure 5.10
The lines appear to be breaking up.

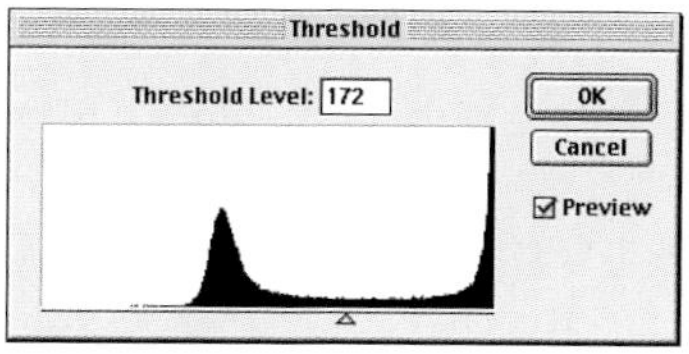

Figure 5.13
Proper threshold setting.

Figure 5.12
This image shows good highlight detail without plugging up the shadow detail.

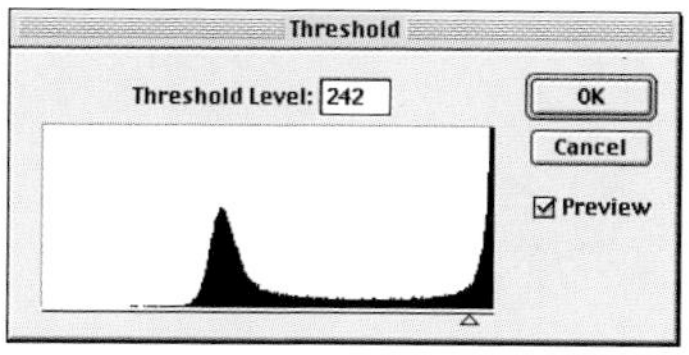

Figure 5.15
The threshold setting is too high.

Figure 5.14
This image has no shadow detail and the lines are too thick.

Refining Areas

To retain additional detail, you must enhance the grayscale image that's below the adjustment layer. To do so, click the name of the layer that contains the original image. There are many ways to enhance the image, including the following:

Increase shadow detail—To bring out detail in shadow areas that originally contained very fine detail, brush across the image with the Sharpen tool.

Fix broken lines—To clean up broken lines, or to make lines thicker, brush across the image with the Burn tool by using the Shadows setting. If the Burn tool doesn't change the image enough, use the History brush with the blending mode menu set to Multiply or Darken to increase the line thickness. Lower the opacity setting if the changes are too extreme.

Figures 5.16 to 5.19 show the quality improvement that is possible by scanning in Grayscale instead of Line Art mode. Even more detail could be brought out of Figure 5.19 by using the enhancement techniques that were applied to Figure 5.20.

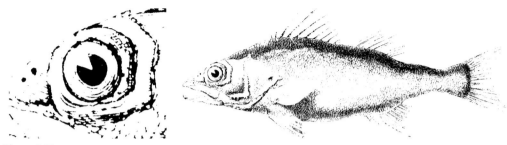

Figure 5.16
Raw line art scan. Same as scanning in grayscale and using the default threshold setting.

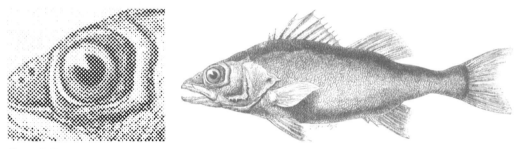

Figure 5.17
Raw grayscale scan. Lines are not crisp, and the file size is very large.

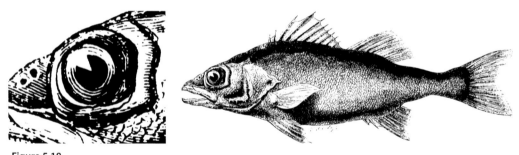

Figure 5.18
Grayscale scan with a proper threshold setting. The shadow detail is plugged up.

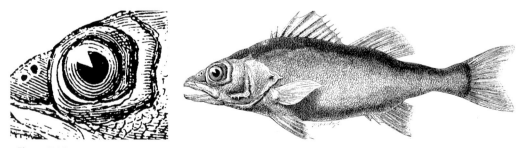

Figure 5.19
Grayscale scan with sharpening and a proper threshold setting. Shows good shadow detail.

Reduce line thickness—To reduce the thickness of lines, brush across the image with the Dodge tool by using the Highlights or Midtones setting. If the Dodge tool doesn't change the image enough, use the History brush with the blending mode menu set to Screen or Lighten to make the lines thinner. Lower the Opacity setting if the changes are too extreme.

If the Dodge and Burn tools don't change the image enough, use the History brush with the blending mode menu set to Hardlight to make lines thinner. Lower the opacity setting if the changes are too extreme.

Control text thickness—If you're scanning text at large point sizes, you can make the text thicker by choosing **Filter>Other>Minimum** or thinner by choosing **Filter>Other>Maximum**. If the adjectives used in these menu options seem contrary to common sense, well, they are. Just remember to apply reverse logic when dealing with text thickness.

NOTE

You can change the current brush at any time by typing [or]. This will cycle through the choices available in the Brushes palette.

Figure 5.20 shows examples of these settings.

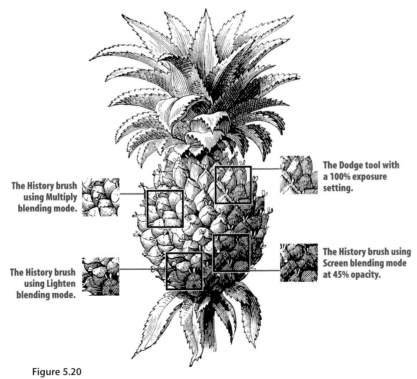

The History brush using Multiply blending mode.

The Dodge tool with a 100% exposure setting.

The History brush using Lighten blending mode.

The History brush using Screen blending mode at 45% opacity.

Figure 5.20
Refining the image.

Minimizing File Size

Nobody likes dealing with big, bloated files. They're greedy resource hogs that slow down your system and wreak havoc on your ability to work quickly and efficiently. Any extra white space around the image makes the file size larger than needed, because it's not necessary for printing the image. To further simplify the image, choose Flatten Image from the side menu of the Layers palette and then use the Eraser tool to clean up any stray pixels in the white area that surrounds the image.

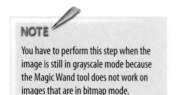

NOTE

You have to perform this step when the image is still in grayscale mode because the Magic Wand tool does not work on images that are in bitmap mode.

Cropping the Image

Select the white areas surrounding the image by double-clicking the Magic Wand tool and setting the tolerance to 0; then click on the white area that surrounds the image. Next, choose **Select>Inverse** to select everything except the white space. To crop the image, it's helpful to use guides. Turn on the rulers by choosing **View>Show Rulers** and then pull out a guide for each side of the image. The guides will snap to the edges of the selection you just made. After you've created a guide for each side of the image, choose the Marquee selection tool and click the upper-left corner of the guides and then drag to the lower-right corner. Finally, choose **Image>Crop** to discard the white areas that surround the image.

Converting to Bitmap

The image is now pure black and white, but the file itself is still in grayscale mode. The image must be converted to bitmap mode in order to save disk space and make sure that any final editing does not produce unwanted shades of gray. Convert the image from grayscale to bitmap by choosing **Image>Mode>Bitmap**. This brings up the Bitmap dialog box (see Figure 5.21). Make sure the input and output resolution numbers match and use the 50% threshold method, which will ensure that shades of gray are converted into smooth lines and won't look noisy. In bitmap mode, the image can only contain pure black and

Figure 5.21
The Bitmap dialog box.

pure white; therefore, the file size is much smaller than one for a grayscale image. In fact, grayscale images are eight times larger than bitmap images.

Saving As EPS or TIFF

Save the image in EPS or TIFF format. The EPS file format allows you to specify whether the white areas should be solid or transparent (see Figure 5.22).

Figure 5.22
The EPS Options dialog box.

Closing Thoughts

Lately I've been noticing that a lot of the line art out there is inferior to what I used to see only a few years ago. Check it out for yourself! Pick up any magazine (even the high-end ones sometimes) and look through it for line art images. If your experience is anything like mine, you'll probably be surprised to see some really mediocre stuff—edges are jagged, lines are broken up, and patterns look clogged. My theory is that people stopped sending out for line art scans and started performing them in-house.

That's fine, but only if you're not sacrificing quality for convenience. After reading this chapter, I hope you'll agree with me that you can have both. As long as you know how to get a good scan that captures the right amount of detail, and then know how to enhance the scanned image in Photoshop, there's no reason why you can't end up with exquisite line art.

Ask Adobe

Q: Why do they call it "Bitmap mode" instead of Line Art mode?

A: Two reasons: First, because that's what it was initially called in the Macintosh OS. Second, because "Line Art" would cause confusion with programs dealing with vector graphics.

Q: Why are most editing tools not available in Bitmap mode?

A: Most of the editing tools need a more or less continuous range of values with which to work. Bitmap mode doesn't provide that because every pixel is either black or white. Consider, for example, the Dodge tool, which wants to progressively lighten pixels. There isn't

NOTE

If you resize an image that's already in bitmap mode (pure black and pure white), the individual pixels in the image become large black squares. To maintain quality, convert the image to grayscale mode and then use the Gaussian Blur filter with a setting just high enough to introduce shades of gray (see Figure 5.23). Now you can use the techniques listed in this chapter to enhance the image and convert it back to bitmap mode.

Figure 5.23
The Gaussian Blur dialog box.

much it can do that is interesting when all it can do is change a pixel from black to white. For similar reasons, a lot of operations aren't available in indexed color mode because, though there is a range of color values, it doesn't necessarily have any order to it.

Ben's Techno-Babble Decoder Ring

Line Art—Any artwork that consists of pure black lines on a pure white background. Line art images always contain extremely crisp edges and do not contain any shades of gray or color.

Threshold—An adjustment that converts all shades of gray to pure black and pure white. Any shades of gray brighter than the threshold value will become white, and any shades darker than the threshold value will become black.

Resample—The process of changing the total number of pixels in an image without cropping or adding empty space.

Courtesy of Nik Willmore.

Courtesy of Nik Willmore.

6 Optimizing Grayscale Images

If you go through life convinced that your way is always best, all the new ideas in the world will pass you by.
—Akio Morita,
Founder of Sony

Courtesy of David Plunkert, www.spurdesign.com.

When inexperienced users first try to adjust a grayscale image, they usually look for something familiar and easy; and the Brightness and Contrast dialog box is frequently where they end up. With a mere flick of the mouse, they can dramatically improve their image. Big results, little effort. At first glance, Brightness and Contrast seem to hold great promise. But does it *really* do the job?

If you were to compare images adjusted with Brightness and Contrast with the images you see in high-end magazines and brochures, you'd notice that the quality of the Brightness and Contrast images is inferior. Why? Because the Brightness and Contrast dialog box adjusts the *entire* image an *equal* amount. So, if you increase the brightness until an area that was 10% gray becomes white, then areas that are black will also be changed the same amount and become 90% gray. By using controls like these, it is extremely hard to achieve professional quality. When you correct one problem, you usually introduce another.

Common adjustment complaints include:

Images appear flat (lacking contrast)

Images print overly dark

Blown out detail in the highlights (bright white areas in the middle of people's foreheads)

Lack of detail in the shadows

All of these problems and more can be solved in one dialog box.

Levels Is the Solution

The Levels dialog box (choose **Image>Adjust>Levels**) is the cure for most common complaints about image quality (see Figure 6.1). It offers you far more control and feedback than Brightness and Contrast. Instead of having only two sliders to adjust, Levels offers you five, as well as a bar chart that indicates exactly what is happening to the image. And unlike the sliders in Brightness and Contrast, the Levels sliders don't change the entire image an equal amount.

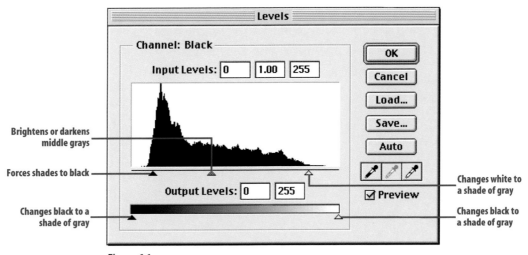

Brightens or darkens middle grays

Forces shades to black

Changes black to a shade of gray

Changes white to a shade of gray

Changes black to a shade of gray

Figure 6.1
Understanding the Levels sliders.

It might take several pages to describe all the controls in the Levels dialog box, but once you know how to use them it will take you less than a minute to optimize an image. Just remember to apply each of the controls in Levels because each builds on the last. You can liken the steps in Levels to the ingredients in créme brülé. Leave one out and you might end up with pudding instead of perfection.

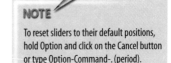

NOTE

To reset sliders to their default positions, hold Option and click on the Cancel button or type Option-Command-. (period).

The Histogram Is Your Guide

You can use the bar chart (histogram) at the top of the Levels dialog box to determine if the adjustments you're making are going to harm the image or improve it. The histogram indicates which shades of gray are in your image and how much space they take up. If you find a gap in the histogram, you can look at the gradient directly below it to see which shade of gray is missing from your image.

The height of the bars indicates how much space the shades take up in the image. The height doesn't indicate an exact number of pixels; instead, it measures how much space the shade takes up *compared* to the other shades in the image. It's as if everyone in a room stood up and you compared how tall each person was without using a ruler.

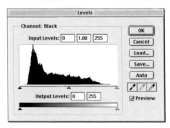

Figure 6.2
This histogram indicates that the shades between 90% and 75% take up a lot of space (tall bars) and the shades between 5% and 15% take up little space (short bars).

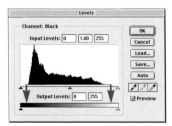

Figure 6.3
Look directly below the ends of the histogram to determine the brightest and darkest shades present in the image.

WARNING

If you are using Photoshop with default settings, the histogram in the Levels dialog box will not be accurate. Choose **File>Preferences>Image Cache** and turn off the Use Cache for Histograms setting. If you leave this setting turned on (default setting) then the histogram will be accurate only when you are viewing your image at 100% magnification. This setting was designed to speed up the creation of histograms, but it also makes them less accurate.

You wouldn't know exactly how tall anyone was, but you'd have an indication of how tall each person was compared to the others. (See Figure 6.2.)

By looking directly below the *first* bar that appears on the left end of the histogram you can determine the darkest shade of gray in the image. By looking directly below the *last* bar that appears on the right end of the histogram you can determine the brightest shade of gray in the image. So if you look at Figure 6.3, you might notice the image contains no pure blacks or pure whites. The darkest shade of gray is about 95%, and the brightest shade is about 6%.

Evaluate and Adjust Contrast

The brightest and darkest areas of your computer monitor are nowhere near as bright or dark as the objects you'll find in the real world. It's even more extreme when you look at the brightest and darkest areas of a printed brochure—the paper is actually pretty dull and the ink isn't all that dark. Because of this, you'll need to use the full range of shades from black to white in order to make your photos look as close to reality as possible.

By adjusting the upper right and upper left sliders in the Levels dialog box, you can dramatically improve the contrast of an image and make it appear more lifelike. When you move the upper left slider in the Levels dialog box, you'll be forcing the shade of gray directly below it, and any shade darker than it, to black. If you move the left slider until it touches the first bar on the histogram, you'll be forcing the darkest shade of gray in the image to black, which should give you nice dark shadows.

By moving the upper right slider, you will force the shade that appears directly below the slider (see the gradient), and any shade brighter than it, to white. If you move the right slider until it touches the last bar on the histogram, you'll be forcing the brightest shade of gray to white, which should give you nice white highlights.

By adjusting both sliders, your image will be using the full range of shades available to a grayscale image (see Figure 6.4). If you move the sliders past the beginning and end of the histogram, you will get even more contrast; but you will risk losing important detail in the process.

Hidden Features to the Rescue

To achieve maximum contrast without sacrificing detail, Adobe created a hidden feature in the Levels dialog box. It's known as Threshold mode because it acts like the Threshold dialog box. This feature allows you to see exactly which areas are becoming black or white and is the key to ensuring that you don't sacrifice detail. To get to the hidden feature you first have to turn off the Preview checkbox in the Levels dialog box, then hold down the Option key when you move the upper right and upper left sliders.

When you move the upper left slider with the hidden feature turned on, the entire screen should turn white until the slider touches the first bar on the histogram; then small black areas should start to appear. These are the areas that will become pure black. You want to make sure you don't force a large concentrated area to black, so move the slider until only small areas appear. You also want to make sure the areas that are becoming black still contain detail. Detail will show up looking like noise (not the kind you hear, the kind you see on television when you don't have an antenna hooked up), so make sure those small areas also look noisy. You'll need to repeat this process with the upper right slider to make sure you get maximal contrast (see Figures 6.5 to 6.15).

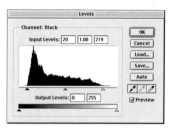

Figure 6.4
The shades that are beyond the upper right and left triangles will become pure black and pure white.

NOTE

The middle slider will move when you adjust the upper right or upper left slider. This happens because Photoshop is attempting to keep the middle slider in the same position relative to the other two sliders. So if the middle slider was centered between the other two, it will remain centered when you move one of the outer sliders.

WARNING

Threshold mode works only when the Use Video LUT Animation option is on (choose **File>Preferences>Displays & Cursors**) and is not available when using adjustment layers. If you want to use an adjustment layer, the technique in the following section shows you how to use the Threshold dialog box as a substitute.

Figure 6.5
Original. (© 1998 PhotoDisc)

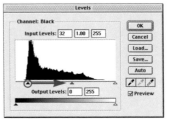

Figure 6.6
Way too far.

Figure 6.7
Large areas lose detail and become
pure black.

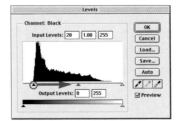

Figure 6.8
Just right.

Figure 6.9
Small areas become black, but still
contain detail (noise).

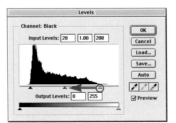

Figure 6.10
Way too far.

Figure 6.11
Large areas lose detail and become
pure white.

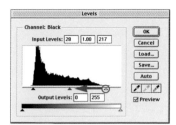

Figure 6.12
Too far.

Figure 6.13
Small areas lose detail.

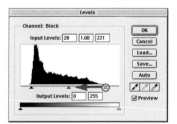

Figure 6.14
Just right.

Figure 6.15
Small areas become white, but still contain detail (noise).

Threshold as a Substitute

As mentioned in the last section, this hidden feature works only on computers that have video cards supporting Video LUT Animation. The majority of Macintosh systems support this feature, but it is only supported on a handful of Windows systems. Use the following technique on Windows systems that don't support Video LUT animation.

Choose **Image>Adjust>Threshold** and move the slider all the way to the left of the histogram; then slowly move it to the right until an area appears that is not a large, concentrated area, and make sure it looks noisy. Record the number at the top of the Threshold dialog box. Repeat the process, this time on the right side of the histogram. Then to make sure you don't turn the entire image to black and white, click the Cancel button. Now, choose Levels and enter the numbers from the Threshold dialog box at the top of the Levels dialog box. The end result will be exactly the same, you just have to use two dialog boxes instead of just one (see Figures 6.16 to 6.18).

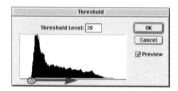

Figure 6.16
Write down the proper Threshold setting for the shadow, then click Cancel.

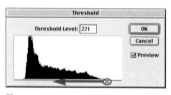

Figure 6.17
Write down the proper Threshold setting for the highlight, then click Cancel.

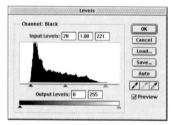

Figure 6.18
Transfer the Threshold settings into the upper left (shadow) and upper right (highlight) text fields in the Levels dialog box.

The Histogram Gives You Feedback

Once you have applied an adjustment to your image, you can see an updated histogram by choosing **Image>Adjust>Levels** again. That way you can see exactly how your adjustments affected the image. You should notice that after adjusting the upper right and upper left sliders, the histogram will stretch all the way across the area available. It's just like stretching out a slinky (you remember, "it walks down stairs alone or in pairs"). As you pull on the ends of the slinky, the loops stretch out and start to create gaps. The same thing happens to a histogram because Photoshop cannot add more bars to the histogram; it can only spread out the ones that were already there. And remember, gaps in the histogram mean that certain shades of gray are missing from the image. So, the more you adjust an image using Levels, the more you increase the possibility that you'll lose some of the smooth transitions between bright and dark areas (see Figure 6.19).

If you see large spikes on either end of the histogram, as shown in Figure 6.20, it's an indication that you've lost detail. That's because you forced quite a bit of space to white or black using Levels. But you'd know you did that because you were using the hidden feature, right? Or maybe you couldn't control yourself and were using that Brightness and Contrast dialog box where you can't tell if you damage the image! You might also get spikes on the ends of the histogram if you scan an image with a brightness setting that is way too high or too low.

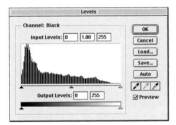

Figure 6.19
After adjusting the top two sliders, your image should use the full range of shades available.

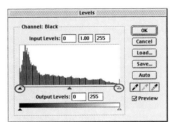

Figure 6.20
Spikes on the end of a histogram usually indicate lost detail.

Improve Brightness

After you have achieved good contrast, your image might look too dark. The middle slider in the Levels dialog box can fix that (Techies love to call this the gamma setting, but us plain folks call it the Midpoint), as shown in Figure 6.22. If you move the middle slider to the left, the image will become brighter without messing up the dark areas of your image. Black areas will stay nice and black. Or, you can move the middle slider to the right to darken the image without messing up the bright areas of the image. White areas will stay bright white.

If you want to know what this adjustment is doing, just look directly below the middle slider; the shade of gray below it will become 50% gray. If you look at an updated histogram of the image, it will look like you stretched out a slinky, then grabbed one side and pulled it to the middle. Some bars will get scrunched (is that a technical term?) together, while others get spread apart.

NOTE

If you find evenly spaced spikes in the histogram of an unadjusted image, it usually indicates a noisy scan (see Figure 6.21). I know, noise is something you hear, not see. Well, just think of the static you see when you don't have an antenna attached to your television—that's visual noise.

Spikes that show up after an image has been adjusted with Levels do not indicate noise. It's as if you took your trusty slinky and tried to squish it down to a centimeter wide. Something would have to budge. The only way I can do it is to bend the slinky into a "V" shape where the loops start piling up, one on top of the other. Otherwise, the loops just line up in a nice row and limit how much I can compress the slinky. Well, the same thing happens with the histogram. Let's say you try to squish 20 bars into a space that is only 15 pixels wide on the histogram. Well, five of the bars have to disappear. They are going to just pile on top of the bars next to them and make those bars about twice as tall. When this happens, you get evenly spaced spikes across part of the histogram.

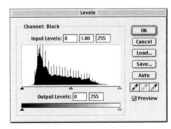

Figure 6.21
Noise.

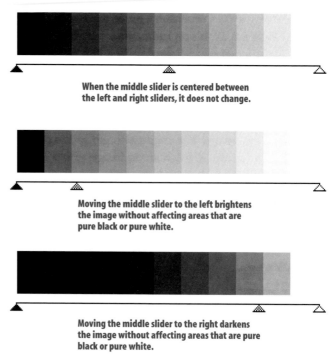

When the middle slider is centered between
the left and right sliders, it does not change.

Moving the middle slider to the left brightens
the image without affecting areas that are
pure black or pure white.

Moving the middle slider to the right darkens
the image without affecting areas that are pure
black or pure white.

Figure 6.22
Understanding the middle slider.

Setting Up Your Images for Final Output

If your images are printed, especially with ink on paper, chances are they will end up looking a lot darker than they did when you viewed them on screen. This darkness is a result of dot gain; and, fortunately, Photoshop allows you to compensate for it. By telling Photoshop ahead of time how you intend to output your images, you'll be able to adjust the on-screen appearance of your image to look as dark as it should be after it's printed.

You can prevent this from happening by telling Photoshop exactly how much darker the images will become when printed. This is known as dot gain. This setting is one you want to ask your printing company about; otherwise, you'll just be guessing and you might not like your end result. But just in case you're working at midnight or don't have time to ask your printing company, I'll give you a table of generic settings. You can type this setting into the **File> Color Settings>CMYK Setup** dialog box, shown in Figure 6.23.

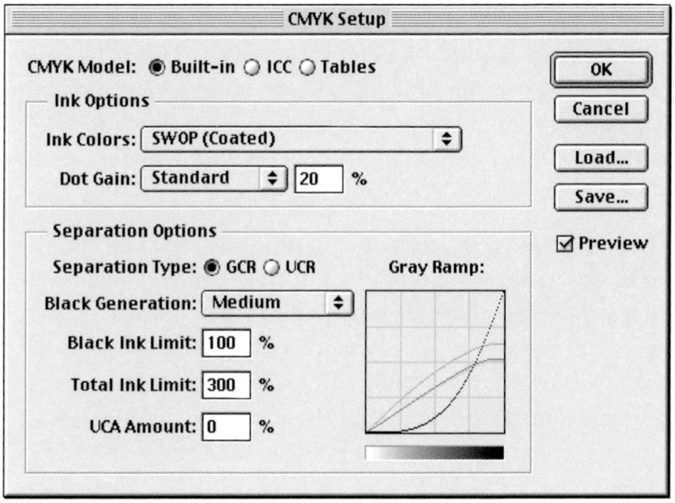

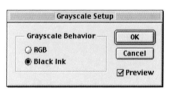

Figure 6.23
CMYK Setup dialog box.

Dot Gain Settings

Newspapers	30%
Magazines and brochures	15%
High-end brochures	10%

The second thing you need to do is set up Photoshop so that you'll be able to display your images properly (suggested settings are shown in the table to the right). Choose **File>Color Settings>Grayscale Setup** and turn on the Preview checkbox. Choose RGB if your end result will be displayed on a computer monitor or television set (television and computer monitors use Red, Green, and Blue light to display everything, even grayscale images); choose Black Ink if the image will be printed. By choosing Black Ink, Photoshop knows to display your images darker than they really are to simulate what will happen when they are printed (see Figure 6.24).

Figure 6.24
Grayscale Setup dialog box.

Prepare for a Printing Press

When you give your printing company your original output, they will have to make three copies of it before it becomes a printed piece. First, they'll convert the original into a piece of metal called a printing plate (first copy). Then they will put the plate on a big, round roller on the printing press and flood it with water and ink. The ink will stick to the plate only where your images and text should be; the water will make sure it doesn't stick to the other areas. Next to that roller is another one known as a

NOTE

If your images are destined for multimedia output (web, video, animation, etc.) then you can skip over the next few steps and go directly to the Sharpening section later in this chapter.

blanket; it's just covered with rubber. The plate will come into contact with the blanket so the ink on the plate will transfer over to the blanket (second copy). And finally the blanket will touch a sheet of paper and transfer the ink onto it (the last copy). Each time a copy is made, you lose some of the smallest dots in the image.

Before I show you how to compensate for the loss of detail in the bright areas of your image, let's look at what happens to the darkest areas. When you print with ink on paper, the ink always absorbs into the paper and spreads out. Just as when you spill coffee on a sheet of paper, it spreads out as it absorbs into the paper. This will cause the darkest areas of an image (97%, 98%, 99%) to become pure black. If you don't adjust for this, you will lose detail in the shadows of your image.

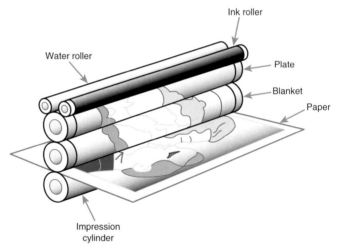

Figure 6.25
Three copies are made before your image turns into a printed page.

Most printing companies create a simple test strip that they print on the edge of your job in the area that will be cropped off after it's printed. This test strip contains shades of gray from 1% to about 5% so they can determine the lightest shade of gray that doesn't disappear and become pure white. Of course, your printing company doesn't just use plain English to describe it; instead, they invented the term *minimum highlight dot reproducible on press.* On the same sheet of paper they will also add shades of gray from 99% to about 75% so they can see the darkest shade of gray that doesn't become pure black. They came up with the term *maximum shadow dot reproducible on press* for that one. If you ask your printing company, they can usually tell you exactly which settings to use. I know you don't always know who will print your images or don't have the time to ask, so I'll give you some generic numbers to use. But, first, let's find out how we compensate for this.

Here's where you come in. By moving the lower right slider in the Levels dialog box, you will change white to the shade of gray the slider is pointing to. You want to move this slider until it points to the lightest shade of gray that will not disappear and become white (known as the minimum highlight dot).

You don't want to just eyeball this setting; so instead of just looking at the shades of gray, we'll use the numbers that are in the Levels dialog box (the ones labeled Output Levels). There is one problem with the numbers: they range from 0-255 instead of 0-100%! Well, this is because you can have up to 256 shades of gray in a grayscale image and Photoshop wants you to be able to control them all. When you're using this numbering system, think about light instead of ink. If you have no light (0), then it would be pitch black; if you have as much light as possible (255), you could call that white. So that you won't need a calculator, I'll give you a conversion table and a special technique just in case you don't have this book around when you need to make conversions.

NOTE

To better understand the effect on quality, try photocopying one of the images from this book. Next, make a copy of the copy, and then a copy of that copy. When you compare the original image to the one that has been copied three times, you'll notice that the brightest part of the image is now pure white. The same thing happens when you give your image to a printing company. Until you learn to compensate for this, you're likely to end up with pictures of people with big white spots in the middle of their foreheads.

Percentage Conversion Table

Percentage	#	Percentage	#	Percentage	#
100%	0	66%	87	32%	173
99%	3	65%	89	31%	176
98%	5	64%	92	30%	179
97%	8	63%	94	29%	181
96%	10	62%	97	28%	184
95%	13	61%	100	27%	186
94%	15	60%	102	26%	189
93%	18	59%	105	25%	191
92%	20	58%	107	24%	194
91%	23	57%	110	23%	196
90%	26	56%	112	22%	199
89%	28	55%	115	21%	202
88%	31	54%	117	20%	204
87%	33	53%	120	19%	207
86%	36	52%	122	18%	209
85%	38	51%	125	17%	211
84%	41	50%	128	16%	214
83%	44	49%	130	15%	217
82%	46	48%	133	14%	219
81%	49	47%	135	13%	222
80%	51	46%	138	12%	224
79%	54	45%	140	11%	227
78%	56	44%	143	10%	229
77%	59	43%	145	9%	232
76%	61	42%	148	8%	235
75%	64	41%	150	7%	237
74%	66	40%	153	6%	240
73%	69	39%	156	5%	242
72%	71	38%	158	4%	245
71%	74	37%	161	3%	247
70%	77	36%	163	2%	250
69%	79	35%	166	1%	252
68%	82	34%	168	0%	255
67%	84	33%	171		

Here's how to turn Photoshop's palettes into a number conversion tool. Open any color photo and choose **Window>Show Color** to open the color palette. Next, choose Grayscale Slider from the side menu of the palette (see Figure 6.26). Now enter the percentage you would like to convert into the 0-255 numbering system. Finally, choose RGB Sliders from the side menu, as in Figure 6.27, and... Bingo, you have three copies of the number that should be used in Levels! This numbering system is used for the outer four sliders in the Levels dialog box.

By moving the lower left slider in the Levels dialog box, you will change black to the shade of gray the slider is pointing to (see Figure 6.28). You want to move this slider until it points to the darkest shade of gray that will not plug up and become black (known as the maximum shadow dot).

Common Minimum Highlight Settings

Newspapers	3%
Magazines & Brochures	3%
High-end Brochures	3%

Common Maximum Shadow Settings.

Newspapers	75%
Magazines & Brochures	90%
High-end Brochures	95%

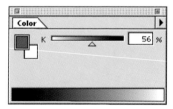

Figure 6.26
Choose Grayscale Slider before entering the number you would like to convert.

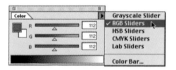

Figure 6.27
Choose RGB Sliders to transform your percentage into the 0-255 numbering system.

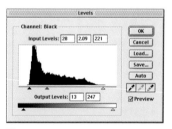

Figure 6.28
The bottom sliders reduce image contrast to compensate for the limitations of the printing press.

At first glance this stuff might seem complicated, but it is really quite simple. All you do is use the numbers from the tables, or ask your printing company for settings; then look them up in the Conversion Table. If you always print on the same kind of paper, you'll always use the same numbers, so you'll end up remembering them.

A Quick Recap

The Levels dialog box contains five sliders, so there are five quick steps to adjusting your grayscale image. The whole process takes less than a minute once you get used to it.

1. Move the upper left slider until it touches the first bar on the histogram to force the darkest area of the image to black (use the hidden feature to go as far as possible without damaging the image). (See Figure 6.29.)

2. Move the upper right slider until it touches the last bar on the histogram to force the brightest area of the image to white (again, use the hidden feature to go as far as possible without damaging the image). (See Figure 6.30.)

3. Move the middle slider to the right until the image looks nice and bright. (See Figure 6.31.)

Figure 6.29
Result of adjusting upper left slider.

Figure 6.30
Result of adjusting upper right slider.

Figure 6.31
Result of adjusting middle slider.

4. Move the lower left slider to make sure the shadows won't plug up and become pure black on the printing press (use the tables for settings or ask your printer for more precise ones). (See Figure 6.32.)

5. Move the lower right slider to make sure you don't lose detail in the highlights when the smallest dots in your image disappear on the printing press (use the tables for settings or ask your printer for more precise ones). (See Figure 6.33.) I usually adjust all five sliders before clicking OK to apply them.

Figure 6.32
Result of adjusting lower left slider.

Figure 6.33
Result of adjusting lower right slider.

Post Adjustment Analysis

Any time you adjust an image, you run the risk of introducing some artifacts that might not be all that pleasant. But in Photoshop there is usually at least one "fix it" for just about every artifact. So let's take a look at what can happen to your image after applying Levels.

Adjustment Artifacts

After you've adjusted an image and you look at an updated histogram, you might find wide gaps in the histogram—this indicates posterization (see Figure 6.34). Posterization is when you should have a smooth transition between areas and instead you see a drastic jump between a bright and dark area. Some call this banding or stair stepping. As long as the gaps in the histogram are smaller than three pixels wide, you probably won't notice it in the image.

Adjusting the image usually causes these gaps. As you adjust the image, the bars on the histogram spread out and gaps start to appear (remember the slinky). The more extreme the adjustment you make, the wider the gaps appear.

NOTE

If you own a 30-bit or higher scanner and your scanning software contains a histogram and has the same adjustment controls available, you can make adjustments within your scanning software. Most scanners can deliver a histogram without gaps because they can look back to the image and pick up extra shades of gray that would fill the gaps. For this to work, you have to own a 30-bit scanner or above. These days almost all scanners are 30-bit or higher. If your scanner is more than two years old, there is a chance you might own a 24-bit model. If you are using one of those 24-bit scanners, there is no advantage to making the adjustments within your scanning software.

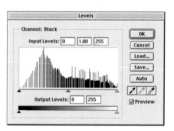

Figure 6.34
Gaps in a histogram indicate Posterization.

NOTE

To see an updated histogram after adjusting the image, you must first apply the adjustment, then open the Levels dialog box again.

NOTE

I don't use this technique on every image. Just on those that have extremely noticeable posterization.

Eliminating Posterization

If you get huge gaps in the histogram, you will probably be able to see the posterization, which usually shows up in the dark areas of the image. Here is a trick that can minimize the posterization. The only problem is that you have to apply this technique manually to each area that is posterized. Although it might take you a little bit of time, the results will be worth it.

To begin, double-click the Magic Wand tool, set the Tolerance setting to zero, and click on an area that looks posterized. Next, choose **Select>Modify>Border**, and use a setting of 2 for slight posterization, or 4 for a moderate amount of posterization. Now apply **Filter>Gaussian Blur** until the area looks smooth (see Figures 6.35 and 6.36). Repeat this process on all the areas that are posterized until you no longer notice any posterization.

Figure 6.35
Click on the preview image, or lower the Radius setting to see the edges of the posterized area.

Figure 6.36
Increase the Radius setting until the posterized area appears smooth.

Sharpening

By now your image should have great contrast and should reproduce nicely on a printing press. But, almost all images that are scanned need to be *sharpened*. First I'll show you the controls available when sharpening; then I'll show you exactly how I go about sharpening an image.

To sharpen an image, choose **Filter>Sharpen**. Photoshop will present you with a pop-out menu of choices. The top three might sound friendly (Sharpen, Sharpen More,

Sharpen Edges), but you need to use the bottom one (Unsharp Mask). The reason you need to use Unsharp is because it is the only choice that allows you to control exactly how much the image will be sharpened. You can think of the other choices as being simple presets that just enter different numbers into the Unsharp Mask filter.

The reason it has the scary name is because before people used desktop computers, they sharpened images in a photographic darkroom. They would have to go through a process that involved a blurry (unsharp) version of the image. This would take well over an hour (don't worry, in Photoshop it only takes seconds) and would not be much fun. The process they'd go through in the darkroom was known as making an Unsharp Mask, so Adobe just borrowed that term when they made the Unsharp Mask filter.

The Unsharp Mask filter increases the contrast where two shades of gray touch in the image so their edges become more prominent and therefore are easier to see. To easily view the effect of the Unsharp Mask filter (see Figure 6.37), I'll demonstrate a document that contains only three shades of gray (20%, 30%, and 50%), as shown in Figures 6.38 to 6.41. When you choose Unsharp Mask, you'll be presented with three sliders: Amount, Radius, and Threshold.

> **Amount**—How much the contrast will be increased and, therefore, how obvious the sharpening will be.

> **Radius**—How much space will be used. If you use too much, it will be obvious.

> **Threshold**—How different two touching shades have to be in order to be sharpened. As you increase this setting, only the areas that are drastically different will be sharpened.

Now that we've explored all the options that are available with the Unsharp Mask filter, let's get down to business and find out how to apply it to an image.

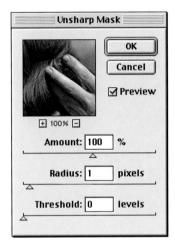

NOTE

You must view your image at 100% magnification in order to get an accurate view of your image while you are applying the Unsharp Mask filter. A quick way to view an image at 100% is to double-click the Zoom tool.

Figure 6.37
Unsharp Mask.

Figure 6.38
The simple document.

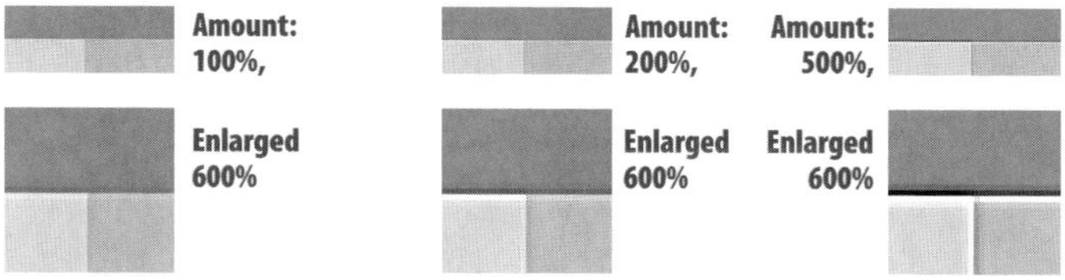

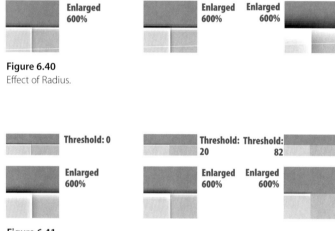

Figure 6.39
Effect of Amount.

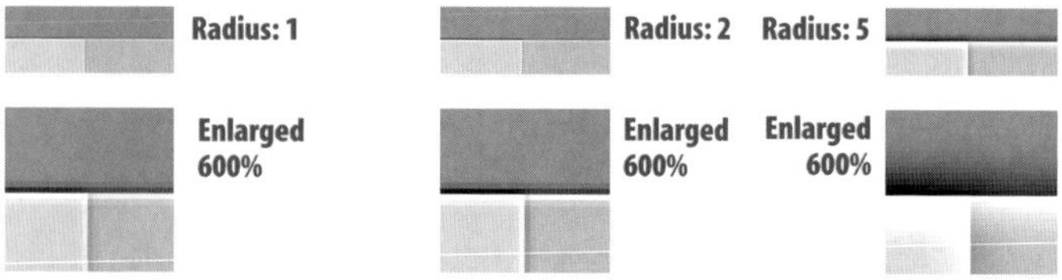

Figure 6.40
Effect of Radius.

Figure 6.41
Effect of Threshold.

> **NOTE**
>
> If you read other books, you'll run across a bunch of "Magic Formulas" that instruct you to multiply the resolution of the image by anywhere from 150 to 225. Supposedly, this will provide you with the ideal Radius setting for your image. I just don't buy it—each image needs to be sharpened a different amount and the amount depends on the content of the image. Whenever the fine detail starts to fall apart, stop! Or, if you are using one of these magic numbers and the image still doesn't appear sharp, then go ahead and use a higher setting. But for all the images I've ever adjusted, I've always used a setting below 2. Anything over 2 just always seems to trash the fine detail in the image.

> **NOTE**
>
> To gain more control over the sharpening process, duplicate the main image layer before sharpening the image. Sharpen this duplicate layer, then duplicate the sharpened version and set one of the sharpened layers to Darken and the other to Lighten. Now the bright part of the sharpening can be controlled separately from the dark part by lowering the opacity setting of these two new layers. I'd use this technique only when the halos are too distracting.

Each time you apply the Unsharp Mask filter, it will remember the last settings you used. Because this filter is used on a wide variety of images (remember we used it for line art scanning), the first thing we'll need to do is make sure it isn't using an extreme setting. So choose **Filter>Sharpen>Unsharp** Mask and type in the generic numbers of Amount=100, Radius=1, Threshold=0.

Now, I know you're not going to want to hear this, but I'll mention it anyway. If you are going to print this image, you can sharpen the image until it looks just a little bit over-sharp.

Figure 6.42
Adjust the Amount setting until the image looks nice and sharp. You'll know this setting is too high when the white halos that appear become overly dominant or when the fine detail in the image starts to break apart into pure black and pure white.

Figure 6.43
If the Amount setting does not make the image look sharp enough, adjust Radius a small amount (1.1, 1.2, 1.3). I always use a very low setting, (though this slider can go up to 250). Go ahead and any setting above 2—your image will look ridiculous.

Figure 6.44
If your image contains skin tones or other areas that should look very smooth, increase the Threshold slider until those areas do look smooth. I usually use Threshold settings between 0 and 9.

NOTE

On the CD-ROM accompanying this book, you'll find a PDF file that supplements this chapter. The file, called extras.pdf, contains the following topics:
    Using the Levels dialog box Save and Load buttons
    Using the Levels dialog box and eyedroppers
    Using the Levels dialog box Auto button
    Using Brightness and Contrast

Closing Thoughts

We've covered two main dialog boxes, Levels and Unsharp Mask. Remember, after you've practiced a few times, the whole process takes about a minute. When you feel that you have mastered Levels, you will be ready to take on the ultimate adjustment tool—Curves. Curves is equipped to do the same basic corrections as Levels, but can also do much, much more. In general, I always start out using Levels with grayscale, and then move on to Curves to fix grayscale problems that Levels can't handle, or to work with color. It's like graduating from a Chevette to a Ferrari. The Ferrari takes more skill and coordination to master, but you get one hell of a ride. But that's another chapter.

Ask Adobe

Q: Why is Photoshop's adjustable sharpening filter called Unsharp Mask?

A: "Unsharp Mask" is the traditional prepress term for a sharpening operation based around using a blurred (unsharp) version of the image.

Q: What's the idea behind the Black Ink setting in the Grayscale Setup dialog box, and why does it occasionally brighten the image instead of darken it (when the image would really get darker on a printing press)?

A: This control is used to indicate whether grayscale images should be treated as an RGB gray (that is, R=G=B=gray value) or as the black plate of a CMYK image. The reason images would actually get lighter sometimes when using the Black Ink setting is that the darkening effect of ink dot gain could be less significant than the darkening effect of RGB gamma.

Q: What the heck does "gamma" mean? And what exactly does the gamma number mean?

A: Gamma curves are curves of the form y = x raised to the gamma power. The use of the term "gamma" in this context is an old colorimeter term. The key thing to remember for Levels is that a gamma value of 1.0 means "no change." For RGB spaces, a gamma value of 1.0 is generally undesirable because, while this makes the space behave uniformly from the standpoint of light energy, the human eye actually perceives things as behaving uniformly when the gamma value is closer to somewhere between 2.2 and 3.0. Another thing to remember in the context of RGB Setup is that lower gamma values give more emphasis to highlight detail, while higher values give more emphasis to shadow detail.

Ben's Techno-Babble Decoder Ring

Unsharp Mask—A term used to describe the traditional process of sharpening an image by combining a blurry version of the image (unsharp) with a normal version. The idea behind Unsharp Mask is to increase contrast and therefore detail.

Minimum Highlight Dot—The smallest halftone dot that is reproducible using a particular printing process. This is usually measured as a percentage and reflects the lowest percentage of ink that will not lose detail when printed.

Maximum Shadow Dot—The largest halftone dot that will not combine with the surrounding halftone dots to become pure black. This is usually measured as a percentage and reflects the highest percentage of ink that could be used without losing detail when printed. The type of paper usually determines what the Maximum Shadow Dot setting will be.

30-bit—Designates how many colors a scanner can capture. 10-bits of Red plus 10-bits of Green plus 10-bits of Blue equals 30-bits total. So, 10-bits per channel (RGB) is the same as 30-bits total. 10-bits=2 to the tenth power, which equals 1024. So a 30-bit scanner can capture 1.1 billion colors (1024×1024×1024=1.1 billion), whereas a 24-bit scanner can only capture 16.7 million colors. When scanning in grayscale, a 24-bit scanner captures 256 grays and a 30-bit scanner captures 1,024 grays.

Keyboard Shortcuts

Levels	Command-L
Auto Levels	Shift-Command-L
Re-apply Previous Setting	Option-Command-L

7 Understanding Curves

Have patience.
All things are difficult
before they become easy.
—Saadi

Courtesy of Michael Slack, www.slackart.com.

If I were going to be dropped on a deserted island and could bring only one thing with me, I might choose a Swiss army knife. With that knife, I could cut firewood, spear fish, and clean my teeth (remember the toothpick?). Much like a Swiss army knife, **Image>Adjust>Curves** can be used for just about anything. In fact, if I had to pick just one adjustment tool to use all the time, it would definitely be Curves. By mastering the Curves dialog box, you have so much control over your images that you might wonder why you would ever need to use the Levels or Brightness and Contrast dialog box. Let's take a look at some of the things you can do with the Curves adjustment tool:

You can pull out far more detail than possible with the sharpening filters (see Figures 7.1 to 7.3).

Figure 7.1
The original image. (© 1998 PhotoDisc)

Figure 7.2
The "unsharp" mask.

Figure 7.3
After a simple Curves adjustment.

You can lighten or darken areas without making selections (see Figures 7.4 and 7.5).

Figure 7.4
The original image. (© 1998 PhotoSpin)

Figure 7.5
After a simple Curves adjustment.

You can turn ordinary text into *extraordinary* text (see Figures 7.6 and 7.7).

Figure 7.6
The original text effect.

Figure 7.7
After a simple Curves adjustment.

You can color-correct your images without guesswork (see Figures 7.8 and 7.9).

Figure 7.8
The original image. (© 1998 Corel Corporation)

Figure 7.9
After a simple Curves adjustment.

None of these changes could be made by using Levels or Brightness and Contrast (that is, without making complicated selections or losing control over the result). Now you can see why you'll want to master Curves!

Using Curves, you can perform all the adjustments available in the Levels, Brightness and Contrast, and Threshold dialog boxes and much, much more. In fact, you can adjust each of the 256 shades of gray in your image independently (see Figure 7.10).

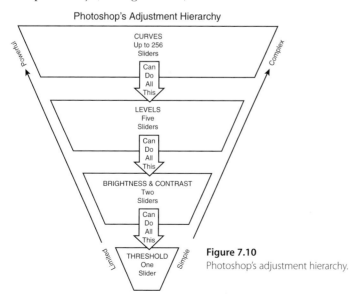

Figure 7.10
Photoshop's adjustment hierarchy.

With Power Comes Complexity

I find that the majority of Photoshop users never truly master (or even become comfortable with) Curves, just like some people never drive cars with manual transmissions. Perhaps the first time they tried to drive with a clutch, they drove up a really steep hill and encountered a stop sign at the top. Then, maybe a big garbage truck pulled up behind them within what seemed like an inch of their bumper. Well, you know what I'm getting at if you've ever driven a car with a clutch. When you're not comfortable with something and are forced to use it in a challenging situation, the tendency is to just give up. However, if you've spent enough time getting comfortable with using a manual transmission, you don't even think about it when you're driving. Curves works the same way. If you just play around with it, you might get scared away. However, if you hang in there, it becomes easier to use, and you'll find yourself doing some amazing things to your images.

But First, a Test!

Before we delve too far into Curves, I want to test your present knowledge of the Curves dialog box. Don't worry, though, because the lower you score, the more you should enjoy this chapter.

Look at the curve shown in Figure 7.11 and see if you can answer the following questions:

Which areas of the image will lose detail from this adjustment?

Which areas of the image will become brighter?

What happened to 62% gray?

What happened to the contrast of the image?

If you truly understand the Curves dialog box, then you found these questions extremely easy to answer. However, if you hesitated before answering any of these questions or couldn't answer them at all, then this chapter was designed for you.

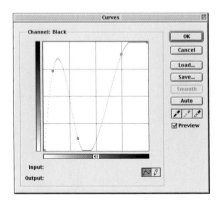

Figure 7.11
Can you figure out exactly what this curve will do to an image?

Working with the Curves Dialog Box

Because the Curves dialog box allows you to adjust every shade of gray in an image (256 in all), it works quite a bit differently than the other adjustment tools. Instead of offering you a few simple sliders (like Levels and other dialog boxes), Curves presents you with a graph. This graph consists of a grid and a line that you can bend into different shapes. When you attempt to bend a line, Photoshop tries to keep it looking like a nice smooth curve (hence the name). This graph is really like having one slider for each shade of gray in your image, which is why it takes a little longer to get used to. However, by the time you make it to the end of this chapter, you should be able to do some amazing things to your images. Let's jump in (head first) and look at one of Photoshop's most powerful tools.

The Gradients Are Your Guides

By looking at the two gradients in the Curves dialog, you can find out exactly what's happening to your image. The bottom gradient represents the shades of gray that were in your image before using Curves. The gradient on the left indicates what you're going to get after you apply Curves.

Try this: Pick any shade of gray from the bottom gradient. Now look straight above it until your eye hits the curve. This is the part of the curve that's affecting that shade of gray. To find out what's happening to it, just look directly to the left of that part of the curve. The shade on the left gradient directly beside that area of the curve shows you what the shade will become (see Figures 7.12 and 7.13). I don't use this method very much, because it's hard to be precise (you're just eyeballing it). However, this gives you your first glimpse into how to think about Curves.

The Big Picture

To find out what a curve is doing to an image, you must compare it to the original unchanged line. After you change the original line from a straight one into a curved one, the original line will no longer be visible. I usually just hold a pen up to the screen and use it as the original

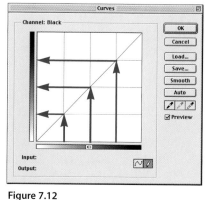

Figure 7.12
The original line is always a 45 degree angle because that's the only kind of line that won't change the image.

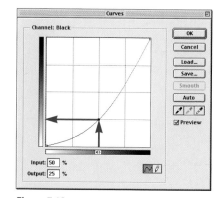

Figure 7.13
Among other things, this curve is changing 50% gray into 25% gray.

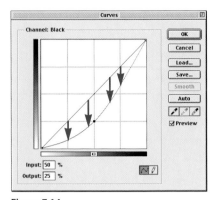

Figure 7.14
Almost all shades of gray were lightened.

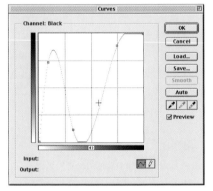

Figure 7.15
Your cursor must be close to the line to be able to add points.

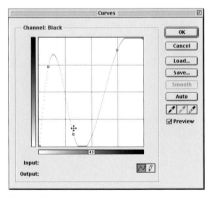

Figure 7.16
Click and drag a point to move it around the grid area.

line. The original line always starts in the lower-left corner and ends in the upper-right corner.

By comparing the two lines (your pen and the curve), you'll notice that almost the entire line has been moved down (see Figure 7.14). Now look at the gradient on the left. Remember, this gradient indicates what happens to your image *after* applying Curves to it. Dark shades are at the top, and bright shades are at the bottom. Because almost the entire line has moved down (and white is at the bottom of the gradient), most of the image will become brighter. The farther the line moves, the more pronounced the change will be. The only shades that did not change in this case are pure black and pure white.

Editing Curves

Before you try to adjust an image, you first have to know how to create and edit a curve, which means understanding how to work with points.

You should try the following steps to really get a feel for how it works. So, go ahead and open an image; then choose **Image>Adjust>Curves**. Add some points, move them around the grid, and then get rid of them:

Adding Points—To add a point to a curve, move your cursor close to the curve until it changes into a cross-hair, then click to add a point (see Figure 7.15).

Moving Points—If you move your cursor close to a point that already exists, your cursor will change into a crosshair cursor with arrows on each end. If you click and drag, you'll move the point that's directly above or below your cursor (see Figure 7.16).

Deleting Points—To remove a point from a curve, either Command-click it or just drag it off the grid area.

Improving Dark Images

Try this: Open any grayscale image you think is too dark (we'll work on color images later), as shown in Figure

7.17. Next, choose **Image>Adjust>Curves** and add a point by clicking the middle of the line. Pull the line straight down and see what happens to your image. Compare the curve to the gradient at the left of the Curves dialog box (see Figures 7.18 and 7.19). The farther you move the curve down, the closer it gets to becoming white. If part of the curve bottoms out, that area will become pure white.

NOTE
You can press the Option key when choosing **Image>Adjust>Curves** to apply the last settings used on an image.

Figure 7.17
The original image. (© 1998 PhotoSpin)

Figure 7.18
After a Curves adjustment.

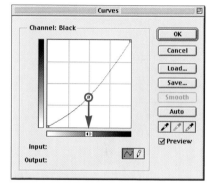

Figure 7.19
The Curves dialog box.

NOTE
If you're attempting to follow along with the steps presented in this chapter, you should know one thing: The gradients in the Curves dialog box can be reversed by clicking the arrows that appear in the middle of the bottom gradient. I'll be using the default settings (black on top for grayscale, CMYK, and lab mode; white on top for RGB mode) unless I mention that I've changed them. Therefore, if you open Curves and find that your gradients look different than the ones shown in this book, just click the arrows. These arrows are discussed in more depth later in this chapter, so by the time you finish, you'll know why you would change them.

Any part of a curve that's below the original line indicates an area that has been brightened. Look at the gradient directly below those areas to determine which shades of the image were brightened. The farther the line is moved down from its original position, the brighter the image will become (see Figures 7.20 and 7.21).

The Grid Shows You the Way

The grid can show you how much brighter or darker you made your image. The default grid lines are at 25% increments. This gives you a nice, uncluttered look, but it's not all that useful. You can change the grid by clicking anywhere on the grid area while holding down the Option key. This changes the grid so that the lines are at 10% increments—much more useful! Every time you Option-click the grid, it toggles between 25% and 10% grids (see Figures 7.22 and 7.23).

NOTE
You can reset the Curves dialog box back to the default line by pressing the Option key and then clicking the Cancel button.

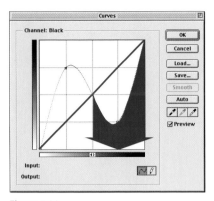

Figure 7.20
Everything between 50% and 100% was brightened.

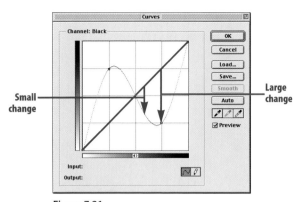

Figure 7.21
A small change versus a large change.

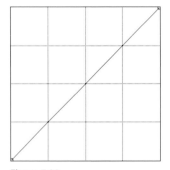

Figure 7.22
A grid with 25% increments.

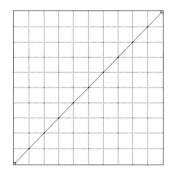

Figure 7.23
A grid with 10% increments.

By using the grid, you no longer have to eyeball the curve. Instead, you can measure how close the curve is to one of the lines in the grid and then follow that line over to the gradient on the left. Knowing that the grid is in 10% increments, you can then count the lines from the top or bottom of the gradient to find out exactly which shade of gray you've ended up with.

Concentrate on the gradient at the left side of the Curves dialog box. This gradient indicates the shades of gray you'll have after applying Curves to your image. Pick a shade of gray from that gradient (such as 90%); then look directly to the right of it to determine if you'll have any areas that shade of gray. Pick another shade and do the same thing. As long as the curve starts in the lower-left corner and ends in the upper-right corner, each one of the shades should be used somewhere in the image (see Figure 7.24). However, there might be a few shades that are used in more than one area of the curve.

Grid Size

To get a larger grid, click on the zoom box, also known as the "grow box," within the title bar of the Curves dialog box. Each time you click this symbol, it toggles between a grid that's 171 pixels wide and one that's 256 pixels wide (see Figure 7.25). I generally use the large grid because it shows more pixels, which makes it easier to be precise. In fact, if you use the small version, you can't control every shade of gray in an image (your image contains 256 shades of gray, and the smaller grid is only 171 pixels wide). I only use the 171-pixel version when working on a small screen, because the large version covers up too much of the image.

Improving Bright Images

Go ahead and try this: Open any grayscale image that you think is too bright (remember, we'll work on color images later). Now choose **Image>Adjust>Curves** and add a point by clicking the middle of the line. Pull the line straight up and see what happens to your image. Compare the curve to the gradient on the left of the Curves dialog box. The farther up you move the curve, the darker the image becomes. If part of the curve tops out, then that area will become pure black. (See Figures 7.26 and 7.27.)

Any part of the curve that's above the original line (your pen in this case) indicates an area that has been darkened (see Figure 7.28). Look at the gradient directly below those areas to determine which shades of the image were darkened. The farther the line is moved up from its original position, the darker the image will become (see Figure 7.29).

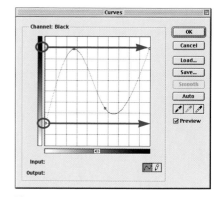

Figure 7.24
After this adjustment, the image should not contain any areas that are darker than 90% or brighter than 20%.

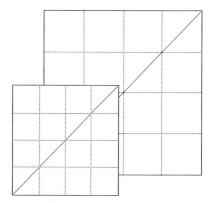

Figure 7.25
The 171- and 256-pixel grids.

Figure 7.26
The original image. (© 1998 PhotoSpin)

Figure 7.27
After a Curves adjustment.

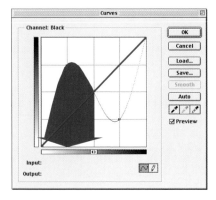

Large change

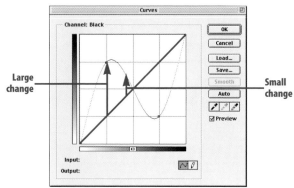

Small change

Figure 7.28
Shades between white and 50% gray were darkened.

Figure 7.29
A small change versus a large change.

Input and Output Numbers

The Input and Output numbers at the bottom of the Curves dialog box allow you to be very precise when adjusting an image. When the points on the curve appear as hollow squares, the Input and Output number will relate to your cursor.

Try it. First, however, make sure that none of the points on the curve are solid. Do this by moving your cursor around until it looks like a white arrow; then click the mouse button. Now move your cursor around the grid area. You'll notice the Input and Output numbers

> **NOTE**
>
> Clicking the Save button brings up a standard Save dialog box, which allows you to save the current settings for future use. The file that's created contains the Input and Output settings for each of the points used on the current curve. To reuse a saved setting, click the Load button.

changing. The Input number tells you which shade of gray is directly below your cursor—go ahead, look at the bottom gradient directly below your cursor. The Output number tells you which shade of gray is directly to the left of your cursor—just glance over at the side gradient. If you trace over the shape of a curve, the Input and Output numbers will show you exactly what the curve is doing to all the shades of gray in your image (see Figure 7.30).

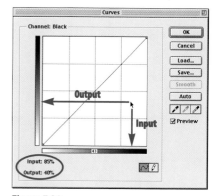

Figure 7.30
Input and Output numbers indicate the location of your cursor.

Entering Numbers

After you've created a point, it will appear as a solid square. This represents the point that's currently being edited. The Input and Output numbers at the bottom of the dialog box indicate the change this point will make to an image. The Input number represents the shade of gray that's being changed. The Output number indicates what's happening to the shade of gray. As long as the point appears as a solid square, you can type numbers into the Input and Output fields to change the location of the point (see Figure 7.31).

Ghosting an Image

Curves can also be helpful when you're planning on adding text to a photograph. When you place text on top of a photo, it's often difficult to read because there isn't much contrast between the text and the image. However, if you lighten the photo, the text will be easier to read. This is known as *ghosting*, or *screening back*, an image.

Try this: Open any color photo (make sure it's in RGB mode); then use the Marquee tool to select about half the image. Choose **Image>Adjust>Curves** and click the point in the lower-left corner of the grid area (use the upper-right point for CMYK images). Now change the Output number from 0 to 100. (I know, it's using the 0–255 numbering system, but we'll talk about that in a minute.) You have just lightened (or *ghosted*) the dark part of the image. This technique is often used to lighten a photo so that any text placed on top of it is easier to read. (See Figures 7.32 and 7.33.)

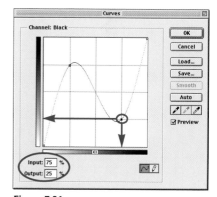

Figure 7.31
To alter the position of a point on the curve, just change one of the numbers.

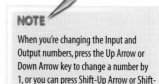

NOTE
When you're changing the Input and Output numbers, press the Up Arrow or Down Arrow key to change a number by 1, or you can press Shift-Up Arrow or Shift-Down Arrow to change a number by 10.

Figure 7.32
Ghosted image. (© 1998 PhotoSpin)

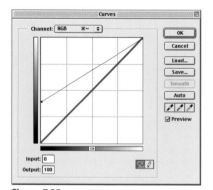

Figure 7.33
Curves dialog box.

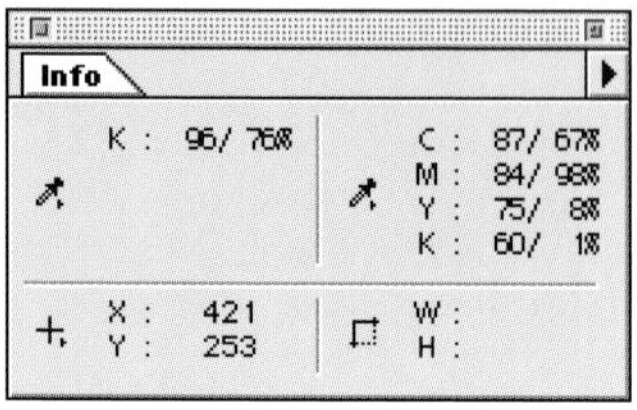

Figure 7.34
The first number is what you have before using Curves; the second is what you get after using Curves.

Compare the line you just made to the original (remember to use your pen). See how the dark areas of the image have changed a large amount, and the bright areas have not changed as drastically.

This is how a printing company ghosts an image. This technique is much better than placing a white box on a layer and lowering the image's opacity setting—that would change all the shades in the image an equal amount.

The Info Palette

The Info palette can also show you how Curves affects your image (see Figure 7.34). When you move your cursor over the image and click, the Info palette indicates what's happening to that area of the image. (If you want a more precise cursor, press the Caps Lock key to change your cursor from the default eyedropper to a more precise crosshair.) The first number in the Info palette tells you how dark the area is before using Curves. The second number tells you how dark it will become after applying Curves.

Two Numbering Systems

Two different numbering systems can be used in the Curves dialog box. You can switch between 0–100% and the 0-255 numbering system (remember Levels) by clicking the little arrows that appear in the middle of the bottom gradient (see Figure 7.35). Go ahead and give it a try.

If you're working on an image that's in RGB mode, Photoshop assumes you're going to use the image onscreen instead of printing it. Therefore, when you open Curves, it uses numbers ranging from 0 to 255. These numbers represent the amount of light your monitor will use to display the image onscreen (0 = no light, or black; 255 = maximum light, or white). You can be more accurate by using this numbering system because images in Photoshop contain 256 shades of gray, and you therefore have control over each shade.

If you're working on an image that's in grayscale or CMYK mode, Photoshop assumes you'll be printing the image (your monitor always uses RGB to display all images). Therefore, when you open Curves, it uses numbers ranging from 0% to 100%. These numbers represent the amount of ink that will be used to reproduce the image (0% = no ink; 100% = solid ink).

When you click the arrows that switch between the two different numbering systems, Photoshop also reverses the gradients at the bottom and left of the graph. It does this to keep the zero point of each numbering system in the lower-left corner of the graph, just like most business and scientific graphs. Zero in the 0–255 numbering system indicates no *light* is present, which means areas look black. Zero in the 0–100% numbering system means no *ink*, which leaves a sheet of paper white. You don't have to remember or understand why this happens, it's just nice to know there's a reason behind it.

Figure 7.35
Click the arrow symbol to switch numbering systems.

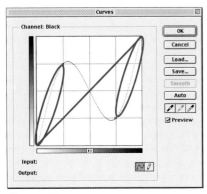

Figure 7.36
Areas between white and 25% as well as between 75% and black have increased contrast.

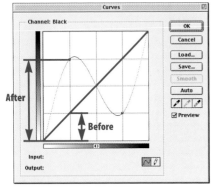

Figure 7.37
Before the adjustment, there's not much contrast; after the adjustment, you can see much more contrast.

NOTE

If you're trying to exaggerate the detail in the darkest areas of an image, you'll have to be very careful not to force areas to pure black. You can do this by making sure no part of the curve bottoms out or by being careful to only brighten areas.

When you switch the numbering system, this also changes the gradient on the left side of the Curves dialog box. Therefore, if you're using the 0–255 numbering system, you have to move a curve up to brighten the image and down to darken it (the exact opposite of what you do in the 0–100% numbering system). I always look at the gradient on the left to remind me; if black is at the top of the gradient (the 0–100% system), moving a curve up will darken the image. If white is at the top of the gradient (the 0–255 system), moving a curve up will brighten the image. It's actually a lot easier than it sounds.

Increasing Contrast and Detail

Any part of the curve that's steeper than the original line indicates an area where the contrast has been increased. Look at the gradient directly below these areas to determine which shades of the image were changed. The steeper the line becomes, the more contrast you'll see in that area of the image. (See Figures 7.36 and 7.37.)

You can exaggerate the detail in an area by increasing the contrast of that area. This makes the bright areas of the detail even brighter (and easier to see) and the dark areas darker (and easier to see).

Open any grayscale image and choose **Image>Adjust> Curves**. Move your cursor over the image and then click and drag across the area where you want to exaggerate the detail. You'll notice that a circle appears in the Curves dialog box. Photoshop is simply looking at the bottom gradient to find the shade of gray under your cursor; it then puts a circle on the curve directly above that shade. This circle indicates the area of the curve that needs to be changed in order to affect the area you're dragging across. Add a point at the highest and lowest ends where the circle now appears. Next, move the top point you just added upward. This will darken these areas, making them easier to see. Also, move the bottom point you added downward. This will brighten these areas, also making them easier to see. The area you dragged across should appear to have more detail. (See Figures 7.38 to 7.40.)

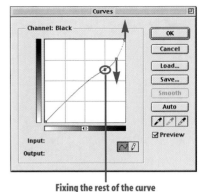

Fixing the rest of the curve

Figure 7.38
The original image. (© 1998 PhotoSpin)

Figure 7.39
After a simple Curves adjustment.

Figure 7.40
Curves dialog box.

You might also need to fix the rest of the curve. Do this by adding another point and moving it so that the majority of the curve looks normal (that is, diagonal).

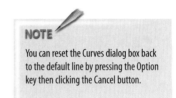

NOTE
You can reset the Curves dialog box back to the default line by pressing the Option key then clicking the Cancel button.

Previewing the Changes

You can compare the changes you've made to the original image in two ways. If you're using a Macintosh (and haven't turned off the Video LUT Animation setting in your preferences), you can turn off the Preview check box and click the title bar at the top of the Curves dialog box. As long as your mouse button is held down, you'll see what the image looked like before the adjustment. When you release the mouse button, you'll see the changes you just made. If you're using Windows, you can just turn the Preview check box off and on. As long as the check box is off, you'll see what the image looked like before the adjustment. When you turn it back on, you'll see the changes you just made. If you have a video card that supports video LUT animation, you should be able to use the first method instead of this one.

Decreasing Contrast and Detail

Any part of the curve that's flatter (more horizontal) than the original line indicates an area where the contrast has been reduced. Look at the gradient directly below these areas to determine which shades of the image were

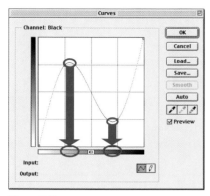

Figure 7.41
The areas between 25% and 35% as well as between 65% and 75% lost contrast.

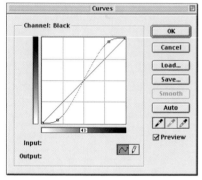

Figure 7.42
A classic S curve.

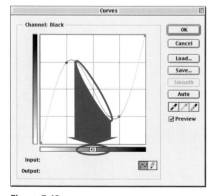

Figure 7.43
Areas between 30% and 70% have been inverted.

changed. The flatter the line becomes, the less contrast you'll see in that area of the image. When you lower the amount of contrast in an image, it becomes harder to see any detail. This can be useful if you *want* to make it harder to see detail in an area. If the curve becomes completely horizontal in an area, you've lost all detail in that area—in other words, it all became a single shade of gray (see Figure 7.41).

Let's Analyze a Classic Tip

Have you ever heard the tip "make an S curve"? Well, let's explore exactly what an S curve does (see Figure 7.42).

Remember, to find out what a curve is doing to your image, you should compare the original line to the curve. I usually use my pen to indicate the original line, but in this case I've added a line so you can see both the original and changed curve at the same time. Now look at the areas of the curve that are steeper than the original line. These steeper areas appear to have more detail. Whenever you pull detail out of one area, you'll also lose detail in another area; therefore, look at the areas of the curve that are flatter than the original line (more horizontal). These areas appear to have less detail. Thus, an S curve attempts to exaggerate detail in most of the image. However, it also gives you less detail in the highlights and shadows of your image.

Inverting Image

You can think of a curve as a stock market chart that indicates what's happening to the market over a month's time. If you're like most investors, whenever the market's going up, you're happy. However, you're always carefully watching that chart to see if the market starts to dip. If it does, that's when you start to panic. You can think of curves in the same way. As long as the curve is rising, you're fine; however, if the curve starts to fall, you're inverting the image, and that usually looks bad because the dark areas of the image will become bright, and the bright areas will become dark (see Figure 7.43). There might be occasions when you would want this to happen, but usually only for special effects.

Freeform Curves

You don't always have to bend the curve by adding and moving points. Another way to define a curve is to click the pencil icon at the bottom of the Curves dialog box and draw a freeform shape (see Figure 7.44). However, the shape you draw has to resemble a line moving from left to right. Go ahead, just try to draw a circle. You can't do it. That's because you can't have one dot directly above another. Instead, they have to be side by side across the grid. Just for giggles, draw a really wild looking line across the grid area and then look at your image. The Pencil tool is usually better for special effects than simple image adjustments.

Let's take a quick look at some of the things you can do when working with a freeform curve:

Smooth—After creating a curve with the Pencil tool, you can click the Smooth button to smooth out the shape you drew (see Figure 7.45). Go ahead and click it multiple times.

Convert to Path—To convert any line drawn with the Pencil tool into a normal curve, click the curve icon (see Figure 7.46).

Straight Lines—You can also draw straight lines with the Pencil tool (see Figure 7.47). Just Shift-click across the graph area and Photoshop will connect the dots to create a straight line.

Posterize—By drawing a stair-stepped shape with the Pencil tool, you can accomplish the same effect as if you had used the **Image> Adjust>Posterize** command (see Figure 7.48). To create straight lines with the Pencil tool, click once and then Shift-click another area. Photoshop will connect the dots with a straight line.

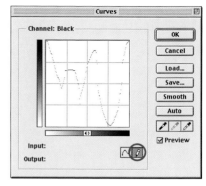

Figure 7.44
A curve created with the Pencil tool.

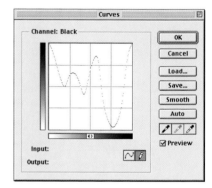

Figure 7.45
A freeform curve after Smooth is applied.

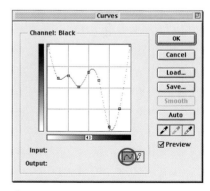

Figure 7.46
The result after converting to a normal path.

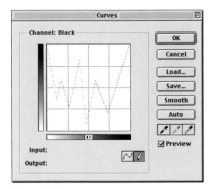

Figure 7.47
Straight lines drawn by Shift-clicking with the Pencil tool.

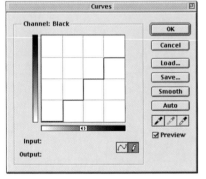

Figure 7.48
Drawing a stair-step is the same as choosing **Image>Adjust>Posterize**.

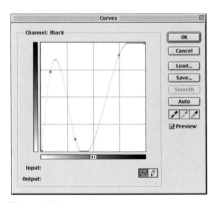

Figure 7.49
Can you figure out what this curve will do to an image?

A Quick Recap

Now, to verify that you're ready to move on, you should make sure you understand the general concepts. Take a look at the curve in Figure 7.49 and see if you can answer the following questions:

Which areas of the image will lose detail from this adjustment?

Which areas of the image will become brighter?

What happened to 62% gray?

What happened to the contrast of the image?

Just in case you couldn't answer all these questions, let's recap what we've covered:

Angle = Contrast = Detail.

Up means *darken* in the 0–100% system.

Down means *darken* in the 0–255 system.

Up means *brighten* in the 0–255 system.

Down means *brighten* in the 0–100% numbers.

Closing Thoughts

My hope is that after you've read this chapter you'll have come to the conclusion that Curves really isn't such a brain twister. And if you came out of it thinking of ways that you might use Curves in the future, even better. The Curves dialog box is one of only a handful of features that really separates the experts from everyone else. But there's no reason why you can't propel yourself into the expert category. Once you get comfortable with Curves (okay, it might take a while), you'll be able to do so much more than you can do by using any other dialog box. So, hang in there and stick with it. The initial learning curve might be somewhat daunting, but the fringe benefits are dynamite.

Ask Adobe

Q: How do the Eyedroppers in the Levels and Curves dialog boxes affect a color image?

A: The black-and-white, point eyedroppers adjust the input and output sliders for the individual color channels so that the color clicked on gets mapped to the target color for the eyedropper.

A couple of common points of confusion should get cleared up regarding these controls:

First, if you are working on an RGB image and you set the target colors using CMYK values, you are still creating a color correction from RGB values to RGB values; hence, when you go to separate the image, you may find that you don't get the same CMYK values. This is more of a "problem" in the shadows than in the "highlights" because the shadows generally afford a lot more ways to express the same color in CMYK; for example, 100% black or 100% cyan, magenta, and yellow and a whole range of options in between.

This issue of having multiple CMYK values for the same color is just an explanation of why mapping adjusting RGB values does not necessarily let you determine the resulting CMYK values when you separate. It is, however, at the crux of the second point of confusion with respect to the eyedroppers, and that is their behavior on CMYK documents. Once again, there are multiple ways to specify the same shadow color; and Levels and Curves just make adjustments on a per-channel basis. Hence, the black point eyedropper is relatively constrained in what it can do. What you will discover if you study the way the controls behave is that the eyedroppers work on the cyan, magenta, and yellow channel but leave the black channel untouched. This works well for correcting color casts, but does not provide as much functionality as is available in RGB.

Finally, the gray point eyedropper adjusts the gamma values to map the color clicked on to a color having the same relative amounts of red, green, and blue (or cyan, magenta, and yellow) as the target color. It attempts to preserve the overall lightness of the image when doing so. The default color for this eyedropper is 50% gray, but all you need to do is find a midrange neutral in the image because this eyedropper is attempting to match relative channel values only instead of exact colors.

NOTE

On the CD accompanying this book, you'll find a PDF file that supplements this chapter. The file, called extras.pdf, contains information about taking what you know about the Curves dialog box and applying it to levels.

Q: Are Curves based on anything used in traditional photography?

A: Curves are just remappings of the color values. They have nothing specific to do with photography.

Ben's Techno-Babble Decoder Ring

Contrast—The range between the brightest and darkest areas of an image.

S-curve—A generic curve used to exaggerate the detail in midtones of an image by suppressing the detail in the highlights and shadows.

Keyboard Shortcuts

Curves	Command-M
Move Point Up	Up Arrow
Move Point Down	Down Arrow
Move Point Left	Left Arrow
Move Point Right	Right Arrow
Select Next Point	Command-Tab
Select Previous Point	Command-Shift-Tab
Deselect All Points	Command-D

Color Correction

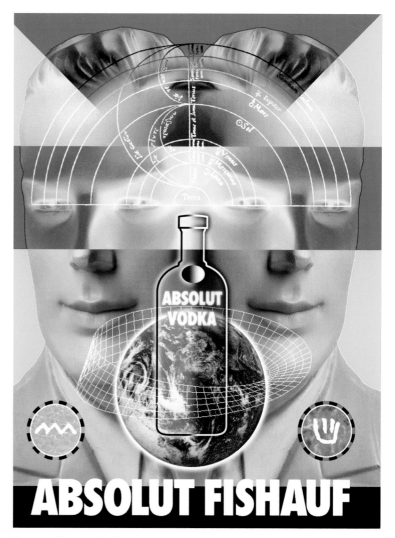

*The camera, you know,
will never capture you.
Photography, in my
experience, has the
miraculous power
of transferring wine
into water.*
—*Oscar Wilde in "Lillie"*

Courtesy of Louis Fishauf, www.magic.ca/~fishauf/.

I'm going to tell you a story about a young man who had a most unfortunate experience with color correction. His name is Andy, and at one time he liked to think of himself as a *serious* photographer. He was very proud that he had just landed his first job as a freelancer. The work involved photographing an author for the cover of a book and scanning the images onto a disk. He was given the whopping sum of $500 and an entire week to do get the job done. "Hah! Piece of cake," thought Andy. "It'll cost practically nothing and I can knock the thing out in a day." Andy wanted to chronicle his first job as a professional so he diligently kept a journal of his efforts:

Monday: Got color film at Safeway, went to the author's house and shot lots of pics (jerk wouldn't let me play with his computer). Ran over to 1-Hour Photo to get film developed. But the prints didn't look so hot. Icky greenish tinge. I asked the counter guy why they looked so crummy. He said there wasn't even a human attending the processing, just a machine that spits out all the rolls with the same settings. And he asked where I got such an old roll of film. (I knew that $1.79 for 36 shots was too good to be true!)

Tuesday: Okay, no more fooling around. Went to Mike's Camera (swankiest camera store in town) and bought pricey film. Ran back to author's house. He was a little surprised to see me again, but let me shoot more pics. Back to Mike's Camera to drop off film, where they have real humans supervising the processing (not cheap!) .

Wednesday: Got the new pics. What's going on! That nasty green tinge is still there! Okay, now I really mean it. This has got to stop. Went to talk to the pro at the camera counter. He totally interrogated me, asked a thousand questions about the lighting conditions, was I using a filter, what kind of film was I using, and all that kind of stuff. He gave me huge list of junk he said I needed to buy. I bought everything he told me to. Cost a ton! But now I've got a bunch of filters, a light diffusion panel (just looks to me like a fancy bed sheet stretched over a frame), some tissue paper to put in front of the lights, and a bunch of little white cards to reflect light. I hope the author doesn't get mad when I show up at his house again.

Thursday: Author guy took it pretty well, but I think he was secretly annoyed with me. (Maybe this time I won't ask to play with that computer.) But I'll bet he was impressed when I walked in with all that extra equipment! I shot up tons of rolls just to be on the safe side.

Friday (Deadline Day): I picked up the prints in the morning and they were awesome! Yah! Just in time, too. Popped open my trusty 1972 Scan-O-Matic and scanned the best picture of the lot. Saw the picture coming up on the screen. "Aaaaaagh!" Another color cast!! Now the author looks murky and brownish. Oh, god. Peeked under the hood of the scanner—bulb flickering. Rushed out the door and spent two precious hours scouring the city for a replacement bulb. Finally found one at the computer salvage place at the edge of town. Only two hours before deadline's up. Replaced the bulb, rescanned the pictures. YES! They look good. Just in the nick of time, too, 'cause the client's calling wanting to know where his scanned images are. Copied images to disk; and just to show my professional courtesy, I decided to make a color printout.

(Courtesy of Andy Katz)

When I saw the printout, I could not believe my eyes. ANOTHER color cast!!! Now the author looks really mad because his face has turned an angry shade of purple. What the devil is going on? The image looks fine on the monitor. Or does it? How do I know the colors on my screen are even accurate? I can't hand over these images. They look awful. Wait a minute, I know what I'll do. I'll just convert it to grayscale and tell the client I was going for an artsy look. Forget the damn color!!!!

Nobody wants to have an experience like Andy's. In a perfect world, there would be no need for color correction. But as Andy so painfully learned, when it comes to reproducing color, our world is far from perfect. Almost all images need some sort of a tweak to get them to look right. Unwanted color casts are the biggest culprits, and they can creep into your image in almost unlimited ways, wreaking havoc with your colors. The good news is that you can fix almost any color cast in less than two minutes, but you have to know what you're doing.

This chapter might seem somewhat long and loaded with nitty-gritty details; but with color correction, the devil really is in the details. I find that most books that include color correction just jump in and start adjusting photos. That's okay, but it doesn't really leave you equipped to understand what is happening to your image. Instead, you get only a few clues about how to fix it. The truth is, the more you understand, the less fixing you'll have to do. This is one of those instances where knowing the mechanics of the process will really pay off later. The fundamental rule of good color management is to take care of any potential color problems as early as possible in the image creation process (from initial photography, developing, scanning, and on up the chain). But if you don't understand the process, you can't do much to control it.

In this chapter we'll find out how to eradicate almost any color cast. And don't panic, this chapter might seem a bit long, but the actual process should go pretty quickly. But we're going to spend some extra time to make sure you really understand this stuff. There are two main approaches to getting great color. Let's take a look at them, and then decide which one will work best for your situation.

Two Approaches to Color Correction

You can manage your color work flow by trying to automate everything (which *sounds* great), or you can do it the old-fashioned manual way (which *sounds* like a pain). At this point, forgive me for some gross generalizations, but I think it will help to get my point across. First, you can divide the world into two groups of Photoshop Users. Group One has an unlimited budget. All of their equipment is state of the art, they hire the best photographers and labs that money can buy and have almost total control over the entire image creation process. Group Two is everybody else (which includes people like Andy). In this section I'll talk about two different scenarios: "Auto Pilot" and the "Manual Route." Group One is more suited to "Auto Pilot" because they are more likely to be able to control their environment. For Group Two I recommend the "Manual Route," which is much more suitable for those who cannot control all of the variables that play into an image. Let's find out how the two different methods work, and you can decide which group you belong to.

Auto Pilot

With the automatic method of color management, you attempt to calibrate and characterize all the equipment used and then let the computer do all the work. The first thing you would need to do is calibrate your equipment to make sure it is working as accurately as possible. Then you'd want to make sure the computer is aware of the limitations of all your equipment. So, if your printer is not capable of reproducing a good blue, then the software would be aware of that and might be able to compensate for it (or at least let you see what it will look like on screen.) Let's take a look at how you'd have to set up your equipment.

Scanner

The first thing you'd have to do is calibrate and characterize your scanner. This is usually done by scanning a special card (known as a color target) that is filled with squares of different colors (the card usually comes with higher-end scanners). By scanning this special image, you would create a special profile for your specific scanner. Then, this profile would be used by your computer to keep track of exactly how your scanner affects the colors in your image.

Monitor

Next, you'd want to calibrate and characterize your monitor. You'd do that by attaching a special color measurement device to your screen and running a special piece of software that displays a bunch of different colors on your screen. By doing this, the software that came with the measurement device would be able to calibrate your screen and create a profile to let the computer know how your monitor displays different colors. (If you're willing to pay the premium, Radius offers a monitor called the Press View that comes with a calibrator.)

Color Proofing Device

Then if you want to print your images on a color printer, you'd need to supply the computer with a profile for that, too. Some color printers come with a pre-made profile and others do not. If your printer didn't come with a profile, then you'd have to make one by printing out a color target and measuring it with a color measurement device, similar to the kind of device used to calibrate your monitor.

Printing Press

If you were planning to print your images on a printing press, the computer would also have to know what happens to colors when they are printed. This can be done just like you do for a color proofing device (like your desktop color printer), or you can use a more generic profile that just includes some basic information about the limitations of the printing press.

The Result

After doing all this work, you should be able to scan an image, press the print button, and see something that looks just like original. Well, that seldom happens due to the limitations of the equipment being used—but it can come pretty close. Then the question is, what happens if the original photograph looks terrible? (Remember Andy's first attempt?) Well, this system (Auto Pilot) does nothing to correct problems with the original photograph.

This system is all very fine and good for large companies that produce very professional results and have most of their equipment in-house. That means they use only professional photographers who know how to light things properly and get great exposure. They own their own equipment (higher-end scanner, color proofing device, and final output device). And, they have the time (and money) to create a profile for all the press conditions they encounter. Then, they don't mess with anything; no playing with those brightness and contrast dials on your monitor, no switching printers for a lower bid, and so on.

Turning Off Profiles

This system is less than ideal if you don't have all the equipment in-house or occasionally send your work to Photoshop users outside of your company, especially with Photoshop 5.0. In earlier versions of Photoshop, you could give a file to anyone you wanted and they could retouch or modify the image and give it back to you. The only areas of the image that would be changed are the ones they changed manually. But now, with Photoshop 5, if they don't have their profiles straight, then the colors will shift, even if you did something as simple as crop the image. Any time you open a file and see the "Converting Colors" progress bar, you know your colors are shifting. If you decide not to go the profile route, you'll definitely want to turn them off. To do that, choose **File>Color Settings>Profile Setup**, turn off all the Embed Profile check boxes, set all the Assumed Profiles to None, and set the Profile Mismatch Handling settings to Ignore, as shown in Figure 8.1.

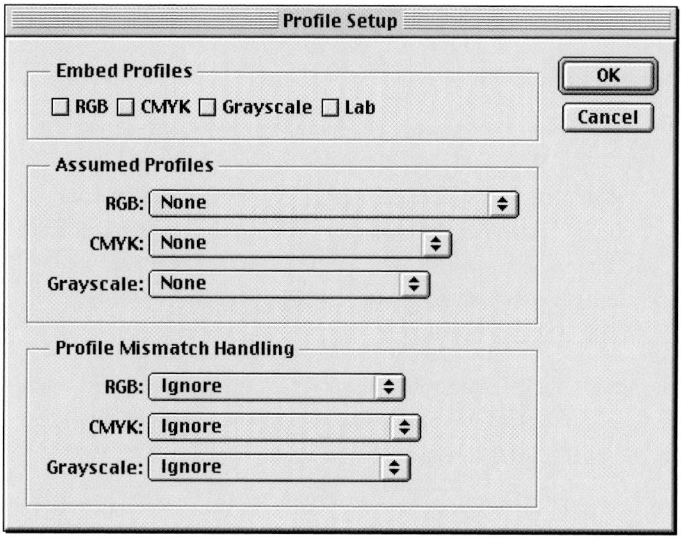

Figure 8.1
The Profile Setup dialog box.

You'll also want to choose **File>ColorSettings>RGB Setup** and set the RGB pop-up menu to Monitor RGB and set the gamma to 1.8. Using profiles can be a really nice way to work, but you have to make sure all who handle your files knows what they are doing, and make sure other programs support them as well (QuarkXPress just ignores them). Turning off profiles will allow Photoshop to work the way earlier versions did, and colors won't shift when you share your files with others. So, unless you have control over the entire process and don't use too many outside vendors, I'd suggest you turn profiles off and manually adjust your images.

The Manual Route

By manually adjusting your images, you'll be able to compensate for a color cast (read: inaccurate reproduction of one or more colors) that was introduced at any point through the image creation process; and you won't have to calibrate all your equipment in the process (except the final output device). And even if you were using the auto pilot method, you'd still want to know about these techniques so you can make up for poor originals. So let's take a look at what is involved.

There are four areas of an image that need to be adjusted to completely remove a color cast. All four of them can be taken care of in just one dialog box—Curves. Before we start adjusting images, let's take a quick look at the areas we will be adjusting:

> **Highlight**—The highlight of an image is the brightest white that should still retain detail. To make something truly white, there shouldn't be any hint of color in it. So we want to make sure the highlight becomes the brightest neutral gray that is capable of retaining detail. Not all photographs contain a highlight that should be white. If you have an image taken at sunset, for instance, you won't want to make the highlight white.

> **Shadow**—The shadow of your image is not the same as a shadow that is cast from on object. Instead, when I say shadow, I mean the darkest area of your image.

> **Neutral Gray**—The third thing you'll need to look for are any areas that should appear as a neutral gray. When I say neutral gray, I mean a gray that has no hint of color in it.

> **Flesh tones**—Finally, you'll need to adjust any flesh tones that are present in your image. Bad flesh tones are one of the most noticeable color problems you see in everyday graphic design. Without adjusting them, you might end up with some very sunburned-looking people.

You might notice a cast in just one area; but if there is one, it will definitely affect the whole image.

Before we jump in and start using Photoshop to adjust images, it's very important to know how color really works in Photoshop. But if you are anxious to start adjusting

NOTE

If you happen to be color blind, that means you are lacking one or more types of cones (RGB) and therefore cannot see all colors.

photographs, you can skip the next section and go direct-ly to the nitty gritty of adjustment. Just be aware that this section is essential to understanding what you are doing and how these adjustments affect your image.

How We Reproduce Color

At the back of your eye (in the retina) are tiny little cones that allow you to perceive color. There are three types of cones and each type is sensitive to a different color of light; one for red, one for green, and one for blue. So all the images you see with your eyes are made out of combi-nations of red, green, and blue light. You could even go so far as to say that humans were designed to see the world with RGB light (see Figure 8.2).

Figure 8.2
Your eye is your own personal RGB light sensor.

Red, Green, and Blue Light

When you use a desktop scanner, you are measuring the amount of red, green, and blue light reflected off an image. That's why your images appear in RGB when they are first loaded into Photoshop. When you view an image on your computer screen or television screen, it is being created by shining red, green, and blue light into your eyes. (Your monitor cannot display all the colors your eye is capable of seeing, however, because it can only get so bright and so dark.) And when you output your image to a 35mm slide, the film is exposed using RGB light. So you see, it really is an RGB world out there (see Figure 8.3).

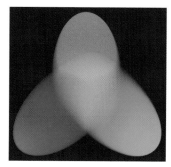

Figure 8.3
All the colors you can see with your eyes are made from a combination of red, green, and blue light.

Surprisingly, I find most people aren't used to thinking in RGB (well, your brain thinks in RGB, but your conscious mind isn't aware of it). Most of us haven't had much experience mixing light. Think about it… when was the last time you were mixing different colored lights together to create anything? Maybe you were in charge of lighting for your high school play? But I bet you can open your desk drawer and find colored pens, pencils, markers, or crayons. Ever since we were kids, we've been messing with ink, toner, paint, and so on to create color, so it's under-standable if you aren't comfortable thinking about mixing RGB light. Well, now's the time to get RGB rooted into your consciousness, so let's take a look at how it works.

200R
200G
200B
150R
150G
150B
100R
100G
100B

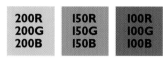

Figure 8.4
Equal amounts of red, green, and blue produce a gray result.

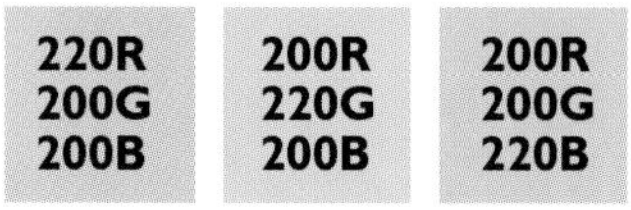
220R
200G
200B
200R
220G
200B
200R
200G
220B

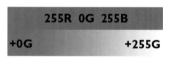

Figure 8.5
When you have unbalanced amounts of red, green, and blue light, you create color.

When you combine red, green, and blue light in equal amounts, you get gray (see Figure 8.4). To create white, you just need to combine red, green, and blue light at high intensities. Black is created from the absence of RGB light—if one of the colors was still present, you'd end up with a dark color instead of black.

Any time the RGB light is not balanced, you create color (see Figure 8.5). You need only one or two colors to create bright, saturated colors (see Figure 8.6). Try this: create a new document in RGB mode, then click on your foreground color. In the Color Picker dialog box, enter the following RGB numbers: 255R 0G 0B. This should produce a bright red color. Now make sure the radio button next to the letter "H" (Hue) is turned on, then drag one of the sliders on the vertical bar up or down. This will change the color you are creating to different bright, intense colors. When you are sliding it around, keep an eye on the RGB settings that are used to create all those colors. It should never need to use more than two.

255R 0G 255B
+0G
+255G

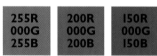

Figure 8.6
You need only one or two of the RGB colors to create bright, saturated colors. Adding the third color just makes the area appear less saturated.

If all three colors are being used, then the color will appear less saturated. Try this one out: back in the Color Picker, choose 255R 0G 255B, then click on the "S" (Saturation) radio button. Now drag the slider on the vertical bar down and see what happens to the RGB settings. As you lower the bar, the third color will start to be used. Remember, when all three colors (RGB) are equal, you have only gray, which means *no saturation.*

255R
000G
255B
200R
000G
200B
150R
000G
150B

Figure 8.7
As you reduce the amount of light, you produce a darker color.

And, if you really want to, you can turn the saturation back up and then click on the "B" (Brightness) radio button to see how it affects the RGB settings. By lowering the brightness, the current RGB numbers get lowered—the less light you have, the darker the color appears, as depicted in Figure 8.7.

I think that should be enough information about RGB, so now let's figure out how things change when you switch to CMYK mode and print your image.

Cyan, Magenta, and Yellow Ink

All the rules that apply to RGB fly out the window when you stop dealing with light and start working with ink. First off, you can't print your images using red, green, and blue ink. It just won't work. Think about it… the light hitting a sheet of paper is made out of RGB light. If you print with red ink, the ink would absorb all the green and blue light that is hitting the paper and allow only the red light to reflect off and enter your eye. Green ink would absorb all the red and blue light, and blue ink would absorb all the red and green light. So if you were to use two colors (red and green), you would end up with pure black because you would have absorbed all the light falling on the paper. (See Figure 8.8.)

We still want to be able to reproduce our RGB images; we just need to take a different approach. We need to find three colors of ink to use: one that absorbs only red light, one that absorbs only blue light, and one that absorbs only green light. To find out exactly which colors are needed, take a peek at Figure 8.9.

Figure 8.8
If you were to use red, green, and blue inks, any combination of the two would produce black.

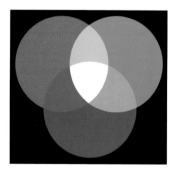

Figure 8.9
Imagine that these three circles were created from three flashlights: one red, one green, and one blue.

Think of the three circles as the output from three separate flashlights: one that has a red bulb, one with a green bulb, and one with a blue bulb. Look in the middle, where they all overlap—remember when you combine RGB light equally, you get gray (white is the brightest shade of gray you can get). Now let's find out which colors we need to

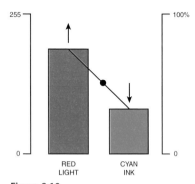

255 ┐   ┌ 100%

0 ┘   └ 0

RED   CYAN
LIGHT   INK

Figure 8.10
The relationship between RGB and CMY is just like a teeter-totter. If you increase red light, you are, in effect, reducing cyan ink.

use when printing an image. Look at the area where the blue and green flashlights overlap (but the red one does not); that's the color of ink you need to control red light. Then look at the area where the red and blue flashlights overlap; that's the color of ink needed to control green light. Finally, look at the area where the red and green flashlights overlap; that's the color of ink you'd need to control blue light.

Cyan ink controls Red light

Magenta ink controls Green light

Yellow ink controls Blue light

You can think of it as a teeter-totter. If you increase the red light, you are reducing the amount of cyan ink needed to reproduce the color (see Figure 8.10).

Process Color Inks

There is just one big problem with printing your images. The people who make ink haven't figured out how to create the exact colors that would be needed to reproduce all the colors you can create in RGB mode. The ink colors that they've come up with are much darker and less saturated than what would be needed to get a really brilliant color. I can't show you the difference between what would be needed and what is available within this book because all the colors shown in this book use the less-than-ideal colors. But you can see the differences on your screen by creating a new document in RGB mode and then clicking on your foreground color. In the RGB area enter 0R 255G 255B, then click on OK. Now click on your foreground color again and click the little triangle (it's known as the out-of-gamut warning) that shows up right next to the colors in the upper right corner (see Figure 8.13). Now compare the two colors shown in the upper right of the Color Picker; the bottom color would be the ideal color for cyan, and the top color is the cyan we're stuck using on a printing press. You can do the same thing to see how far off the magenta and yellow inks are; just use the following RGB numbers: magenta=255R 0G 255B, yellow=255R 255G 0B.

When you combine the ideal CYM inks, you end up with pure black. But when you combine the non-ideal inks, you just get a muddy brown color, as you can see in Figure 8.11. This is one of the reasons why you also use black ink (the K in CMYK) when reproducing an image on a printing press. Without black ink, your shadows would not look nice and black. Black ink is abbreviated as "K" because many people use the word Blue when referring to cyan ink, so the letter "K" (for Key) was substituted for black.

These non-ideal colors (CMYK) are known as the process color inks (see Figure 8.12). So, there really are two sets of CMY colors, the ideal ones, and the real ones known as process colors. Because we haven't figured out how to create ideal inks, we can't reproduce all the colors that you can see in RGB mode. Because of this you might see some colors shift when you convert an image from RGB to CMYK mode.

Figure 8.11
100 percent of cyan, magenta, and yellow produce a dark, muddy brown, so black ink is used to create true blacks.

Figure 8.12
The non-ideal colors of cyan, magenta, and yellow.

Out-of-Gamut Colors

Because your computer monitor cannot reproduce all the colors your eye can see and a printing press can reproduce even fewer colors, there is a term used to describe the colors that are reproducible. All the colors that are reproducible in RGB mode are collectively known as the *RGB gamut*. The colors reproducible in CMYK mode are known as the *CMYK gamut*.

When you are choosing a color in Photoshop you will often see a small triangle appear next to the color you have chosen, as shown in Figure 8.13. This triangle indicates that the color you have chosen cannot be reproduced using CMYK inks (known as the gamut alarm). When the triangle shows up, a small square of color will be displayed directly below it. This is indicating the closest color that can be reproduced; and by clicking on it, you will choose it instead of the color you had originally chosen. So, if the end use of your image is on a printing press, be sure to click that little color swatch whenever it shows up; otherwise, the colors you paint with will end up shifting when you convert your image to CMYK mode.

Gamut Warning

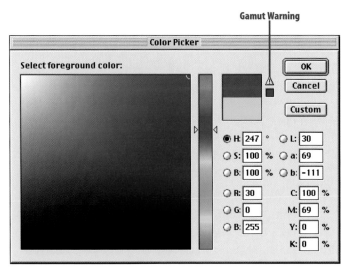

Figure 8.13
The Color Picker's gamut warning indicates a color that cannot be reproduced using CMYK inks.

If you want to see an on-screen preview of what will happen to your image when it is converted to CMYK choose **View>Preview>CMYK**. Or, if you just want to see which areas of the image are going to shift, you can choose **View> Gamut Warning**. This will place gray on top of any areas that will shift in color. These features can be useful after you have adjusted your image and are getting ready to convert it to CMYK.

RGB versus CMYK

You can perform color correction in RGB or CMYK mode. Your choice will depend on your particular work flow:

If your image is already in CMYK mode and you are going to print it using CMYK inks, then you should perform your color correction in CMYK mode.

If your image is in RGB mode and its primary use is onscreen (multimedia, web, video, etc.), then the color correction should happen in RGB mode.

If the image is not yet scanned and will end up being printed using CMYK inks, then the color correction could be performed in either mode.

You'll run into a large number of people who claim color correction should be performed in CMYK mode only. Most people who color correct for a living seem to claim that. These people usually work for very respected service bureaus and printing companies. But there is one thing in common with all of them—they color correct their images for a single purpose (magazine, newspaper, brochure, etc.) and have very little experience working in RGB mode. In fact, most of them have never used Photoshop as a creative tool; all they think about is output (CMYK output, that is).

Well, my take on the whole issue is this: I couldn't care less which mode you use as long as you get the best result possible and get it done in a reasonable amount of time. Or, as Thomas Edison once said, "Hell, there are no rules here, we're trying to accomplish something."

I'll show you how to perform color correction in both RGB and CMYK mode. I think you'll find it much easier (and faster) to correct your images in RGB mode. And if you give your image to someone who says you should only do it in CMYK, that person will never be able to tell the difference. In fact, I did this in a high-end color correction class and the teacher (who says CMYK only) never knew I did it. He even placed my images right next to the work of four other people who did the exact same images in CMYK mode and he couldn't tell I wasn't following his instructions.

Of course, you want your images to look good in CMYK mode; but how you get there is less important than the quality you end up with. And if you need to use your images for more than one type of printing condition (newspaper, magazines, brochures, etc.), then you will definitely want to perform your color correction in RGB mode. When you convert an image to CMYK mode, the settings in the CMYK Setup dialog box get applied to your image. This targets the image for a specific set of print conditions (total ink limit, dot gain, and so on). So, if you perform your corrections in CMYK mode, you are doing it for a specific type of printing. RGB images, on the other hand, are not committed to a specific type of printing.

After correcting your image, all you have to do is enter the proper settings in the CMYK Setup dialog box, then convert to CMYK. In fact, you can duplicate the RGB image and use different settings each time you convert to CMYK for each type of printing condition.

CMYK mode is also a rather lousy mode to work in. When combining images together, running filters, or doing just about anything else, your image will look better if you stay in RGB mode and then convert to CMYK when you're all done. Following are some of the advantages of using RGB mode:

File sizes are 1/4 smaller so your computer runs faster.

It's much easier to produce a neutral gray (that can't be said of CMYK).

Glows fading to black look much better (in CMYK they look washed out).

All the filters work (dozens are diabled in CMYK mode).

Filters work properly and don't produce a brownish result (you'll get brown gunk in CMYK).

Blending modes work better (they are less than predictable in CMYK).

It is impossible to over use ink and create press problems (it's really easy to screw that up in CMYK).

Your scanner scans in RGB, your monitor displays your image in RGB, and your eyes even perceive color in RGB, so why not stick with it as long as you can (then convert to CMYK)?

Okay, I think I've stressed how important RGB mode is, so now let's jump in and find out how you perform color correction in RGB or CMYK mode. Remember we'll end up adjusting four areas of our image: highlight, shadow, neutral grays, and skin tones.

RGB Color Correction

We will look at the process in four parts: achieving good contrast, balancing the colors, sharpening, and converting to CMYK. You don't always have to perform all four parts; but the more you do, the better your result will be.

Achieve Good Contrast

No matter how you reproduce an image, you will not be able to achieve as much contrast as was present when the photograph was taken. The brightest white your computer monitor can produce is nowhere near as bright as the brightest white you'll see in real life. And if you are going to print the image, the paper isn't even as white as your computer screen. The same problem occurs with the dark area of your image; your monitor can get only so dark, and ink on paper is not very dark compared to the real world. So, you will usually want to use the full range of contrast that is available to get your image as close to reality as possible.

Before you attempt to pull out the full contrast of your image, you'll want to discard any information that will not be used in the end result. So, if your image contains a black border or you are going to use only a small portion of it, you'll want to crop the image first (see Figure 8.14). There are many ways to crop an image (Crop tool, **Image>Crop, Image>Canvas Size**, and so on), but I usually just make a selection using the Marquee tool and then choose **Image>Crop** (see Figure 8.15). The reason I don't use the Crop tool is that I might not realize that the Fixed Target size checkbox is turned on; and, therefore, might scale the image at the same time as cropping it. But you can use any method you prefer.

To pull out optimal contrast, you'll need to choose **Image>Adjust>Levels** (see Figure 8.16). Pulling in the upper right and upper left sliders will increase the contrast. But by performing this action to all the color channels in the image (RGB), you will limit the amount of contrast you can get without damaging the image. So, before you start messing with the sliders, change the pop-up menu at the top of the dialog box to Red. Now you can pull in the upper left and upper right sliders until they touch the beginning and end of the histogram. (Some histograms already extend all the way across the area available and therefore already have good contrast and don't need to be adjusted with Levels.)

Figure 8.14
Original image contains lots of space that won't be used, and has white around its edge. (© 1998 PhotoDisc)

Figure 8.15
Crop the image so it contains only the information you want to use.

NOTE

For information about how to work with the Levels dialog box, see Chapter 6, "Optimizing Grayscale Images."

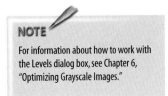

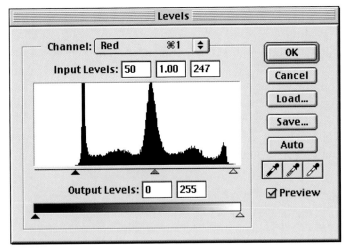

Figure 8.16
Choose Red from the Channel pop-up menu, then move in the upper right and upper left sliders until they touch the histogram.

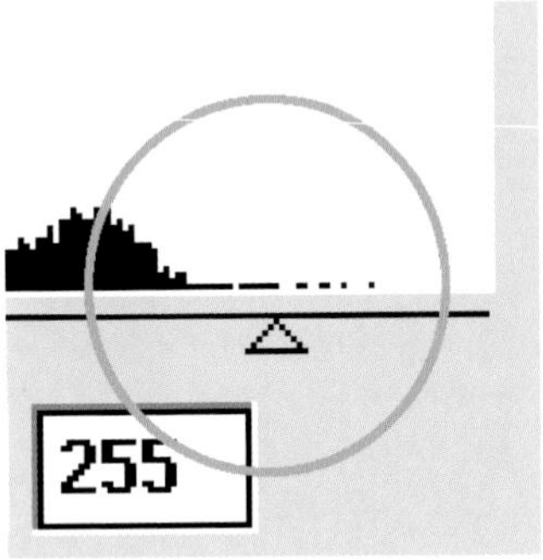

Figure 8.17
If you encounter any stray pixels that are a few pixels away from the main part of the histogram, pass them by.

After you have adjusted the Red channel, you can perform the same type of adjustment to the Green and Blue channels. Occasionally you'll find a histogram that contains a few stray pixels that are not really connected to the main histogram, as shown in Figure 8.17. When this happens, you can ignore them and pass right by them to the first part of the histogram. But be careful, you don't want to damage your image; so make sure the only pixels you pass by are those that really look like they don't belong.

The process you've gone through up to this point should improve the contrast of most images (compare Figures 8.18 and 8.19). If you found yourself moving the sliders quite a distance, then the colors might have also improved. But now we need to make sure the image does not contain a color cast.

Balance Colors

To eliminate any color casts that are present, you'll need to adjust three areas of the image (highlight, shadow, and neutral gray). We'll first locate these areas, then set up Photoshop to monitor what happens to them as we adjust the image. You'll end up using the Color Sampler tool to place "sample points" that look like little crosshairs on each area of the image that is going to be adjusted. (To remove sample points, Option-click them, or drag them to

the edge of the screen using the Color Sampler tool.) So let's find those areas and place some samples.

Figure 8.18
Before adjusting contrast by using Levels.

Figure 8.19
Result of achieving good contrast.

Locate Highlight

First let's locate the highlight. The highlight is the brightest area that should still contain detail. You'll often find it in someone's white shirt collar, a Styrofoam cup, or a sheet of paper. But remember, this is an area that should contain detail, so don't pick the brightest part of a metallic object, a light bulb, or a reflection on the edge of a glass object (those are known as specular highlights and should not contain detail). In Figure 8.19, the brightest white falls on the handlebar grip next to the boy's left hand.

If you are really having trouble finding a highlight, you can choose **Image>Adjust>Threshold** and move the slider all the way to the right; then slowly move it to the left (see Figure 8.20). This will show you where the brightest areas of the image are located.

Once you've found the highlight (if one exists), double-click on the Color Sampler tool and set its sample size setting to 3 by 3 Average, then click on highlight to add a sample point on top of it (see Figure 8.21). Now if you open the Info palette, you will always see what is happening to that area. (See Figure 8.22.)

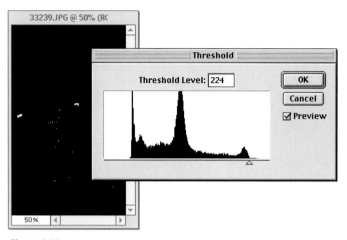

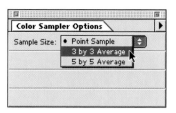

Figure 8.21
Before using the Color Sampler tool, set its Sample Size setting to 3 by 3 Average.

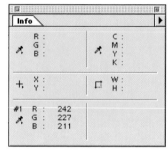

Figure 8.20
You can use the Threshold command to find hard-to-locate highlights. If the brightest area of the image should not be white, then you don't want to adjust the highlight of the image. So, if you have an outdoor scene taken at sunset, I'd bet the brightest area should be orange instead of white and I therefore would not adjust that portion of the image.

Figure 8.22
After using the Color Sampler tool, you should see an additional color readout in the Info palette.

Locate Shadow

Now it's time to locate the shadow of the image. Remember, when I mention the shadow, I don't mean a traditional shadow (the kind cast from an object); instead, I'm talking about the darkest area of the image. All images have a shadow area, but it can sometimes be hard to locate because you'll find multiple candidates.

Well, you can use the same trick I mentioned when we found the highlight—use the Threshold dialog box. The only change you have to make is to start with the slider all the way to the left. This will show you where the darkest area of the image is hiding. You don't want to find the darkest speck (that could be dust), so be sure to look for a general area that is at least five or six pixels in size.

Figure 8.23
The shadow is the darkest area of the image that should still retain detail.

Once you've located the shadow, place a sample point on top of it using the Color Sampler tool (see Figure 8.23). Now you should see two extra readouts at the bottom of the Info palette, one for the highlight and one for the shadow, as shown in Figure 8.24.

Locate Neutral Gray

Now we have one more area to find before we jump in and start making our adjustments. This time we want to find any area that should appear as a neutral gray in the final image; that means the area should not be bluish gray or pinkish gray, but *pure gray*. You might have to really hunt for a gray; it is not always obvious. It could be a gray sweatshirt, the darker area of a white shirt, or the edge of a book. Not every image has a neutral gray; so if you have a photo of a forest, you might not be able to find a gray. If you can't find one, then don't adjust it.

So, once again, when you find what you want, slap a sample point on top of it so you get yet another readout from the Info palette (refer to Figures 8.25 and 8.26).

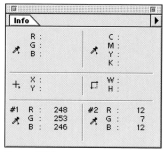

Figure 8.24
After adding a second sample point, you should see two readouts at the bottom of the Info palette.

Figure 8.25
A neutral gray is any area that should appear as just plain gray, with no hint of color.

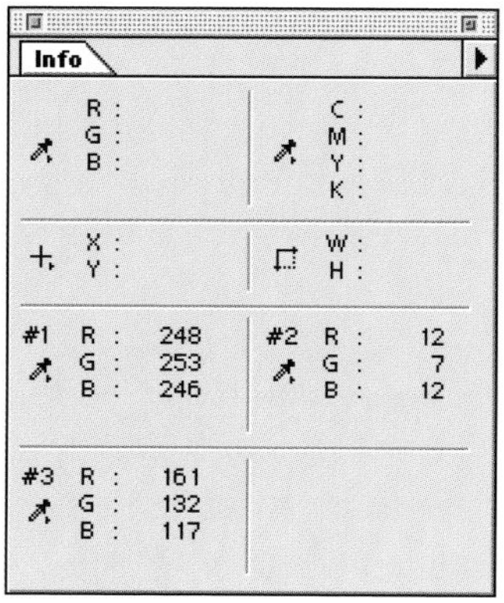

Figure 8.26
After you use the Color Sampler tool to click on a neutral gray, you should find three readouts in the Info palette.

What We're Shootin' For

To make sure that your gray areas don't have a slight color cast, you'll need to adjust their RGB numbers so that they are all equal. Well, that's what we need to do to the three areas (highlight, shadow, neutral gray) we've looked at so far. So if you glance over at the Info palette, you should see three readouts at the bottom of the palette. If the RGB numbers are equal, then the image does not have a color cast (I doubt that is the case). But that's not all we have to think about—we also want the brightest area of the image to be as bright as possible without losing detail and the darkest area to be as dark as possible.

You don't want the highlight to become pure white because it would look too bright. You want to reserve pure white for those areas that shine light directly into the camera lens (light bulbs, shiny reflections, etc.). That means you want the highlight to be just a tad bit darker than white. The lightest shade that can still retain detail is about 3% ink, and that's what we'll use for the highlight setting. But we're adjusting our image in RGB mode, and when you do that, you'll be using a numbering system that ranges from 0-255, not 0-100%. So, let's figure out how to create 3% gray in RGB mode. To accomplish this, click on your foreground color and set the saturation setting (S) to 0, change the brightness setting (B) to 100%, and click on the brightness radio button (B). Now slowly move the slider that is attached to the vertical bar (which should contain grays) down until the magenta (M) and yellow (Y) readouts indicate 3% and then look at the RGB numbers. This will show you exactly what RGB numbers are needed to produce that much ink. So you'll see that we want the highlight to be set to 241R 241G 241B (see Figure 8.27).

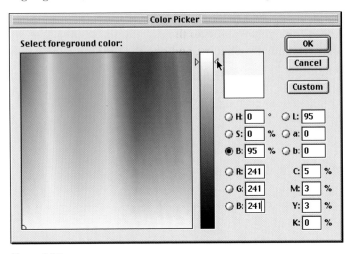

Figure 8.27
A good highlight value is 241R 241G 241B.

We're going to end up making the darkest area of the image pure black (0R 0G 0B) because your computer monitor can display a 99% gray without losing detail. If the image is converted to CMYK mode, we'll set it up so we won't lose detail as well. The setting for the neutral gray area varies depending on how bright the area is. To determine the exact setting needed, all you have to do is analyze the numbers that appear in the Info palette. Since grays in RGB mode contain equal amounts of all three colors, the color that is the farthest off is the one that is creating the color cast. I usually just average the two numbers that are closest together and then set all three RGB numbers to that setting.

Making the Adjustment

Now it's time to make our adjustments. We're going to first get the highlight, shadow, and neutral gray out of the way; then we'll tackle any flesh tone problems with a separate adjustment. To start out, create a new adjustment layer by choosing **Layer>New>Adjustment Layer.** Name the layer something like "Fix up the colors," or "correct color cast," then choose Curves from the Type pop-up menu (see Figure 8.28).

Since we are attempting to balance the red, green, and blue light in these areas, you need to work on the individual color channels by changing the pop-up menu at the top of the Curves dialog box. You'll be adding a total of three adjustment points to the curve: one for the highlight, one for the shadow, and one for the neutral gray. Each time you'll be taking a number out of the Info palette to determine the proper Input setting and then using a preset Output setting for all of them (except the neutral gray).

Figure 8.28
Creating a new Curves adjustment layer.

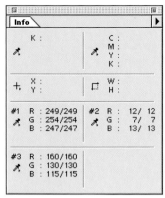

Figure 8.29
The Info palette contains all the Input settings you'll need when using the Curves dialog box to adjust your image.

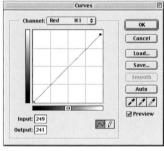

Figure 8.30
Adjust the upper right point until the Input number matches what is in the Info palette, and the output number reads 241.

Let's start with the highlight adjustment. Look over to the first set of numbers at the bottom of the Info palette; they should be for the highlight of the image (see Figure 8.29). You will see that each of the RGB readouts show two numbers separated by a slash. The number on the left is what was in the image before the adjustment (also known as the Input setting), and the number on the right is what you will end up with after the adjustment (also known as the Output setting). The two numbers are identical because you haven't made any changes yet.

To change the amount of red being used for the highlight, change the pop-up menu at the top of the Curves dialog box to Red, then click on the little square that is in the upper right of the grid, as depicted in Figure 8.30. This should make the numbers at the bottom of the dialog box available for editing. Now, click on the Input number (that means before adjustment) and enter the red number that is shown in the Info palette for the highlight of the image. I mentioned earlier that you'll want the highlight to contain 241R, so press Tab to edit the Output number (that means after the adjustment) and type in 241.

Next, click on the square that is in the lower left of the grid (the one on the end of the "curve"), then click on the Input field or just press Tab (see Figure 8.31). Enter the red setting that is listed in the Info palette (from the second set of numbers), and change the Output setting to 0.

Now it's time to create a third point for the neutral gray setting. To add a point to the curve, click near the middle of the curve (see Figure 8.32). Now set the Input number to what you find in the Info palette (third readout). To figure out the Output setting, average the two numbers that are closest to being equal in the Info palette. In my case, red is the farthest off (160 compared to 130 and 115), so I'd average the green and blue numbers to end up with 125.

Now repeat this process for Green and Blue, adding a total of three points for each color. After you have completed this step, any color casts should be removed from your image. Compare Figures 8.33 and 8.34.

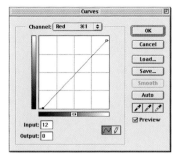

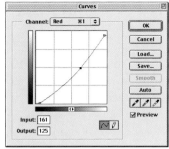

Figure 8.31
Adjust the lower left point until the Input number matches what is in the Info palette, and the output number reads 0.

Figure 8.32
Add a point to the middle of the curve to adjust the neutral gray setting.

Figure 8.33
Before color correction, the image contains a slight red cast (look at the road surface).

Figure 8.34
After correction, the cast has been removed.

Flesh Tones in RGB Mode

Unfortunately, I don't have a magic RGB formula for flesh tones. When it comes to the color of skin, nature has provided a wealth of diversity. That's a wonderful thing, but trying to reproduce them all ain't so easy. But I can give you some guidelines that will help you achieve acceptable results. The rest is up to you.

The guidelines I have come from the prepress industry and are therefore CMYK values. But don't worry, I'll show you how to convert them to RGB numbers so you can continue with your RGB corrections.

Yellow should always be higher than magenta.

1% higher=baby skin.

10% higher=black or Asian skin.

20% higher=a very tanned version of a white skin.

The more cyan you have, the more tanned a person will look.

5%=baby skin.

10%=Asian skin.

20%=skin of a tanned white person.

35%=black skin.

These numbers really depend on how bright the skin appears, so take them as general guides instead of absolute settings. I like to keep a file of images that I have already had printed, then look through and find a flesh tone that is similar to what I'd like. Then I can open the file that image was created from and read the numbers out of the Info palette to find out how to create the same shade.

Now let's find out how to convert from CMYK to RGB numbers. First, I usually click on the flesh tone I'm about to change using the Eyedropper tool (this will change your foreground color). Then I'll click on my foreground color and use the Color Picker to take a peek at the CMYK numbers (even though I'm in RGB mode). I can change these numbers until I think they are within the guidelines listed above, and then I just glance over at the RGB numbers to see how to create the same result.

We adjust flesh tones in the same way we adjusted the rest of the image: create a new adjustment layer and use the numbers from the Info palette for input numbers (assuming you added a sample point), and use the RGB numbers you got out of the Color Picker for the output numbers.

It might have taken me over a dozen pages to describe how to color correct an image; but the actual process, once you're used to it, should hardly ever take more than two minutes. Once you're happy with your colors and have removed any color casts, you'll most likely want to sharpen the image.

Sharpening the Image

It's not very often that I sharpen all the channels in an RGB or CMYK image. When I do, I usually end up with off-color halos around the edges of objects. Well, sharpening is all about halos; but they become rather distracting when they are different in color from the object you are sharpening.

An RGB image is made from red, green, and blue light; and if you sharpen all of those colors at the same time, it is very easy to get some odd-colored halos. The same thing happens in CMYK mode because CMY (cyan, magenta, yellow) are all colors, and the black channel does not contain that much detail. Lab mode, on the other hand, can do wonders for your image. It is the only mode that separates the brightness of your image (known as Lightness) from all the color information (stored in the a and b channels). (See Figures 8.35 to 8.37.)

Figure 8.35
The Lightness channel contains the brightness values.

Figure 8.36
The "a" channel contains colors ranging from red to green.

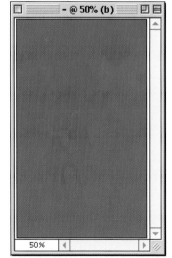

Figure 8.37
The "b" channel contains colors ranging from blue to yellow.

To sharpen just the Lightness information, open the Channels palette and click on the Lightness channel. This will make your image appear as a grayscale image. To view the image in full color, but still edit the Lightness information, turn on the eyeball icon next to the Lab channel by clicking just to the left of its preview thumbnail.

Now you can choose **Filter>Sharpen>Unsharp Mask** and sharpen the image just like we did with a grayscale image. As a result, you should prevent any odd-colored halos. Once you are done sharpening the image, be sure to click on the topmost channel so you are no longer just working on the Lightness channel.

If you are planning on using your image for multimedia (web, video, etc.) or to output to a 35mm slide or a dye-sub printer, you can sit back and smile because you are all done with color correction and can change the mode of your image back to RGB and save it. I'd also leave my images in RGB mode for most desktop color printers. But, if the end use of your image will be a printing press, then you'll need to convert the image to CMYK mode before you send it off to the printer. You can pull up your shirt-sleeves now.

Converting to CMYK Mode

I prefer to work on my images in RGB mode for as long as possible before converting them to CMYK. That's because CMYK mode is a pretty lousy mode to work in, but I mentioned that earlier so I won't drive it into the ground here.

So, even though I'm going to show you how to convert your image to CMYK mode in this chapter, I suggest you wait until you are finished constructing your image. But let's see what is involved and which setting will produce acceptable results. Before converting to CMYK mode, we'll have to choose CMYK Setup from the **File>Color Settings** menu and let Photoshop know what type of printing conditions we plan to use (see Figure 8.38). I find most people think of the CMYK Setup dialog box as some sort of "mystery box" that they should leave alone. But if you leave it alone, especially with Photoshop 5's changes (which we'll talk about later in this chapter), you are really looking for trouble.

If this is the first time you've been in this dialog box, it might seem a overwhelming (it did for me). But stick with me, we'll wade through it together. All the settings in this box have to do with what type of printing you will be using and the limitations of the paper you are printing on. I will say it again because it's so important: this is a dialog box you definitely don't want to ignore. If the settings are wrong, you can end up with lots of problems once your image hits the printing press. If you don't feel like dealing with all these choices, you can ask your printing company for the ideal settings for your specific type of printing. If you plan on going that route, be sure to give them an idea of what type of paper you will be using (coated or uncoated, and the weight) so they can give you accurate settings. Let's take a look at what all this means and figure out what will produce good results.

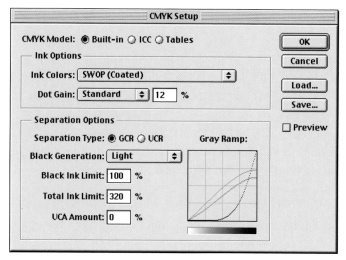

Figure 8.38
The CMYK Setup dialog box determines what will happen to your image when it is converted into CMYK mode.

Ink Colors

The Ink Colors pop-up menu lets Photoshop know the colors of ink you are printing with. Each one of these settings describes a slightly different version of cyan, magenta, yellow, and black ink. In the U.S. we almost always use the SWOP standards; but if you are printing in Asia, you might end up using Toyo inks, or you might use Eurostandard if you are printing in Europe. So, unless I'm sending my image overseas, I usually use one of the SWOP choices. Each one of these choices has different options for printing on coated or uncoated paper.

Dot Gain

Basic Dot Gain Conversions

Photoshop 4	Photoshop 5
10%	-1%
11%	0%
12%	1%
13%	2%
14%	4%
15%	5%
16%	6%
17%	8%
18%	9%
19%	10%
20%	12%
21%	13%
22%	15%
23%	16%
24%	18%
25%	20%
26%	21%
27%	23%
28%	25%
29%	27%
30%	29%
31%	30%
32%	32%
33%	34%
34%	36%
35%	38%
36%	40%

On a printing press, your image will be made from different-sized black circles to simulate shades of gray. When these circles are printed with ink, the ink absorbs into the paper and spreads out, just like when you spill coffee on a paper towel. The Dot Gain setting tells Photoshop how much these dots will gain in size. You need to be aware that Adobe changed the way dot gain is calculated to make it more accurate than older versions of the program, *but* for some reason they didn't document it in the manuals. This could cause quite a few problems for the uninformed. So tell your Photoshop friends and save them some grief. You can use the table to the left to convert between settings you are used to using in Photoshop 4 to the new settings for Photoshop 5.

Or, if you need to convert when you don't have this book around (shame on you), you can open the old version of Photoshop, choose **File>Color Settings>Printing Inks Setup**, and click the Save button. Then open Photoshop 5 and choose **File>Color Settings>CMYK Setup**, and click the Load button. This will cause Photoshop to convert your old settings to the new, more accurate method of measuring Dot Gain.

Now that you know they made some changes, you might want to know which settings I recommend for different printing conditions. Take a glance at the table that follows. You'll find a range of settings for the most popular types of printing conditions. Use the lower end of the range when you are using really nice paper, and use the higher range when you are going the cheap route.

Press and Paper Stock	Dot Gain
Sheetfed coated stock	1-6%
Sheetfed uncoated stock	8-15%
Web press coated stock	8-15%
Web press uncoated stock	15-29%
Web press newsprint	29-40%

Separation Type

Now we're on to the bottom section of the dialog box (whew!). This section determines how Photoshop will limit the amount of ink used on the printing press. If you use too much ink, the paper won't dry fast enough, and that can cause many problems on press. First, wet ink can act like glue and cause your paper to stick to different parts of the printing press. Second, when the paper comes out the end of the press and then a second sheet comes down and touches the first, some of the overly wet ink might transfer and create a ghosted image. And, finally, if the ink is not dry enough, then your paper will wrinkle when it is drying—have you ever read a book in the bathtub? That's what happens when paper gets too wet—wrinkle-mania. So let's see what's needed for different kinds of paper stocks.

If you remember our little talk about how RGB works (or did you skip over that part?), equal amounts of red, green, and blue create a neutral gray. You need only one or two of the colors to create bright, saturated colors. If you add the third color to a saturated color, all it does is lower its saturation. Well, if you convert the RGB numbers into a bar chart, you might notice that most of the colors in your document use all three RGB colors and therefore are not completely saturated (see Figure 8.39).

Remember how I said the relationship between RGB and CMY is like a teeter-totter? If you use more red light, you'll be using less cyan ink in CMYK mode. Well, it would work that way if we could come up with ideal CMY inks, but it's pretty close to correct with the inks we're stuck with. So you could convert your RGB bar chart into an equivalent CMY bar chart; and with ideal CMY inks, equal amounts would create gray (see Figure 8.40).

WARNING

No matter what you do, do not ignore the fact that the Dot Gain default settings have changed with Photoshop 5. Adobe changed the way dot gain is measured, but did not change the default setting! The default in Photoshop 4 was 20%, but in Photoshop 5 the equivalent would be only 12%. Because they didn't change the default setting to 12% (they left it at 20%), they did the equivalent of changing the default to 25% in Photoshop 4. So if you want consistent results between the two versions, be sure to use the preceding table. Also, beware that when you change the Ink Colors pop-up menu, Photoshop will also change the Dot Gain setting. So, if you change the Ink Colors, be sure to re-enter the Dot Gain setting you need because the defaults often create problems.

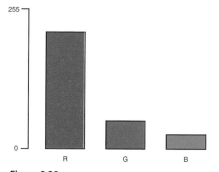

Figure 8.39
Most colors will contain all three RGB components.

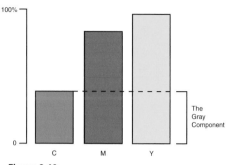

Figure 8.40
If you convert the RGB color into its CMY components, all three colors will still be used.

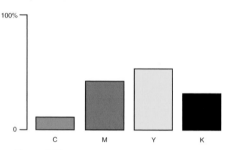

Figure 8.41.
By removing the gray component and replacing it with black ink, you will reduce the total amount of ink used.

So if you look at Figure 8.40, the part of the color that uses equal amounts of CMY is making the color darker (it just adds gray). You could remove all the "gray component" and replace it with some black and you'd end up with better-looking shadows (remember, non-ideal CMY produces brown instead of black) that use less ink (see Figure 8.41). That's what GCR (gray component replacement) is all about.

But you probably don't want to remove all of the gray component; otherwise, your shadows would look flat and lifeless. So you also have a choice of how much you want to replace. That's known as the Black Generation setting. Try this out: choose **File>Color Settings>CMYK Setup** and set the Separation Type to GCR and the Black Generation to None. Now look at the little grid in the left of the dialog box. (See Figure 8.42.) This shows you how you would create all the neutral grays in your image. You should see three lines: one for cyan, one for magenta, and one for yellow. Well, there are actually four lines (one for black), but the black one is all the way against the bottom of the grid.

Now change the Black Generation to Light and see what happens to the grid (see Figure 8.43). Do you notice that you are replacing some of the CMY ink with black?

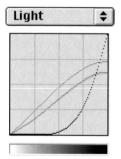

Figure 8.42
When black generation is set to None, gray will be created without black ink.

Figure 8.43
The Black Generation setting determines how much of the CMY ink will be replaced with black.

Now watch the grid and try out the other Black Generation settings. The more black ink you use, the less CMY you need. If you just used CMY ink to create your shadows, you'd end up with dark, muddy-brown shadows and an awful lot of ink. But you don't want to use too much black; otherwise, the shadows will appear flat and lifeless. This setting also determines how easily the person adjusting the printing press can shift the colors in your image. The more color ink you use, the easier it is to get it to shift on the printing press. The amount of black you use depends on the content of the image you are creating and how you are planning to print it.

Light—Use for the majority of jobs. It produces nice, rich shadows and gives the press operator lots of control over the colors in your image.

Medium—Use for newsprint (because you don't want lots of ink) or when the subject of your photo is mainly neutral grays (like a pile of silver dollars).

Heavy—Don't use it because the shadow appears to be lifeless and loses detail.

Maximum—Use for screen shots because you want nice black lines.

I use GCR with a Light Black Generation setting for the majority of my images. But I find some printing companies prefer to use UCR (which stands for Under Color Removal). So, let's take a look at how UCR reduces the amount of ink in your document. Try this: open the CMYK Setup dialog box once again, set the Separation Type to GCR and the Black Generation to Medium (see Figure 8.44). Now watch how the grid changes when you change the Separation Type to UCR (see Figure 8.45). It mainly pulls out black in the darkest areas of the image.

Now compare GCR with Light Black Generation to UCR. They should look almost the same. Well, UCR is attempting to replace only CMY with Black in the neutral gray areas of your image. (GCR takes it out of the color areas as well.) This will usually produce a bit less black ink than do the GCR settings.

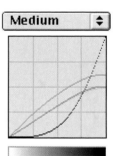

Figure 8.44
Medium Black generation starts removing CMY ink at around 30% gray.

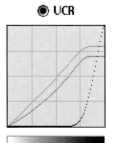

Figure 8.45
UCR removes CMY ink in the darkest areas of the grays.

I use this setting when the dark areas of an image are most important because it will pull out some additional contrast from the shadows. UCR can also do a decent choice when printing on newsprint. But for the majority of my jobs, I stay with GCR. Okay, enough about UCR and GCR. Now let's move on to the other settings in this dialog box.

Black Ink Limit

The Black Ink limit settings determine the maximum amount of black ink that will be used anywhere in your image. Because ink absorbs into paper and spreads out, the darkest shades of gray (99%, 98%, 97%, 96%, and so on) usually become pure black by the time your image comes out the end of the printing press. You probably don't want any important detail in those shades; otherwise, you'll lose it all when the image is printed. So, you will usually want to type in the darkest shade of gray that doesn't become black. You can ask your printing company for this info (it would be known as the maximum shadow dot reproducible on press—I'd subtract about 3% from the number they give you just for a safety net), or you can use the settings in the following table. Photoshop's default setting of 100% almost ensures that you'll lose detail in the shadows of your image.

> **NOTE**
>
> You can use a black ink limit of 100% if you don't need to retain any detail in the dark areas of the image. I use this setting when I want to create a nice black background to place a type effect on top of (like a green glow fading to black).

Recommended black ink limit settings

Press and Paper Stock	Black Ink Limit
Sheetfed coated stock	94%
Sheetfed uncoated stock	90%
Web press coated stock	90%
Web press uncoated stock	86%
Web press newsprint	80%

Total Ink Limit

Thankfully, Total Ink Limit is rather straightforward; it determines the maximum amount of ink you can use in any area of your image. This is where you are really controlling exactly how much ink will be on the press. If you get this number too high, you're looking for problems—remember the wrinkles, ghosted images, and sticking I mentioned earlier. I'd suggest you ask your printing company what setting to use because it is so dependent on the paper you are using. There are hundreds (if not thousands) of different papers out there, so all I can give you is a general guide. Use the upper end of the range when you are using really nice paper, and use the lower range when you are going the cheap route.

Press and Paper Stock	Total Ink Limit
Sheetfed coated stock	320-340%
Sheetfed uncoated stock	285-300%
Web press coated stock	300-320%
Web press uncoated stock	280-300%
Web press newsprint	220-280%

UCA Amount

Sometimes when you replace the color inks with black, your shadows start to look drab and lackluster. If you start noticing this unwelcome phenomenon, UCA can come to the rescue. UCA stands for Under Color Addition. It will attempt to add some additional CMY into your shadows to richen them. I only use this setting when I notice my shadows looking a wee bit weak because it really is a poor fix. It just dumps more cyan, magenta, and yellow into the shadows. If you do decide to use it, use a low amount of around 10%. But whatever you do, leave the UCA setting at 0% if you are printing your image on newsprint (you don't want to shove more ink onto that cheapo paper).

Saving Your Preferences

Now that you have all your CMYK Setup settings perfected, you might as well save them by clicking on the Save button. I'd name them something that reminds you of what type of printing conditions they are to be used for, such as "Sheetfed coated stock." That way you can set up a

NOTE

On the CD accompanying this book, you'll find a PDF file that supplements this chapter. The file, called extras.pdf, contains the following topics related to CMYK color correction:

Calculating highlight settings
Calculating neutral grays
Flesh tones
Curves

In the same file, you'll also find information about

Correcting for scanner only
Using unwanted colors
Matching color between documents
Repairing blue skies
Sharpening black channels

few settings, just open the dialog box, and use the Load button instead of thinking about each individual setting every time you are using a different printing condition.

Converting to CMYK

Warning: Before you convert the image to CMYK mode, you'll want to merge any adjustment layers you have created into the main image. If you don't merge them, then the adjustments will look quite different in CMYK mode.

Now, if you have all those settings typed in, you can convert your color-corrected image to CMYK mode by choosing **Image>Mode>CMYK** color. When you convert to CMYK, Photoshop does a bunch of work behind the scenes to ensure that your image conforms to the settings you specified in the CMYK Setup dialog box. It does not merely attach those settings, it actually changes the image as if you had gone in and messed with Curves.

Closing Thoughts

There's no question that being introduced to color correction for the first time can be a little overwhelming. But look at it this way. If you were five years old and were just learning how to write your name, the effort of that simple task would seem Herculean. But by the time you're five and a half, writing your name is as easy as pie. So it will be with color correction after you've been through the process a few times. The techniques described in this chapter are the very same ones used by the high-paid color maestros who put out all of those ever-so-perfect glossy magazine ads. It will take you a while to really get the hang of these techniques; but once you do, it should take you less than two minutes to correct most images.

There's one last bit of advice. Make sure to always correct your images separately before blending them together. That way you will be able to maintain the color integrity of each component of your big picture. And remember— you're infinitely better off if you can fix color problems at an early stage in the image creation process. And the more you understand about that process, the less fixing you'll have to do.

Ask Adobe

Q: What mode should I color correct my images in, and why?

A: This is a matter of personal preference as much as anything; and you may find yourself doing some work in RGB, converting to CMYK, and then doing final tuning. Color correcting in RGB before separating allows one to address issues with out-of-gamut colors before the colors have been clipped. Many color corrections also behave a bit more predictably. On the other hand, you may frequently want to do some tweaking after a separation to improve the results; and there are some who argue that certain color moves are easier in CMYK. In particular, because the detail is preserved in the black plate, you may be able to get away with more dramatic moves in cyan, magenta, and yellow than you could in RGB.

Q: Why do certain effects like Glows fading to black look better when created in RGB mode? And why do I have to flatten the image when converting to CMYK to maintain the quality of the effect (if I don't flatten it, it looks washed out)?

A: Color blending in CMYK is simply less reliable than it is in RGB. Darkening modes like Multiply generally behave more or less the same in both modes, so shadows will frequently work well in CMYK. But other modes are far less likely to work quite the way you'd expect simply because the interaction of the four color components in CMYK is more complex than the three components in RGB. For example, for a glow to lighten an area it needs to do the "right" thing in the black component along with the cyan, magenta, and yellow components. This is why effects that depend on particular blend modes have more trouble in CMYK and why one generally should flatten an image before converting it.

Q: Why do many of the filters (Emboss, etc.) produce a brownish result when applied in CMYK mode?

A: Because CMYK is actually a relatively bad color model for a wide variety of operations. This is because it uses four components to specify something that is really just a three-component process. It also generally lacks the reliable behavior for neutrals that Photoshop imposes on the RGB spaces it supports. In the case of Emboss, for example, non-edge areas end up at 50% in all of the channels. In RGB, this corresponds to middle gray. In CMYK, printing 50% for each of the inks is likely to produce a color cast because the inks do not behave identically.

Q: Why aren't all the filters (such as Artistic, Brush Strokes, Sketch, and Texture) available in CMYK mode?

A: Some filters, such as Lens Flare and Lighting Effects, depend on particular parts of the behavior of RGB. Others just simply did not initially support CMYK and haven't been subject to enough demand to make adding CMYK support a priority.

Ben's Techno-Babble Decoder Ring

Sheetfed Press—A printing press that is fed one sheet at a time. Sheetfed presses are typically slower and produce higher-quality results than a web press. They are used to print the majority of brochures and annual reports.

Web Press—A printing press that is fed with one continuous roll of paper. This allows for much higher speed than sheetfed presses and is typically used when printing newspapers and magazines. Web presses usually include in-line folding and trimming equipment.

Neutral Gray—A pure gray that does not have any hint of color.

Specular Highlight—An intense reflection that contains little or no detail. You'll find specular highlights in jewelry, metallic objects, and very shiny surfaces.

Dot Gain—The process of a round dot (usually measured at 50% gray) gaining in size as the ink it is created from absorbs into a sheet of paper and spreads out. This phenomenon causes images to darken when printed using ink on paper.

Total Ink Limit—The maximum amount of CMYK ink that should be used in any one area of an image. Calculated by adding together the percentages of the four CMYK inks. This setting is used to prevent drying problems due to excessive ink concentrated on an absorbent paper.

Black Ink Limit—The maximum amount of black ink that should be used in the darkest areas of an image. This setting is used to prevent the loss of detail in the darkest area of an image. Dot gain usually causes the darkest shades of gray (95-99%) to become pure black on the printing press.

GCR—Gray Component Replacement is a method of reducing the amount of ink used when converting to CMYK mode by replacing CMY ink with black.

UCR—Under Color Removal is a method of reducing the amount of ink used when converting to CMYK mode. UCR attempts to replace CMY ink with black in the shadows and neutral gray areas only.

UCA—Under Color Addition attempts to add CMY ink to the shadows of an image to make them appear richer. This is usually used to maintain rich, deep shadows when applying GCR to an image.

SWOP—Specifications for Web Offset Publication are specifications used in the printing industry to maintain consistency between all the vendors involved in producing a printed page. SWOP standards are maintained and updated by a non-profit organization formed to maintain technical standards in the graphic arts industry.

9 Channels

Why take the escalator when I have a perfectly good canoe right here? — Austin Powers in the movie "Austin Powers, International Man of Mystery."

Courtesy of Robert Brünz, www.brunz.com.

If you just did a double take on that quote and said, "huh, what?" you just reacted the same way that most people do the first time they hear about channels. Okay, at first glance, channels might be a little confusing. Let's just get that out in the open. But let's also not forget that confusion is not a fatal disease; and in this chapter, hopefully, you're going to get the cure. With the help of some plain, everyday language, we'll take a tour through channels; and you can see for yourself that there are no exotic mysteries, puzzles, or riddles about them.

To get to the root of all this confusion, you have to go back to when channels were first conceived and given their misbegotten name. The very name "channels" breeds confusion because it doesn't relate to anything in the real world, and so it doesn't mean anything to anybody. As a result, most people just give it a nickname. I've heard them called stencils, masks, friskets, rubyliths, and amberliths, to name a few. I don't know about you, but in the course of normal conversation (as opposed to Photoshop-speak), when you talk about channels, things like HBO, NBC, and CNN are the first things that come to mind.

So, taking all of that into consideration, you might wonder what in blazes was Adobe thinking when they came up with that name? I can't answer that. But I can tell you that regardless of the hopeless misnomer, channels are absolutely essential to your work in Photoshop. Once you you've mastered them, you will have one of Photoshop's most powerful tools at your beck and call.

Channels are Worth The Pain!

To be fair, I have to tell you that a lot of people who try channels for the first time throw their hands up in the air and give up. They convince themselves that they don't really need channels, and they learn how to patch things up in other ways. But I believe that if they really knew what they were missing, they'd take another crack at it.

Let's say you just met a secretary named Minnie. In her office there are two pieces of equipment, an old IBM Selectric typewriter and the best personal computer that money can buy. Whenever Minnie's boss gives her a memo to type, she immediately loads up the Selectric with a fresh piece of paper and starts rat-tatting away. "Minnie!," you ask, "why don't you use the computer for that?" Minnie just gives you a dirty look over her bifocals. So you try to reason with her, "But, Minnie, what if you make a mistake, or the boss changes his mind? Wouldn't it be easier to have that memo stored in your computer?" Minnie lets out a long impatient sigh (the kind of sigh that only mothers can do justice to). Then she gives it to you straight: "Look here, smartypants, maybe it *would* be easier, maybe it *wouldn't*, but whichever way you look at it, that thing is just too doggoned hard to learn." And with that, she swivels around, hunches over her beloved Selectric and finishes her memo.

Of course, everybody knows that Minnie is crazy as a loon not to use the computer. And anyone who uses a computer knows that, yes, it might have been a little challenging at first, but once you've learned it, how could you possibly live without it? That's exactly how it is with channels! Channels are so completely integrated into Photoshop that there's hardly anything you can do to your image without affecting the information that's stored in the channels palette. And if it has that much influence on your image, wouldn't you want to know what they are all about? Of course you would.

Without channels, it's impossible to save the shape of a selection so that you can get it back later. It would also be impossible to force a shadow to print with only black ink (which makes them look better). And you'd have terrible troubles working with metallic or florescent inks without the help of channels. So, let's take a headlong plunge into the not-so-mysterious world of channels. And for the purposes of this chapter, when we talk about them, we're going to be using just two terms: channels and masks.

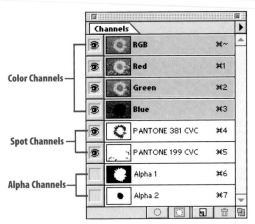

Figure 9.1
Channel types.

Three Varieties of Channels

There are three varieties of channels: color, spot, and alpha channels (see Figure 9.1). They all look about the same, but they perform completely different tasks. However, they do have some things in common: they have the same dimensions as the document that contains them, they can contain up to 256 shades of gray, and Photoshop treats them as if they were individual grayscale documents. Let's take a surface look at them; then we'll explore each one in depth.

Color Channels

The topmost channels in the Channels palette are known as color channels because they keep track of all of the colors that will be printed and displayed. The names of these channels correspond to the mode your image is in (an RGB image will contain Red, Green, and Blue color channels, a CMYK image will contain Cyan, Magenta, Yellow and Black channels.). So, when you paint, edit, or apply a filter to your image, it is the information in the color channels that you are really changing.

Sample Use: You've got an image taken by a digital camera. It's not just any image; it's your Granny blowing out candles on her 90th birthday. You know that pictures from digital cameras are notorious for looking "noisy," but this one takes the cake. Your beloved Granny looks like her face is covered with blackheads. If you didn't know better, you'd probably just try to blur the image to get rid of the noise. But you do know better, because you know that if you did that, you'd end up removing the majority of the detail in the image. So instead, you switch over to color channels and start working on your image "under the hood." In just a few moments you've gotten rid of the noise and sharpened the overall image as well. Granny looks much better.

Spot Channels

Directly below the color channels are the spot channels. This type of channel is used for creating documents that will be printed using colors other than (or in addition to) cyan, magenta, yellow, and black. The name of a Spot Channel is usually the name of the ink that will be used (like PANTONE 185 CVC). Only documents that have been specifically set up for spot color work will contain this type of channel.

Sample Use: You're asked to create a "look" that resembles the cover of *Wired* magazine. You thumb through a few copies and notice that they go for the big eye-stopping colors: neon, florescent, metallic. You know, disco colors. You go to the standard Color Picker and choose a far-out shade of metallic purple not seen since the days of "Saturday Night Fever." But you get flagged down by the CMYK Police: "Gamut Warning! Color Cannot Be Reproduced in CMYK, you idiot!" Nooo problem. Like a flash, you switch over to Spot channels, where you confidently create your spaced-out colors, knowing that you are also creating the necessary information needed by your printer to reproduce them accurately. Groovy.

Alpha Channels

Channels that appear at the bottom of the Channels palette are called alpha channels. This is the real McCoy—the stuff people are usually talking about when they bring up channels. Alpha channels have user-defined names; or if a name isn't supplied when a channel is created, Photoshop uses a generic name like "Alpha 1." An alpha channel is a saved *selection*—it's that simple (well, almost that simple).

Sample use: You just spent the good part of an hour making an eyestraining selection of every curl and wisp of hair on a model who's got a mane bigger than Tina Turner's. You're doing this because your client requested a redhead when you only had a blonde; but you're on to this guy and justifiably suspicious that in the end he'll probably want a brunette. So, as usual, you outsmart him and save that selection as an alpha channel, knowing that you will be prepared for anything, even zebra stripes if necessary. Then you have the option of charging the client for all the time you saved, or not.

Navigating the Channels Palette

Okay, you've been briefly introduced to the channels family. You know their names (color, spot, and alpha); and you know, in the most general sense, what they're intended for. Before we look at them any closer, let's take a moment and get familiar with their place of residence, the Channels palette.

If you've read the Layer Primer chapter (I hope you did) and now you're sitting there staring at the Channels palette, you'll probably notice that channels look almost identical to layers. Well, Adobe did this for a good reason. They want you to get used to one style of palette. They assumed that if you became comfortable with one kind of palette, you would quickly adapt to other palettes that were similar in design and function. So, the Layers, Channels, and Paths palettes look almost identical (see Figures 9.2 to 9.4). Just a few of the icons at the bottom of each palette are different. And even with these they tried to be consistent. For instance, the icon you use to create a new layer looks the same as the one you use to create a new channel or path.

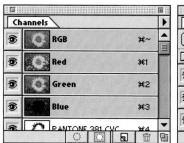

Figure 9.2
Channels palette.

Figure 9.3
Layers palette.

Figure 9.4
Paths palette.

As with layers, the eyeballs control what is being displayed within the main image window. Just click in the column that contains the eyeballs to toggle them on or off. The channels that are active for editing are the ones that are highlighted. Click the name of a channel to make it active; or to activate more than one channel at a time, Shift-click their names (I wish I could do that with layers). To change the stacking order of the channels, drag the name of a channel up or down within the channels stack (you can't change the order of the color channels). To create a new empty channel, click on the icon that resembles a piece of paper with a folded corner. To change the name of a channel, double-click on its name. And, to delete a channel, drag it to the little trashcan icon (see Figure 9.5).

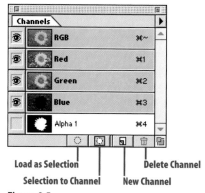

Figure 9.5
The Channels palette.

Okay, that's enough for now. We'll cover the rest of the palette as we go through the different types of channels. So put on your thinking cap and let's get started.

Understanding Color Channels

Using color channels is like peeking behind the scenes and seeing how Photoshop is creating your image. You might think of color channels as the engine in your car. When you push the gas pedal, you are causing a whole chain reaction of events under the hood. In this case, while you are working in layers, the chain reaction is occurring in the color channels. They store up-to-the-minute information about RGB colors (Red, Green, and Blue light), CMYK colors (Cyan, Magenta, Yellow, and Black ink), or any other color modes you are using. If you don't tamper with the channels, Photoshop will assume that whatever you're doing, you want it to affect all of the channels at the same time. But, if you pop the hood and designate specific channels, you can do some very precise sculpting and manipulations in ways that would be virtually impossible without using color channels.

You'll need to choose a color mode to work in; but before you do, you might want to know a little something about your options.

Choosing a Color Mode

In RGB mode, Photoshop constructs your image out of Red, Green and Blue light (see Figure 9.6). This is the mode most images start in because all scanners and digital cameras use RGB light to capture images, and all computer monitors use RGB light to display images. Some fancy (and very expensive) high-end scanners might deliver a CMYK result, but that conversion occurs in software after the RGB scan. This mode is ideal for images that will be displayed using light; this includes images that will be used on-screen for multimedia or the Internet, or those that will be output to video. You'll also want to use RGB mode when outputting images to 35mm slides because the output device (a film recorder) will use RGB light to expose the photographic film. And since you view all your images on an RGB monitor while you are editing them, this mode turns out to be an excellent "working mode." Once you have finished editing the image, you can convert it to any mode you desire (CMYK for publishing, Indexed color for Internet, etc.).

CMYK mode creates your image out of Cyan, Magenta, Yellow, and Black ink, also known as process colors (see Figure 9.7). This is the mode that your image should end up in if your final destination is a printing press. When

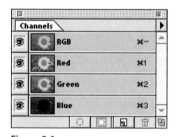

Figure 9.6.
RGB Channels.

Figure 9.7
CMYK Channels.

you convert an image to CMYK mode, Photoshop compensates for many factors (dot gain, total ink limit, etc.) that are specific to the type of paper and press that will be used. I recommend that you perform most editing and adjusting in RGB mode. This will allow you to adjust an image once and use it for multiple types of printing.

The Lab mode is a different animal. It separates your image into lightness, which means how bright or dark the image is, and two channels called A and B (see Figure 9.8). The A and B channels are weird because they don't contain just one color. The A channel contains colors that are between green and red, and the B channel contains colors that are between blue and yellow. This makes it the only mode that separates how bright your image is from the color information, and that's what makes it so useful. Lab mode safeguards your colors so you can just adjust how bright or dark the image is without shifting its colors. Whereas with RGB and CMYK mode, if you tried to do the same adjustments, the colors would probably shift. Lab mode is usually a temporary stop on your way to one of the other modes. It's not usually your final destination.

WARNING

Due to impurities in the CMYK inks, the CMYK mode cannot reproduce all the colors available in RGB mode. When using the Color Picker to choose a color, a small triangular warning symbol (known as the gamut warning) will appear next to the color you have chosen if it is one of the colors that are not reproducible in CMYK mode. Clicking on the triangle will give you the closest reproducible color.

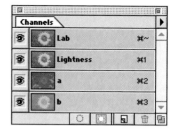

Figure 9.8
Lab Channels.

How Channels Relate to Layers

All of the information in the color channels is assembled from the elements in the Layers palette. If you view a single layer, the color channels display just that particular layer's content, as shown in Figure 9.9. If you view multiple layers, the color channels show the result of combining those layers, as shown in Figure 9.10. Because you can edit only one layer at a time, any changes made using the color channels will affect the currently active layer only.

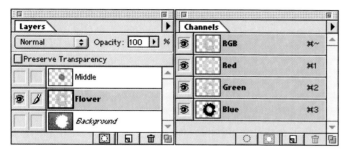

Figure 9.9
If a single layer is visible, the channels indicate what is contained in that layer.

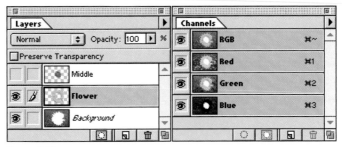

Figure 9.10
When multiple layers are visible, the channels reflect the combination of those layers.

The Composite Color Channel

If the image contains more than one color channel (RGB, CMYK, or Lab), then the topmost channel will be a special one known as the composite channel (see Figure 9.11). This composite channel does not contain any information; it is just a shortcut to make all the color channels visible and active for editing, which is their default state if you haven't been editing the individual channels. So, in effect, this is how you get things back to normal after messing with the individual channels.

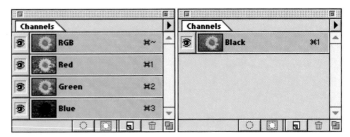

Figure 9.11
When multiple color channels are present, the topmost channel is known as the composite channel.

Viewing Channels in Color

When viewing a single-color channel (by clicking on its name in the Channels palette), it will appear as a grayscale image. This was done on purpose to make it easy for you to see exactly what the channel contains. If you view more than one color channel at a time (by turning on more eyeballs in the palette), the channels will appear in color.

You can force Photoshop to display individual channels in color (instead of grayscale) by choosing **File>Preferences> Displays & Cursors** and turning on the Color Channels in Color checkbox (see Figure 9.12). I don't find this all that useful because it becomes much harder to see exactly what is in each channel, especially when viewing the yellow channel of a CMYK image (it's just so light!). Go ahead and try it: open an image, convert it to CMYK mode, and take a peek at the yellow channel; then turn the preference on and off (see Figures 9.13 and 9.14). Then you'll understand why they chose Grayscale as the best way to view a channel.

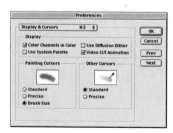

Figure 9.12
Displays & Cursors dialog box.

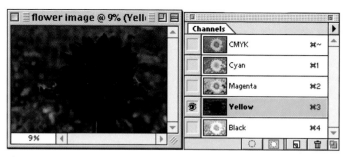

Figure 9.13
Color Channels in Color checkbox off. (© 1998 PhotoDisc)

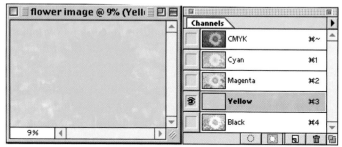

Figure 9.14
Color Channels in Color checkbox on.

Editing Multiple Channels

When you are adjusting an image using Levels or Curves, you'll notice a pop-up menu at the top of the dialog box such as the one in Figure 9.15. This little menu determines which color channels you are editing (you can either edit a single channel or all of them).

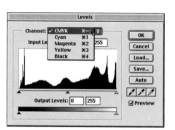

Figure 9.15
When applying Levels, you can either adjust a single color channel or all of them.

By using the Channels palette, you can force Levels or Curves (or any control for that matter) to affect more than one channel (see Figure 9.16). Just click on the channel you would like to change, then Shift-click on another channel, and finally turn on the eyeball of the composite channel (the topmost one). This can be extremely useful when working on fleshtones because they are mainly made from magenta and yellow ink.

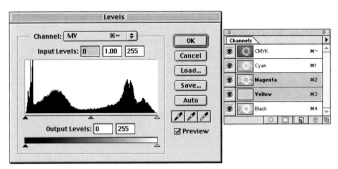

Figure 9.16
By messing with the Channels palette, you can get the Levels dialog box to affect multiple channels.

Applying a Filter to a Single Channel

Without using the Channels palette, it's next to impossible to get a filter to affect only one channel. When you're not using the Channels palette, a filter will always apply to all the color channels that are present in the document.

Figure 9.17
Viewing all the channels, but editing the Blue channel only.

Images taken from digital cameras often appear noisy. If you blur the entire image to get rid of the noise, it usually looks terrible because you discard most of the important detail. But if you click through the channels, you might notice that the noise is most prominent in one channel (usually the blue channel). By blurring just the blue channel, your image will look better without throwing away too much detail. To blur just the blue channel, click on its name in the Channels palette, then apply the Blur filter (see Figures 9.17 and 9.18). If you would like to see the image in full color, turn on the eyeball on the composite channel before applying the filter.

You can also improve the image by sharpening only those channels that do not contain a large amount of noise (usually the red and green channels), as shown in Figures 9.19 and 9.20.

Figure 9.18
Apply the **Filter>Blur>Gaussian Blur** filter to remove noise.

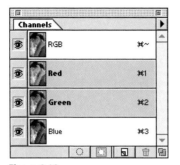

Figure 9.19
Viewing all the channels, but editing the Red and Green channles only.

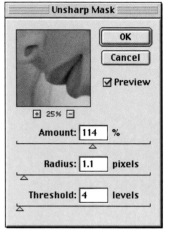

Figure 9.20
Applying the **Filter>Sharpen> Unsharp Mask** filter to bring out detail.

Black-Only Grayscale Images

The most common way to force a portion of an image to black and white is to select the area and choose **Image> Adjust>Desaturate**. On screen this will appear as if the image will be printed with only black ink. But if you open the Info palette and move your cursor over the black and white area, you'll notice that the image still contains all four colors of ink (see Figure 9.21).

To get the image to print with only black ink, you'll need to use the Channels palette. To begin, select the area you want to print with black ink, choose **Edit>Copy**, then click on the black channel and choose **Edit>Paste**. But because you chose Copy instead of Cut, there will still be information left in the other channels, so click on each of the color channels (*except* black) and press the Delete key to remove all information from those areas (see Figure 9.22).

There are many more uses for the color channels, and we'll get to some of them in later chapters.

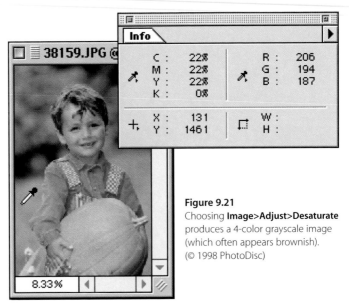

Figure 9.21
Choosing **Image>Adjust>Desaturate**
produces a 4-color grayscale image
(which often appears brownish).
(© 1998 PhotoDisc)

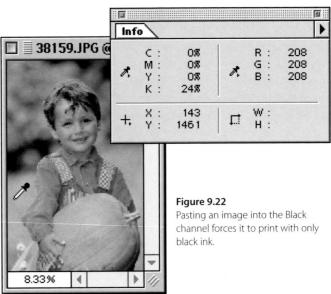

Figure 9.22
Pasting an image into the Black
channel forces it to print with only
black ink.

Understanding Spot Channels

Remember when you got your first box of crayons? I'll bet
you that it was the standard issue 8-color box from
Crayola. I remember mine vividly. I thought it was great—
that is, until the rich kid from across the street swaggered
over and showed me his box. It was the gigantic 64-color
model with the built-in sharpener. My box was limited to

black, brown, blue, red, purple, orange, yellow, and green, which seemed adequate until I discovered Periwinkle, Prussian Blue, and Raw Sienna in his huge set. Well, you can think of spot channels as a way to get all those colors that don't come in the standard (CMYK) box.

It all comes down to this. If you are planning on printing an image using inks other than cyan, magenta, yellow, and black (such as florescent orange), you'll need to use one or more spot channels. These channels will allow you to paint with PANTONE colors (the most popular brand of spot color ink). They also allow your image to look correct on screen and print correctly from both Photoshop and your page layout program. This is a new feature that is just making its debut in Photoshop 5. Before Photoshop 5 came along, it was very difficult to use spot colors in a way that you could really see what the end result would look like. Heck, in my seminars, I used to spend almost an hour demonstrating what now takes just a few seconds.

No Layers Support

Just because Photoshop has direct support for spot color doesn't mean it's easy to use. The information you add to a spot channel will not appear on any layer, not even the background layer (see Figure 9.23). It's as if they're sitting in an invisible "layer" slapped on top of everything else. Hopefully, when Adobe releases Photoshop 6, spot colors will be accessible within the normal layers.

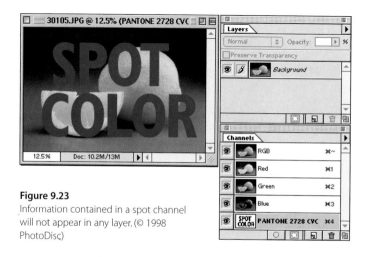

Figure 9.23
Information contained in a spot channel will not appear in any layer. (© 1998 PhotoDisc)

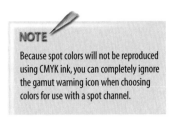

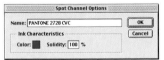

Figure 9.24
Spot Channel Options dialog box.

Creating Spot Channels

You'll need to create one spot channel for each PANTONE color you would like to use. To create one, choose New Spot Channel from the side menu of the Channels palette. A dialog box will appear asking for the specific color you would like to use and its Solidity setting (see Figure 9.24). To specify the color you would like to use, click on the color swatch at the left of the dialog box. This will bring up a standard Color Picker dialog box. To get to PANTONE colors, click on the Custom button.

Unlike process colors, which are transparent, many PANTONE inks are almost completely opaque. Certain PANTONE colors will completely obstruct the view of colors that appear underneath them (like the metallic inks), while others will allow you to see a hint of the colors that are underneath. The Solidity setting controls how translucent these inks will appear on screen in Photoshop (see Figures 9.25 and 9.26). Unfortunately, Photoshop does not automatically supply a setting for you, and there is no resource I can think of that will give you great settings. I contacted both Adobe and PANTONE and neither of them could supply recommended settings. So, this is a setting you have to guess at unless you have a lot of experience with the inks you are using.

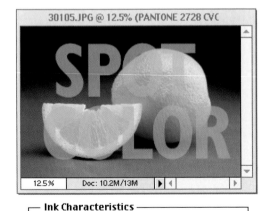

Figure 9.25
Solidity: 100%.

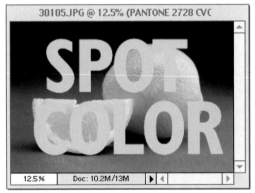
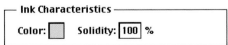

Figure 9.26
Solidity: 40%.

After you have created some spot channels, you can view those channels at the same time as the normal color channels by turning on the eyeball icon next to the composite channel as well as the ones next to each spot channel.

Painting with Spot Colors

To paint with a spot color, you must first click on the name of the color you would like to use from the Channels palette. Next, open the Color palette and choose the percentage of this ink you would like to use (from the grayscale slider), then paint away (see Figure 9.27). Photoshop acts as if you are working on a separate grayscale image when you paint in one of the spot channels. So if you attempt to paint with a color chosen from the Color Picker, Photoshop will convert it to a shade of gray when you are painting.

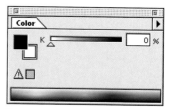

Figure 9.27
Color palette.

When you paint in a spot channel, Photoshop leaves the color channels unchanged. That means if you don't want the spot color you are painting with to print on top of the CMYK image (knock out as opposed to overprint), you'll have to manually switch to the color channels and delete the areas you painted across with the spot color. This can take a tremendous amount of time and isn't always the easiest thing to accomplish.

You can also paste images into the spot channels or apply any filter or adjustment that is available to grayscale images.

Proofing on CMYK printers

Most desktop printers use cyan, magenta, yellow, and black (process colors) to output an image. Since the spot channels don't change the information in the CMYK color channels, you'll need to do a few things to get your image to print correctly on a desktop color printer (see Figure 9.28). To start with, you don't want to mess up the document you've worked so hard creating, so choose **Edit>Duplicate** to work on a duplicate image. Next, click on one of the spot channels and choose Merge Spot Channel from the side menu of the Channels palette, shown in Figure 9.29. Repeat this process with all of the spot

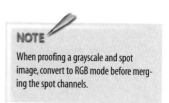

NOTE

When proofing a grayscale and spot image, convert to RGB mode before merging the spot channels.

channels in your document. This will make your image printable on a desktop color printer by simulating the look of the spot colors using cyan, magenta, yellow, and black ink. After the image has been printed, you can discard this file and go back to editing the original image.

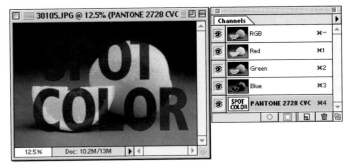

Figure 9.28
Information in the spot channels is difficult to print on desktop color printers.

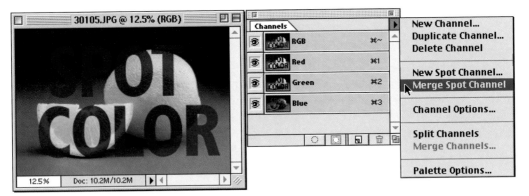

Figure 9.29
Merging the spot channels will simulate the look of spot colors using CMYK inks.

Saving the Image

There are only two file formats that support spot channels, Photoshop and DCS 2.0 (DCS is short for Desktop Color Separations). Since most page layout programs can't deal with images in the Photoshop file format, you'll have to use DCS 2.0. The DCS file format is really part of the EPS file format, which is supported by most (if not all) page layout programs. In order to be able to save your image in the DCS 2.0 format, the image must be in Grayscale or CMYK mode. When saving a DCS 2.0 file, you will be offered a bunch of options; and, unfortunately, most of them aren't all that straightforward. So let's take a peek at them (see Figure 9.30).

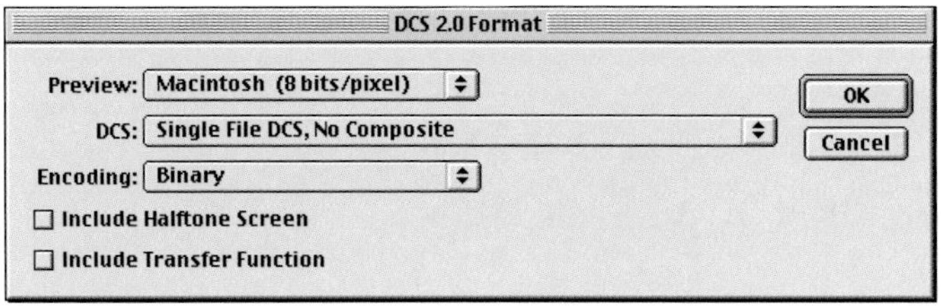

Figure 9.30
DSC 2.0 Save dialog box.

The preview menu determines what will be seen on-screen in your page layout program. Your choices are: TIFF (1 bit/pixel), TIFF (8 bits/pixel), Macintosh (1 bit/pixel), Macintosh (8 bits/pixel), and Macintosh (JPEG)—why can't they use English! Let's try to decipher these choices. Use the TIFF options when the image will be used on the Windows platform, and use the Macintosh options for a Mac (duh). 1 bit/pixel means pure black and pure white (that looks terrible), 8 bits/pixel means 256 colors (that looks okay), and JPEG means full color (that looks great). These choices only affect the on-screen image that appears in other programs, not the printed version. No matter which option you choose, the printed version of the image will look great. So, what do I use? I always use the JPEG choice because it looks great and doesn't make the files overly large (see Figure 9.31).

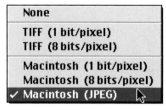

Figure 9.31
A JPEG preview usually produces the best on-screen preview image.

The DCS menu determines how many files you will end up with (see Figure 9.32). Unless you really know what you are doing and have a good reason to mess with this (some people can come up with one), leave it set to Single File with Color Composite. I haven't needed to use the other options for any of the files I've output.

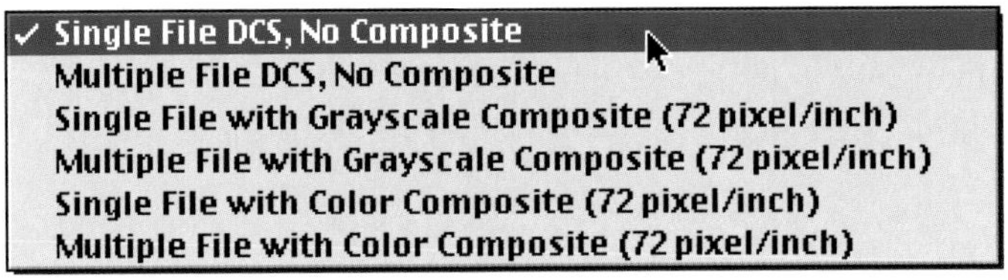

✓ Single File DCS, No Composite
Multiple File DCS, No Composite
Single File with Grayscale Composite (72 pixel/inch)
Multiple File with Grayscale Composite (72 pixel/inch)
Single File with Color Composite (72 pixel/inch)
Multiple File with Color Composite (72 pixel/inch)

Figure 9.32
Single file DSC documents are the easiest to keep track of.

ASCII
✓ Binary
JPEG (low quality)
JPEG (medium quality)
JPEG (high quality)
JPEG (maximum quality)

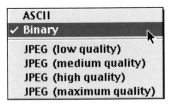

Figure 9.33
Use Binary for Macs and ASCII for Windows.

The Encoding menu determines how the information that will be printed (as opposed to the on-screen preview) will be stored. Macintosh users should use the Binary option, and Windows users should use ASCII (see Figure 9.33). Some really old Mac programs and printers cannot handle Binary files; so if you run into a problem, resave your image using ASCII encoding. The JPEG choices will degrade the quality of the printed image and deliver a dramatically smaller file. JPEG should be used only if the image will not need to be resaved and if quality is not your first concern. (JPEG degrades the image each time it is saved.)

Understanding Alpha Channels

Alpha channels is like a big storage bin for selections. Whenever you spend more than a few minutes creating a selection and there's the remotest chance that you might need it again, you should transform it into an alpha channel for safekeeping. That way it will be available for you to use again and again. And the great thing about alpha channels is that they're not limited to being just a storage device; the channels are also malleable like modeling clay so that you can sculpt and manipulate your selections in ways that are not possible with mere mortal selection tools. Mastering alpha channels is the mark of a true Photoshop virtuoso.

Loading and Saving Selections

If you make a selection, then choose **Select>Save Selection**. Photoshop stores the selection at the bottom of the Channels palette (see Figure 9.34). Go ahead and try it.

Make a selection, open the Channels palette (so you can see what's going on), then choose **Select>Save Selection**. An alpha channel is a saved *selection*—it's that simple (almost).

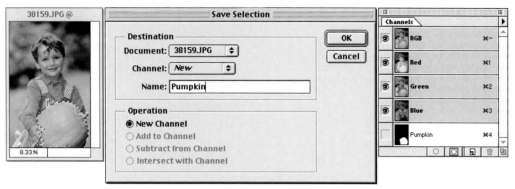

Figure 9.34
Choosing **Select>Save Selection** will produce a new Alpha Channel.

Now let's find out how to reload the selection you just saved. But first, choose **Select>Deselect** to get rid of the selection that is currently active. As long as you saved it, you should be able to get it back at any time by choosing **Select>Load Selection**, as shown in Figure 9.35.

Now let's try the same thing using the Channels palette. To save a selection, Option-click on the Save Selection icon at the bottom of the Channels palette (it's the second from the left). This does the same thing as choosing **Select>Save Selection** (see Figure 9.36). If you click on the Save Selection icon without holding down the Option key, Photoshop will assign the new channel a generic name such as "Alpha 1."

To get the selection back, drag the name of the channel onto the selection icon at the bottom of the palette (it's the far left icon). That does the exact same thing as choosing **Select>Load Selection** (see Figure 9.37). The advantage to using the Channels palette is that you get a visual preview of the shape of the selection.

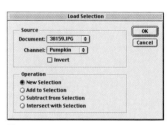

Figure 9.35
Choose **Select>Load Selection** to reload a saved selection.

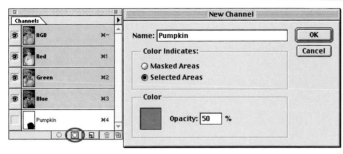

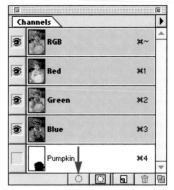

Figure 9.36
Option-clicking on the new save selection icon is the same as choosing **Select>Save Selection**.

Figure 9.37
Dragging the name of a channel onto the selection icon is the same as choosing **Select>Load Selection**.

NOTE

You can also Command-click on the name of a channel to load it as a selection.

Deleting Alpha Channels

There is no way to delete a saved selection (channel) when using the Select menu. Instead, you need to open the Channels palette and drag the name of a channel onto the right-most icon (the one that looks like a little trashcan).

Viewing Individual Channels

If you would like to see what a channel contains without loading it as a selection, you can simply click on the name of the channel in the Channels palette. This will display the channel in the main image window, as seen in Figure 9.38. White areas in the channel indicate areas that will be selected, and black areas indicate non-selected areas. After you're done looking at a channel, just click on the composite (topmost) channel to get back to editing all the color channels.

New Channel

So far, all we've been doing is saving and reloading selections that we've made with the normal selection tools. You can also create a selection by creating a brand new (empty) channel and editing the channel. Try this—click on the second icon from the right at the bottom of the Channels palette (the one that looks like a sheet of paper

Figure 9.38
Click on the name of a channel to view it in the main image window.

with a folded corner). This action will create a new, empty channel and display it in the image window. Now change your foreground color to white, choose the Paintbrush tool and a hard-edged brush, and sign your name in the channel. If you're using a mouse it might not look like your signature, but that's okay. Once you're finished, click on the topmost channel to get back to the main image, and drag the name of the channel you were messing with to the selection icon and Bingo!—the shape of your signature is selected. Photoshop can't tell the difference between a channel that was created by saving a selection and one that was created from scratch (see Figure 9.39).

Figure 9.39
Result of painting in a new channel, then loading the channel as a selection.

Feathered Selections

Now let's see what feathered selections look like when saved as a channel. Make a selection using the Lasso tool, then save it as a channel. Next, choose **Select>Feather** and use a setting of 10, then again save the selection as a channel. Now click on the name of the first channel and take a look at it, then click on the name of the second one to see the difference, as demonstrated in Figures 9.40 and 9.41. Feathered selections appear with blurry edges in the Channels palette. This happens because shades of gray in a channel indicate an area that is partially selected (50% gray means 50% selected).

But when you look at the marching ants that appear after the channel has been loaded as a selection, they only show you where the selection is at least 50% selected. That isn't a very accurate picture of what the selection really looks like (see Figure 9.42). But if you save the same selection as a channel, you can see exactly what is happening on its edge. So, if you want to create a feathered selection when editing a channel, just choose a soft-edged brush to paint with.

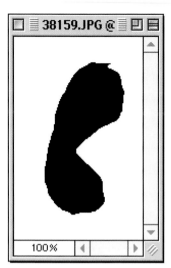

Figure 9.40
Normal.

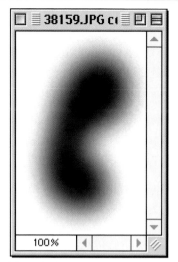

Figure 9.41
Feathered.

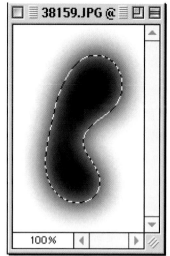

Figure 9.42
The marching ants show up where an
area is at least 50% selected.

Shades of Gray

Try this out. Create a new channel, then paint in it with
20% gray, then load that as a selection and paint in the
selected area with bright red. Now choose **Select>Deselect**,
lower the opacity of the painting tool to 80%, and paint
with bright red. They should look exactly the same. That's
how Photoshop makes a selection fade out, by simply lowering the opacity of the tool you are using. The only problem is that the marching ants show up only where an
image is at least 50% selected. So, try this one on for size.
Create a new channel and paint with 49% gray, then paint
in another area with 51% gray, then load the channel as a
selection and paint across the area. Only the areas that
are at least 50% show up, but the other areas are still
selected (see Figure 9.43). Try creating a channel and
then paint with 55% gray. Now load that one and you'll
even get a warning message, pictured in Figure 9.44.

We really haven't done anything fancy yet, so let's try
something fun. To start with, you have to remember that
when you are editing a channel, Photoshop treats the
channel as if it is a grayscale image. That means you can

use any tool that is available when working on grayscale images. So give this a try: Select an area using the Marquee tool, then save it in the Channels palette. View the channel, then choose **Filter>Distort>Ripple** and mess with the settings until you've created something that looks a little kooky (see Figure 9.45). Finally, click on the composite (topmost) channel, then load that channel as a selection. You can create infinite varieties of fascinating selections with this simple technique.

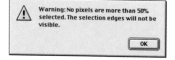

Figure 9.44
When you load a channel that does not contain any shades brighter than 50% gray, a warning will appear.

Figure 9.43
When painting in a channel, only the areas that contain less than 50% gray will be visible when the channel is loaded as a selection.

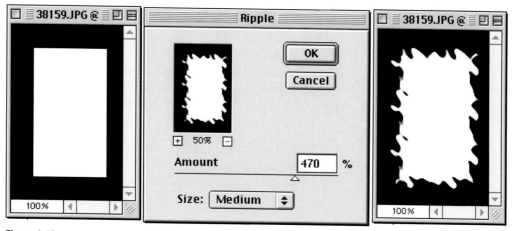

Figure 9.45
Applying the Ripple filter to a channel.

You can also "unfeather" a selection using the Channels palette (see Figure 9.46). Remember, a feathered edge looks like a blurry edge when saved as a channel. Well, all you have to do to remove that blurry look is to save the selection as a channel, then choose **Image>Adjust>Threshold**. This will give the channel a very crisp edge and therefore an unfeathered edge.

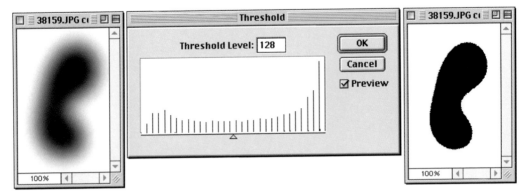

Figure 9.46
Unfeathering a selection using Threshold.

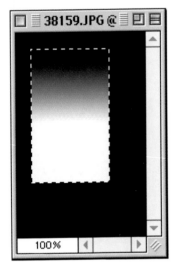

Figure 9.47
Using a selection within a channel to restrict which areas can be edited.

Selections within Channels

You can even use a selection to isolate a particular area of a channel, as shown in Figure 9.47. A selection within a channel can help you create a selection that is only feathered on one side. To accomplish this, first create a new empty channel. Next, choose the Marquee tool and select an area. Now use the Gradient tool set to Black to White and create a gradient within the selected area. Once you're done, switch back to the main image (by clicking on the topmost channel) and load the channel you just created. Now to see exactly how this selection will affect the image, choose **Image>Adjust>Levels** and attempt to lighten that area by dragging the lower left slider.

View with the Image

We've covered some ideal uses for alpha channels, but their usefulness is very limited if you can't see how the channels line up with the main image. At any time, you can overlay a channel onto the main image by simply turning on the eyeball icon next to the composite channel while you are editing an alpha channel (see Figure 9.48). This enables you to see exactly which areas of the image will be selected. When you do this, the dark areas of the alpha channel will be overlaid onto the main image. Photoshop substitutes a color for the shades of gray in a channel to make them easier to see. You can change the color that is used by double-clicking on the name of the alpha channel (see Figure 9.49).

WARNING

Keep an eye on the Channel Options dialog. Since the dark areas of a channel are the only parts that show up when overlaying it onto the main image, this setting also changes what black means in an alpha channel. When viewing a single channel, just substitute the words "black indicates" where it says "color indicates," and it should make a lot more sense.

Figure 9.48
Viewing a channel at the same time as the main image. (© 1998 PhotoSpin)

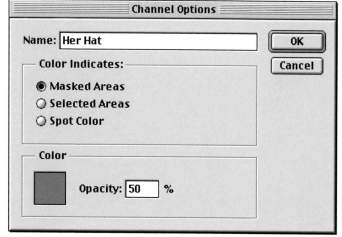

Figure 9.49
Channel Options settings used.

Photoshop also allows you to switch *where* the color shows up. You can specify whether you want the selected or unselected areas to show up. To change this setting, double-click on the name of the alpha channel and change the Color Indicates setting (see Figures 9.50 and 9.51). Photoshop uses the term Masked Areas to describe areas that are not selected.

The Opacity setting determines how much you will be able to see through the overlaid channel.

Figure 9.50
Changing the Color Indicates setting changes where the color overlay appears.

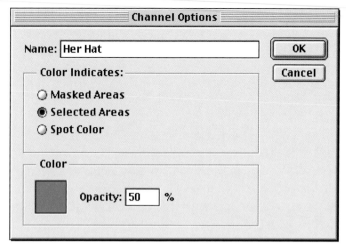

Figure 9.51
Channel Options settings used.

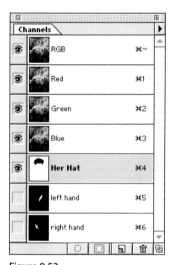

Figure 9.52
When viewing multiple channels, the channel or channels that are highlighted are the only ones being edited.

When you are viewing an alpha channel at the same time as the main image, you'll need to keep track of exactly what you are editing. The channel or channels that are highlighted in color are always the ones that you are currently editing, as shown in Figure 9.52. Other channels might be visible; but if they aren't highlighted, you won't be able to change them.

Quick Mask Mode

If alpha channels are like a storage bin and some modeling clay, then Quick Mask is just the clay without the storage ability. With Quick Mask you can quickly sculpt and manipulate a selection without storing it. It's like a temporary channel you can play around with. This can come in handy when you want to create or view a feathered selection (see Figures 9.53 and 9.54).

Let's say that you have a selection you made with the Marquee tool and want to quickly change the edge to one of those wacky ones used by running a filter on a channel. Well, just turn on Quick Mask mode and

Photoshop will create a temporary channel and even view it with the main image. Now you can run your filter and quickly turn off Quick Mask mode and you have the selection you envisioned.

Turning on Quick Mask mode does the exact same thing as saving a selection in the Channels palette and viewing it with the main image. Turning Quick Mask off is the same as loading that channel as a selection and throwing it away.

We'll end up using Quick Mask mode any time we need a quick change that would not be possible with the normal selection tools. In the meantime, here are a few examples of how you might use Quick Mask:

Unfeathering a selection

Viewing a feathered selection

Applying a filter to a selection

Creating a selection using the Gradient tool

Figure 9.53
You can't tell if this selection has a feathered edge. (© 1998 PhotoSpin)

Figure 9.54
In Quick Mask mode you can easily tell if a selection has a feathered edge.

Selecting Complex Objects

Because the three types of channels (color, spot, and alpha) are stored within the same palette, you can cheat by stealing information from one type of channel and using it in another. Let's try this by using one of the color channels to create a very useful alpha channel.

Look for Contrast

The first step in selecting a complex object is to flip through the color channels to find the one that has the most contrast between what you would like to select and its background (see Figures 9.55 to 9.57). If you don't find a great candidate, you can also choose **Edit>Duplicate** to make a second version of your file, then convert that image to the other modes (RGB, CMYK, LAB, etc.) and look for contrast in those channels.

Figure 9.55
Red channel: low contrast. (© 1998 PhotoSpin)

Figure 9.56
Green channel: medium contrast.

Figure 9.57
Blue channel: high contrast.

Once you've found some good contrast, you'll want to duplicate that channel by dragging its name onto the new channel icon. When you duplicate a color channel, the duplicate is one of the alpha channels (it just happens to have a picture pasted into it). If you found your good contrast channel in a duplicate of the document, you can copy it between documents by dragging its name in the Channels palette on top of another document.

Adjust the Channel

In order to transform this raw channel into a useful alpha channel, we'll need to get rid of most of the shades of gray it contains. But before we get to that, you'll need to be sure the area you want selected is the bright part of the channel. If it appears dark, then choose **Image>Adjust>Invert** before adjusting the image. To adjust the image, choose **Image>Adjust>Levels** (see Figures 9.58 and 9.59).

Moving the upper right and upper left sliders will force areas of the channel to pure black and pure white. You'll want to get the area you want selected to become pure white and the area that should be not selected to pure black. After you have done this, you can load the channel as a selection—and Wow!—you'll have the object selected!

Figure 9.58
Result.

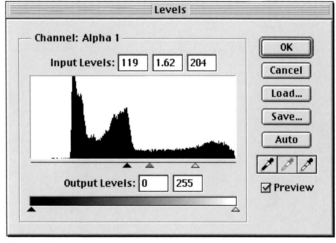

Figure 9.59
Levels adjustment being applied.

Complex Backgrounds

If the image you are working on contains a multi-colored, complex background, you'll need to modify this technique. After you have found the channel that contains good contrast and duplicated it, you'll need to do the following: Double-click on that channel and set its color to a bright color with a 100% opacity setting, then view it at the same time as the main image. Now when you adjust the image using Levels, you'll see an exact preview of what will happen when you delete the background (see Figures 9.60 and 9.61).

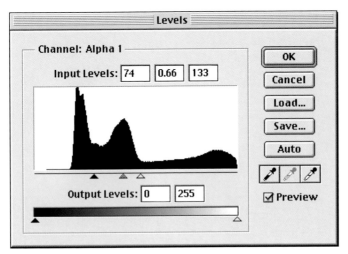

Figure 9.60
Levels adjustment being applied.

Figure 9.61
Viewing the channel at the same time as the main image.

If there are areas that don't quite work out (you can't quite get the edge to look right), then you might need to select a specific area, copy information from a different color channel and paste it into the alpha channel you've been using. Just remember, the channel that is highlighted is the one you are editing; so click on the channel that has good contrast in a particular area, choose Copy, then switch back to the alpha channel and choose Paste. You can also select areas before applying levels to use different settings for different parts of the image, as depicted in Figures 9.62 to 9.64.

After you have created a good alpha channel, you might need to clean it up by selecting areas and filling them with white or black to fine tune the result (see Figure 9.65).

You can also view the main image and select areas that are missing from the alpha channel (see Figure 9.66), then switch to the alpha channel and fill those areas with white or black (see Figure 9.67).

After you have perfected the alpha channel, drag its name to the selection icon at the bottom of the Channels palette and click on the topmost channel to view the main image. Now you can press Delete to remove the background of the image, as shown in Figure 9.68.

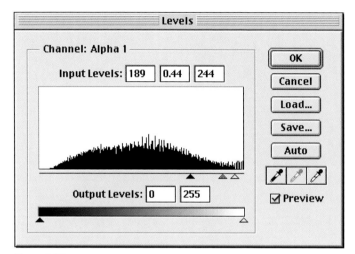

Figure 9.62
Result.

Figure 9.63
Levels being applied to top portion of the channel.

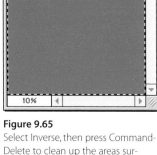

Figure 9.64
Select the area around the subject of the photo.

Figure 9.65
Select Inverse, then press Command-Delete to clean up the areas surrounding the image.

Figure 9.66
View the main image and select any areas that are missing from the channel.

Figure 9.67
Click on the channel, then press Option-Delete to fill the area with white.

Figure 9.68
Result of loading channel as a selection and pressing Delete.

Saving Channels with your Image

If you want to save your spot or alpha channels with your file, you'll have to use a file format that understands them. First of all, the Photoshop file format completely supports all kinds of channels, which makes it a great working file format. But unfortunately, most other programs can't understand images saved in the Photoshop format. The TIFF format also supports alpha channels, but does not know the difference between spot and alpha channels, so it is not usually used for spot channels. The DCS 2.0 format supports spot channels and is compatible with the majority of publishing programs, so it is usually used for spot color work. Most of the other formats do not support alpha or spot channels, so they appear grayed out when attempting to save an image that contains those types of channels. If you need to save your image using a format that does not support spot or alpha channels, choose **File>Save A Copy** when saving the file. This dialog box will automatically discard channels if the format you choose does not support them.

Closing Thoughts

I truly hope that after going through this chapter you've come to terms with channels. They don't really deserve the mind-boggling reputation that seems to follow them. I like to think of them as three friendly little dogs: Spot, Color, and Alpha. They will be loyal to you throughout your lifetime as a Photoshopper and will take care of all sorts of special needs, especially when you're working with color or with complex selections (or, for that matter, *any* selection that you'd like to save for later). So, if for any reason, you're still one of those people who want to throw their hands up in the air when the subject of channels comes up, think twice. It's worth the pain, and believe me when I tell you that the pain will turn into pure pleasure once you've realized what a gem the Channels palette is.

Ask Adobe

Q: When I want to save a selection, should I use a channel or a path, and why?

A: Use a channel because it can precisely capture the contents of the selection mask. A path can capture an approximation only. If the selection is such that it could be well approximated using a path, then it will probably also produce a channel that compresses well when saved in Photoshop format.

Q: Why are saved selections called "alpha" channels? Where did the "alpha" in alpha channels come from?

A: Alpha channel is the traditional term used in the computer graphics industry for extra channels. Sometimes they are assigned the specific interpretation of meaning transparency information, but they also frequently just mean "non-color" channels.

Q: When creating a spot channel, what does the Solidity setting mean, and what number should I use?

A: Solidity is used to tune how the screen preview looks for the ink. Referring to paints instead of inks, we can consider a range from watercolor to acrylics. Watercolor paints are generally relatively translucent. You can put down watercolors with full coverage and still see through them. The colors underneath are just filtered by the newly applied color. In Photoshop, this corresponds to low solidity.

Acrylics, on the other hand, tend to completely obliterate the colors below them. This corresponds to a high solidity value in Photoshop. The process inks (cyan, magenta, and yellow) generally have low solidity. The best way to determine what value to use is to run a press check and tune the values to match the results of your proof.

Ben's Techno-Babble Decoder Ring

Mask—Any time you view a selection as a grayscale image (as opposed to a "marching ants" selection), it is also called a mask. That means it's okay to call a channel a mask if you'd like. And when you see features like Quick Mask and Layer Masks mentioned in Photoshop, those are things that will also be stored in the Channels palette.

Bits—In Photoshop, 256 shades of gray is known as 8-bits. This describes how much memory Photoshop uses to keep track of all those shades. So if you find a setting in your scanning software that is called "8-bit grayscale," it just means a normal 256 shade grayscale scan. Or, if you hear someone say, "I have a 24-bit color image," that means they have an image that is in RGB mode (three channels) and each channel is 8-bits (8+8+8=24). Or, if you hear about a 32-bit image, that just means the image contains four channels; they are either talking about an image that is in CMYK mode (4 channels) or an RGB image (three channels) plus one alpha channel (for a total of four channels).

Color Channel—When you edit an image in Photoshop, you are really editing the color channels. These channels break your image into one or more color components. The mode of the document will determine how many color channels will be present: RGB mode will have three channels (red, green, and blue), CMYK mode will have four channels (cyan, magenta, yellow, and black), and grayscale will contain only one channel (called black).

Spot Channel—Spot channels are a special variety of color channel that allow you to construct your image out of inks other than, or in addition to, cyan, magenta, yellow, and black. Spot channels are usually used when printing with PANTONE inks.

Alpha Channel—Alpha channels are basically saved selections. They do not affect how your image will be printed. Alpha channels can also be used to determine which areas of an image should appear transparent when saving a GIF file.

Composite Channel—The composite channel does not contain any information; in fact, it is simply a shortcut to view and edit all the color channels at the same time. This is often used to return the Channels palette back to its "normal" state after isolating a single channel for editing.

PANTONE—A brand of ink commonly used when printing with fewer than four inks, or when colors are needed that cannot be reproduced using CMYK inks (metallic colors, florescent colors, deep blues, and bright greens cannot be accurately simulated using CMYK inks). PANTONE inks are commonly referred to as Spot Color inks.

Gamut—A term used to describe the entire range of colors that are reproducible using a certain set of inks, dyes, or light. The gamut warning in Photoshop warns you that the currently chosen color is not reproducible using CMYK inks.

EPS—Encapsulated Postscript(EPS) is a file format used to transfer Postscript language page descriptions between programs and output devices. EPS files should be used only with Postscript-aware printers; otherwise, the resulting image will appear with a low resolution "jaggy" appearance when printed.

DCS—Desktop Color Separation(DCS) is a special version of the EPS file format that comes in two versions, DCS 1.0 and DCS 2.0. You can think of DCS 1.0 as the old version of this file format because prior to Photoshop 5 it was the only version available in Photoshop; and it used to be integrated into the normal EPS save dialog box. DCS 1.0 files allow you to save a CMYK image and get five files total, one for each channel in the image, and one preview image. DCS 2.0 is new to Photoshop 5 and is special because it is the only file format (other than Photoshop's own format) that allows you to save spot channels in addition to the CMYK channels.

Keyboard Shortcuts

View composite	Command-~
View channel	Command-channel #
Load channel as a selection	Command-Option-channel#

Part III **Creative Explorations**

Courtesy of Rick Valicenti, Thirst Advertising, and Gary Fisher Bicycle Corporation. Photography by William Valicenti.

10 Shadows

Courtesy of Derek Brigham, www.visi.com/~dbrigham/noctago.home.html.

Imagine a three-layer chocolate cake without the frosting. Everyone would say, "That cake has no frosting!" Imagine the cake with frosting. Nobody would say anything, but they'd eat the cake.
—Liz Allen

Go figure. You spend hours creating a great shadow. You sweat over the minutiae. You listen to an entire CD while you perfect the tiniest details. And when you're done, nobody notices it... Good! You've got the right shadow.

Shadows can make or break an image. It's true. Even though we don't notice them, shadows help create a sense of solidness, of physical existence. Just try this, close your eyes and then think about all the shadows that were present within your field of vision. You probably can't remember a single one. Remove the shadows and you remove the realism of the image. Shadowless images seam to float in thin air. And, if anyone happens to notice a shadow in your image, it's almost surely too dark.

Four Shadow Types

There are many techniques for creating great shadows; the complexity of the image will determine which technique you use.

Natural Shadows—Transforms an existing shadow into one that can be overlaid onto another image. Also removes any grays from beyond the edge of the shadow.

Reconstructed Shadows—Replaces the original shadow with a new shadow so you can remove a complex background and still retain the basic shape of the original shadow.

Cast Shadows—A perspective shadow is designed to exaggerate the height of an object. A cast shadow is based on the shape of the object that is casting it.

Drop Shadows—A simple offset shadow that is the same shape as the object that is casting it.

Ideally, you would simply remove the background of an image and leave its shadow. This is possible if you happen to have a solid-colored background. But if the background is complicated, you'll have to resort to reconstructing a shadow that resembles the original. The farther you get from the original shadow, the less realistic the image will appear.

How to Think About Shadows

Lay your hand on top of the desk you are sitting at (assuming you're not lounging on the sofa). Notice how dark the shadow below your hand appears. Now, slowly lift your hand above the surface and see what happens to the shadow. It should become lighter, and the edge should become softer. You might also notice that the shadow became larger—it's not always easy to see that happening, but it does. If there is more than one light source above your hand, you will most likely see multiple shadows. If you were to draw a line from one of the light sources to the middle of your hand, then continue the line through your hand until it hit the desk, the line should be smack dab in the middle of the shadow.

Finding the light source in the real world is much easier, however, than finding the light source in an image. If you can't see the light source (there's no lamp or ball of fiery sun in the photo), you can instead look at the part of the image that is darker than the rest. This will indicate from which direction the light was coming.

NOTE

If you combine two images that have radically different light sources, it will be difficult to recreate realistic shadows. The dissimilar lighting of the subjects will not relate in a natural way to the new shadows that you are creating, and your mind will know something is not right about the image.

Natural Shadows

Let's start with my favorite technique. We'll simply (well, not quite simply) slip the background out from beneath the original shadow, leaving just the shadow intact. Then we'll make this original shadow transparent so we can overlay it on any other image within Photoshop. This technique works when your image has a solid-colored background; in fact, a white or gray background will give you the best results (see Figure 10.1).

Figure 10.1
Here the shadow under the crab image was made transparent so it could be overlaid onto the dollar bill. (© 1998 PhotoDisc)

Figure 10.2
Isolate the subject onto its own layer.

NOTE

It is important to choose Layer Via Copy instead of Layer Via Cut in order to avoid getting a bright halo around your image. Halos are caused by replacing the underlying image with white, which happens when you cut the subject from its original layer. If you're curious, go ahead and try using **Layer>New>Layer Via Cut** and then look closely at the edge of the subject.

Isolate the Subject

The first thing you need to do is to get the subject of the photo (a crab, in my case) onto its own layer (see Figure 10.2). That way you can isolate the shadow from its background without affecting the subject of the image. Do this by selecting the subject with any selection tool, then choosing **Layer>New>Layer Via Copy**. This will leave you with two layers: one that contains the crab and the other that contains the crab and its shadow. To avoid confusion, whenever I mention the subject of the photo, think of the top layer (the one that contains only the crab); and whenever I talk about the shadow layer, think of the layer that is under the subject (which contains both the crab and its shadow).

Now click on the shadow layer (the "Background" image, in my case). This will allow you to modify the background of the image without messing up the subject of the image.

Find Edge of Shadow

Next, you'll want to find out exactly where the edge of the shadow is and exactly what shade of gray is on the edge. That way, you'll be able to force the rest of the background to white and leave just the shadow remaining. To do this, choose **Image>Adjust>Threshold** and move the slider around until the shadow (which will appear as solid black) is as large as possible without bumping into the edge of the document (that will indicate where the shadow ends and the background begins), as shown in Figures 10.3 to 10.6. You can use the Up Arrow and Down Arrow keys on the keyboard to move the slider small amounts. The shadow will appear black because the Threshold dialog box is designed to convert an image into pure black and pure white. But we are using this tool as a measurement device to indicate exactly where the edge of the shadow appears—it's much too difficult to find it with the naked eye.

When the shadow appears as large as possible without bumping into the edge of the document, write down the number that is shown at the top of the Threshold dialog box, then click the Cancel button. This number represents the shade of gray that is at the edge of the shadow. The Threshold dialog box is using the same numbering system that's used in the Levels dialog box, which we'll use in the next step.

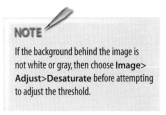

NOTE

If the background behind the image is not white or gray, then choose **Image> Adjust>Desaturate** before attempting to adjust the threshold.

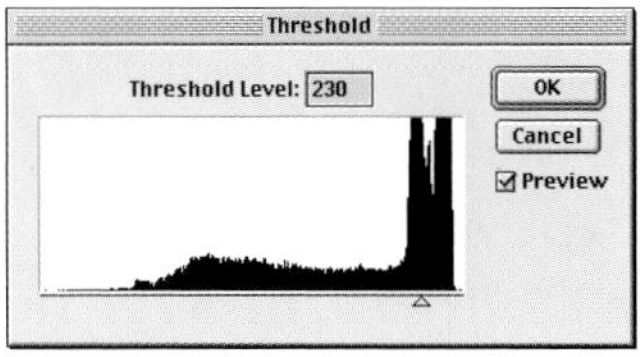

Figure 10.4
Threshold is too high.

Figure 10.3
Shadow is bumping into edge of the document.

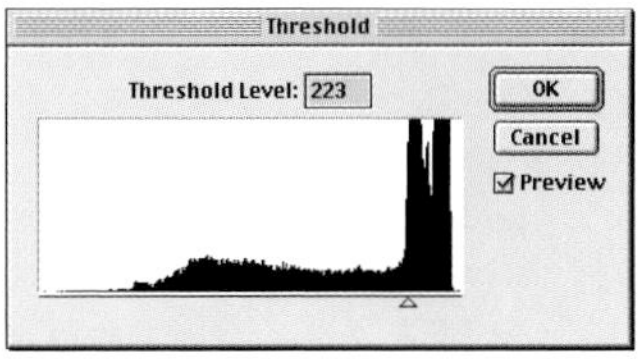

Figure 10.6
Threshold is just right.

Figure 10.5
Shadow is as large as possible without bumping into edge of the document.

NOTE

To make sure there aren't any tiny specks of gray beyond the edge of the shadow, I usually subtract one from the number that was shown in the Threshold dialog box.

Force Edge of Shadow to White

Now to discard the background (force it to white), but keep the shadow, we'll need to force the edge of the shadow to white. So start by choosing **Image>Adjust>Levels** (see Figure 10.7). The upper right slider forces shades to white. The number in the upper right of the dialog box indicates which shades are becoming white. So, all you have to do is replace that number with the number you wrote down from the Threshold dialog box, and bingo! —the shadow fades out to white (see Figure 10.8).

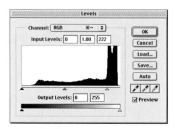

Figure 10.7
Enter the number that was used in the Threshold dialog box into the upper right text field of the Levels dialog box, the one called Input Levels.

Figure 10.8
Discarding the background.

Refine the Result

While you're still in the Levels dialog box, you can control many aspects of the shadow's appearance. If you move the lower left slider, you will lighten the shadow (compare Figures 10.9 and 10.10). Remember to make your shadows a little lighter than you think they should be; otherwise, people might notice them, and that would ruin the realism of the image. Also, if the image will be printed on a printing press, the image will appear darker than it does on screen. And, remember, we don't want anyone to notice the shadow; otherwise, it won't look natural.

You can also control how the shadow fades out by moving the middle slider. If the shadow is not dark enough, you can move the upper left slider over until it touches the beginning of the histogram.

Figure 10.9
Original shadow brightness.

Figure 10.10
Lightened by using Levels.

Clean Up Unwanted Grays

After making the shadow fade out to white, there might still be some unwanted shades of gray near the edge of the document. To find these shades, add a new Threshold adjustment layer above the shadow layer by choosing **Layer>New>Adjustment Layer** and selecting Threshold from the Type pop-up menu. Move the slider in the Threshold dialog box all the way to the right, then click OK (Figure 10.11). Now you should be able to see any extra grays that are present in the image (not all images will have the extra grays). To remove them, click on the shadow layer in the Layers palette and use the Eraser tool to brush over the areas that still have grays. After you've gotten rid of all the extra grays, drag the Threshold adjustment layer to the trash icon at the bottom of the Layers palette.

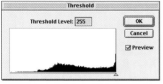

Figure 10.11
Finding unwanted shades of gray.

Control the Shadow's Color

After applying Levels, you might notice some color in the shadow. Most of the time, the color will make the shadow appear more realistic. But sometimes the color is too intense. To adjust how intense the color appears, choose **Image>Adjust>Hue/Saturation** and move the Saturation slider (see Figure 10.12). If you move the slider all the way to the left, there will be no hint of color in the shadow. If you would like to add color to the shadow, turn on the Colorize checkbox in the Hue/Saturation dialog box, then move the Hue slider to pick the basic color, and adjust the saturation slider to change how intense it appears. This can be useful when you have a shiny object that should reflect some of its color into the shadow area.

Figure 10.12
Lower the Saturation setting to reduce the amount of color that appears in the shadow.

Make Shadow Transparent

Using the crab and the two-dollar bill images as an example, we'll make the crab's shadow transparent and then overlay it onto the two-dollar bill. When you place the final image (in my case, the crab) on top of another image, you might want its shadow to appear transparent so that the two images are properly integrated and look like they belong together. To accomplish this, open the image upon which you want to cast the shadow—I'll use the two-dollar bill. Now, switch back to the image that contains the shadow (my crab) and link the layer that contains the subject to the layer than contains its shadow by clicking to the left of each layer in the Layers palette. A link symbol should appear, as shown in Figure 10.13. Now use the Move tool to drag the crab onto the second document. This should copy both layers into that document, as Figure 10.14 depicts.

To make the shadow transparent, be sure you are working on the shadow layer, then use the Layers palette, set its blending mode menu to Multiply, and bingo!—transparent shadow (see Figure 10.15).

NOTE

If you can't tell if the shadow has color in it, just choose **Image>Adjust>Desaturate**. This will remove all the color from the shadow. Then you can choose **Edit>Undo** to see exactly how much color was in the shadow. Or if you want a shadow that has no hint of color, choose **Image>Adjust>Desaturate**, but don't choose **Edit>Undo**.

Figure 10.13
Link the layers by clicking to the left of the layer preview icon.

NOTE
You must drag from the image window to copy linked layers from one document to another. If you drag from the Layers palette, only one layer will be copied.

NOTE
If the edge of the shadow is not soft enough, choose **Filter>Blur>Gaussian Blur** and use a very low setting, such as 1 or 2.

WARNING
It is best to use Multiply mode when your image is in RGB mode. If you use it while in CMYK mode, you can easily create a problem with too much ink on the printing press. This happens when the shadow combines with the underlying image and, in effect, darkens it, producing excessive ink coverage. If you use it *before* converting to CMYK, be sure to choose Flatten Image when converting the image to CMYK mode, or use the black only shadow technique described at the end of this chapter. For more information about potential CMYK problems, see Chapter 8, "Color Correction."

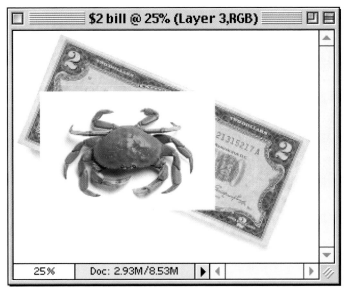

Figure 10.14
Using the Move tool, drag the image on top of another document.

Figure 10.15
Use the Multiply blending mode to make the shadow become transparent.

Reconstructing a Shadow

If the background of an image is complex, then the natural shadow technique described above will not work. It works only with simple, almost solid-colored backgrounds. The natural shadow technique will also get messed up if there is a wrinkle or crease in the background that runs directly under the shadow. If that's the case, I'd completely remove the background on the image and then attempt to recreate new shadows that resemble the originals. (See Figures 10.16 to 10.18.)

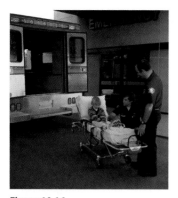

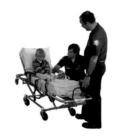

Figure 10.16
Original image.(© 1998 PhotoSpin)

Figure 10.17
Background removed.

Figure 10.18
Shadows added.

Isolate the Subject

As with natural shadows, the first thing you need to do is to get the subject of the photo onto its own layer. That way you can create and edit shadows without changing the subject. Do this by selecting the subject with any selection tool, then choose **Layer>New>Layer Via Copy** (see Figure 10.19).

Trace Shadow Edges

Before removing the background, it will be helpful if you trace the shape of the original shadows. That way any new shadows you create can have the same shape and position. Use the Pen tool to trace around the edges of each shadow that appears in the image (see Figures 10.20 and 10.21). Most images contain more than one shadow, maybe a hard-edged shadow on one object and a softer-edged shadow on another. You want to create a new path for each shadow that is in the image. After you've done that, make a mental note about how soft the edges are and how dark the shadow is. Now you can finally delete the layer that contains the shadows.

Reconstruct Shadows

To recreate the shadows, first create a new layer below the subject of the image. Now set your foreground color to black and drag the first path in the Paths palette to the first icon in the Paths palette. This should fill the shape of the path with your foreground color, which is black (see

Figure 10.19
Isolate the subject onto its own layer.

NOTE

For information about paths, check out my Web site at http:www.digitalmastery.com.

Figure 10.22). The black shape should appear on the layer you just created. This black shape represents one of the shadows. To lighten the shadow, just lower the opacity setting in the Layers palette (see Figure 10.23). To make it look more realistic, you will need to choose **Filter>Blur>Gaussian Blur** and move the slider until the edge is as soft as the original, as shown in Figure 10.24. Repeat this process for each shadow in the image.

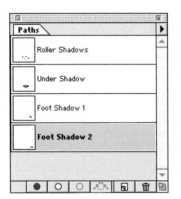

Figure 10.20
Each shadow has its own path.

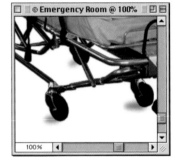

Figure 10.21
Use the Pen tool to trace the shadows.

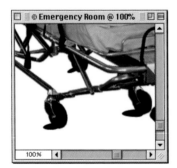

Figure 10.22
Filled with black.

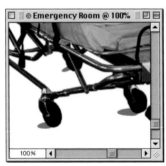

Figure 10.23
Opacity lowered.

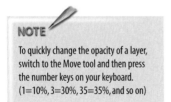

Figure 10.24
Gaussian Blur applied.

NOTE

To quickly change the opacity of a layer, switch to the Move tool and then press the number keys on your keyboard. (1=10%, 3=30%, 35=35%, and so on)

If you need the shadow to fade out in a particular direction, drag the name of a path to the selection icon at the bottom of the Paths palette. Choose **Select>Feather** to soften the edge, and then use the Linear Gradient tool set to Black to White and drag across the selected area (see Figures 10.25 and 10.26).

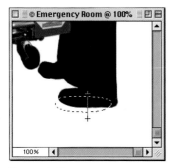

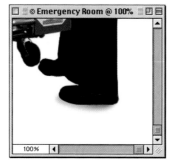

Figure 10.25
Selection.

Figure 10.26
After gradient is applied.

Cast Shadows

You can create a shadow that falls at an angle away from the subject, also known as a cast shadow, to exaggerate the height of an object. The longer the shadow, the taller the object will appear. This will also make it appear that the light source that's hitting the subject is coming from the upper right (see Figures 10.27 and 10.28).

Figure 10.27
Original image. (© 1998 PhotoDisc)

Figure 10.28
Cast shadow added.

Isolate the Subject

To create a cast shadow, you'll first need to get the subject of the photo onto its own layer (see Figure 10.29). That way you can create a shadow without damaging the subject. Do this by selecting the subject with any selection tool, then choosing **Layer>New>Layer Via Copy**.

Figure 10.29
Isolate the subject onto its own layer.

Fill a Duplicate

Cast shadows are usually based on a blatant copy of the shape of the subject. To create a shadow that is the same shape as the subject, duplicate the subject's layer by dragging it onto the duplicate layer icon at the bottom of the Layers palette. Now, fill the shape by choosing **Edit>Fill**, change the Use menu to Black, and turn on Preserve Transparency (see Figures 10.30 and 10.31). Preserve Transparency will make sure the transparent parts of the layer are not modified.

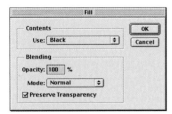

Figure 10.30
The Fill dialog box.

Figure 10.31
Duplicate the layer and fill with black.

NOTE

To create a more natural, less refined edge, choose **Filter>Sylize>Diffuse** and use the default settings. The Diffuse filter will add noise to the edge of the shadow, making it appear less man made.

Distort the Shadow Layer

The shadow should appear beneath the subject, so drag the name of the shadow layer until it is below the subject layer in the Layers palette. To make the shadow fall at an angle, choose **Edit>Transform>Distort** and then move the upper two squares that surround the image around until you have the desired angle, as in Figure 10.32.

Figure 10.32
Distorting the shadow by using **Edit>Transform>Distort**.

Fade the Shadow

You'll need an unusual selection in order to make the shadow fade out as it gets farther away from the subject of the image. So, turn on Quick Mask mode by typing Q, then use the Linear Gradient tool (make sure that the pop-up menu in the Gradient Options Palette is set to black, white), and click on the topmost part of the shadow. Then drag straight down (hold down the Shift key to make sure it's straight) until you hit the bottom of the shadow. Now turn off Quick Mask mode by typing Q. If the selection you get is on the bottom of the document instead of the top (which is what we want), then choose **Select>Inverse**. Finally, press the Delete key to make the shadow fade out (see Figure 10.33).

Figure 10.33
Create a selection by using the Gradient tool while in Quick Mask mode.

Blur the Shadow

Now the shadow is fading out, but it still has a crisp edge. In the real world, shadows become more blurry as they get farther away from the subject of the photograph (or in my case, the feet of 'Zilla). To get a nice, natural-looking fade-out, switch to the Marquee tool, then click and drag the selection until the bottom of the marching ants touches the topmost part of the shadow.

Next, choose **Filter>Blur>Gaussian Blur** and use a setting just high enough to slightly blur the shadow (see Figure 10.34). Now move the selection down by typing Shift-Down Arrow a few times and then blur the shadow again, using the same setting. Repeat this process until the selection is all the way at the bottom of the shadow (see Figure 10.35).

Achieve Proper Brightness

To brighten the shadow, adjust the Opacity setting of the shadow layer in the Layers palette (see Figures 10.36 and 10.37). Make the shadow a little lighter than you think it should be; otherwise, people might notice it.

Figure 10.34
Gaussian Blur filter.

Figure 10.35
Move the selection down before each blur.

Figure 10.36
Shadow is too dark.

Figure 10.37
Shadow after lowering Opacity setting to 30%.

Figure 10.38
Original image.

Figure 10.39
After a drop shadow has been
applied.

Figure 10.40
Isolate the subject onto its own layer.

Simple Shadows

If you have a simple subject like a button, coin, or other relatively flat object, you can use Photoshop layer effects to quickly add a drop shadow, as shown in Figures 10.38 and 10.39.

First you must get the subject of the photo onto its own layer. That way you can create and edit shadows without changing the subject. Do this by selecting the subject with any selection tool, then choosing **Layer>New>Layer Via Copy** (see Figure 10.40). Now choose **Layer>Effects>Drop Shadow** and adjust the controls until the shadow looks appropriate (see Figure 10.41).

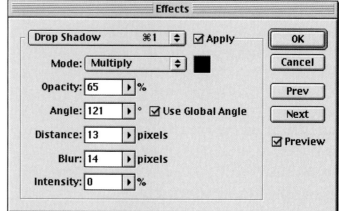

Figure 10.41
Apply a layer effect to add a drop shadow.

RGB versus CMYK

I usually create all my shadows while I'm in RGB mode even if the end result will need to be in CMYK mode. Here are a few reasons I prefer to work in RGB mode:

The natural shadow technique described earlier in this chapter will produce shadows that appear slightly brown if it is performed while in CMYK mode.

Using the Multiply blending mode can cause problems with too much ink in an area if used in CMYK mode.

NOTE
You can adjust the drop shadow settings by clicking on the main image window and dragging the shadow while the Drop Shadow dialog box is still open.

Your file size is smaller with RGB.

All the filters work when in RGB mode.

When you convert an image that contains layers to CMYK mode, a dialog box always appears asking if you would like to flatten the image. I usually choose to flatten it when converting; otherwise, I might run into problems with too much ink coverage (because I used the Multiply blending mode). The only time I don't flatten the image is when I'll be creating black only shadows. There are no problems when using the Multiply blending mode on black only shadows.

Closing Thoughts

If you feel funny taking so much time to perfect some-thing that will never be noticed, don't fret. Shadows are just as important as the light, but the very best shadows are the ones that go undetected. As with everything else in Photoshop, after you've test driven them a few times, the techniques you learned in this chapter should take only a few minutes to perform. And isn't it worth a few minutes to get those subtle, flawless, ethereal shadows that no one will ever notice?

NOTE

On the accompanying CD, you'll find a PDF file that supplements this chapter. The file, called extras.pdf, contains information about creating black-only shadows.

Ask Adobe

Q: Why is the adjustable blur filter called "Gaussian Blur" and what the heck does Gaussian mean?

A: It's named for Carl Friedrich Gauss, a nineteenth-century German mathematician whose name is attached to the Gaussian or bell-shaped distribution curve. It is an approximation of this curve that is used in averaging together pixel values to create the blurred values.

Q: Can I create a transparent shadow that I can use in my page layout program? And if not, why not?

A: PostScript does not support transparency. Hence, there is no way to create a transparent shadow that will interact with other ele-ments on the page in the same way a shadow layer would interact with other elements in Photoshop. There are a wide variety of work arounds for this that are based on giving up some options.

Ben's Techno-Babble Decoder Ring

Rosette—A pattern caused by printing four halftone screens at differing angles. You can see a similar effect by placing two bug screens together at different angles (you know, the kind that is used in the screen door of your house).

Keyboard Shortcuts

New Layer Via Cut	Command-J
New Layer Via Copy	Shift-Command-J
Hue/Saturation	Command-U
Desaturate	Shift-Command-U
Levels	Command-L
Feather	Option-Command-D
Fill Dialog	Shift-Delete
Toggle Preserve Transparency	/
Toggle Quick Mask Mode	Q

Courtesy of Robert Bowen Studio.
Photography by Eric Meola.
Art Director: Bronson Smith,
Schieffelin & Somerset.

11 Image Blending

What you see on these screens up here is a fantasy; a computer enhanced hallucination!
—Stephen Falken in "War Games"

Courtesy of Robert Bowen Studio, Sony Electronics, Inc., and Lowe & Partners/SMS. Photography by Howard Berman. Art Director: Maria Kostyk-Petro. Copywriter: Steve Doppelt.

No matter how many times I see them, I'm always in awe of the amazing special effects you see in big-budget Hollywood flicks. I know it's all man-made digital voodoo, but I still get a thrill when the effects are done so well. Consider *Jurassic Park* when they blended the computer-generated dinos with actors and live-action backgrounds—so incredibly lifelike that you wouldn't be surprised to find yourself standing behind a Velociraptor in the popcorn line.

In Photoshop you can create your own kind of movie magic by blending diverse visual elements into one big picture (the only difference is the pictures don't move). Some people call this compositing or image blending. This is where Photoshop really gets to strut its stuff and where you can put your creative agility to the test. The possibilities with compositing are truly boundless. Where else could you create a passionate embrace between an ugly, smelly, wrinkly bulldog and his arch-rival, a prim and proper kitty-cat. (Robert Bowen did it, and the piece even won the Gold Lion Award in Cannes!) Where else could you put the face of a famous singer onto the body of a goldfish and have her swim around her own fishbowl? Certainly not in real life! But with Photoshop all you need is your imagination and bag full of good blending techniques.

Three Ways to Blend

In this chapter we'll explore the features that allow you to blend multiple images into one seamless composite. We'll cover grouping layers, blending sliders, and layer masks. Once you've mastered all three, you'll be able to blend your images together like magic. But before we start blending some images, let's take a look at how these features work.

Grouping Layers

When two layers are grouped together, the top layer will show up only in those places where there is information on the layer directly below it. This can be useful for simple effects like photographic edges or placing a photo inside of some text.

Sample Use: You've spent hours creating a big retro-looking headline that could have come from the movie poster of *Creature from the Black Lagoon*. Your client, not exactly the king of good taste, calls and says he wants you to put flames inside the headline. You put aside your better judgment and agree to the flames, but only because he pays on time. Then he calls back; he's got some unresolved issues. He doesn't know whether he wants flames or hot lava inside the text, and he's also thinking about changing the headline altogether. He wonders out loud if it will take long or cost much more to do this? "Well," you say, "I think I could wrap this up in about three hours." Greatly relieved, he tells you you're a miracle worker and hangs up. Then you pop open the Layers palette where you've grouped the headline and flames, and faster than you can say hocus pocus you've tweaked the text and are off to the beach for a three-hour (paid) vacation.

Blending Sliders

The blending sliders allow you to make certain areas of a layer disappear or show up based on how bright or dark they are. So, if you want all the dark parts of an object to disappear, you can easily accomplish that.

Sample Use: A big fish prospect that you've been trying to snag for months finally throws you a bone. She's desperate because the super-swanky design studio she usually uses can't meet her deadline. You know she's just using you, but what the hey, it's a shot at a new client. She's given you some images that you've loaded into Photoshop. One is a photograph of some big, fat, billowy clouds; the other is of a bunch of whales. She wants you to make it look like the whales are swimming around in the clouds. In some places she wants the whales to replace the sky that is behind the clouds, but in other places she wants the whales to actually blend in with the clouds. Very surreal. She impatiently bites her nails and wants to know how many hours it will take to get the effect. You know you can nail this job in a jiffy with the blending sliders; so while your hands are busy with the mouse, you give her a fearless look and reply, "I'll do it while you wait." She frowns, "I can't just sit around here for hours!" You smile, "No problem, it's already done." The look on her face delivers the good news— you've got a client for life.

Layer Masks

I consider layer masks to be the most powerful blending function in Photoshop. With layer masks you can make any part of a layer disappear and control exactly how much you'd like its edge to fade out. What you can do with layer masks is infinite.

Sample Use: You're waiting for your biggest client, a twenty-year-old creative genius with a ring in his nose. Although this is just a planning meeting, you know from experience that the genius will want to see some action. Armed with your fastest computer and Photoshop at the ready, you're not surprised when the kid comes in and starts throwing around madcap ideas like they're going out of style. Blending seems to be the theme of the day. First he wants something that looks like a skyscraper growing out of a pencil. Then he changes his mind and decides he wants to fuse together a hippopotamus and a ballerina. But then he gets a funny look on his face and says, "I know! Let's put Godzilla in an Elvis suit!" Ahhh, you think, a perfect day for layer masks. Without batting an eyelash, you go about the business of giving 'Zilla his new look. Six months later you almost choke on your coffee when you find out that your Elvis-Zilla ad got an award.

Now that you have a feeling for the blending options that are available, let's get into the specifics of how this all works.

Grouping Layers

When you group multiple layers together, all the layers within the group will be visible only where there is information in the bottommost layer of the group (see Figures 11.1 and 11.2). You can group layers together by using any of the following techniques:

Figure 11.1
Result of grouping a photo with a type layer. (Original image © 1998 Adobe Systems, Inc.)

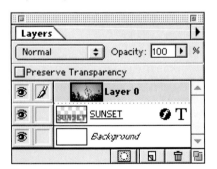

Figure 11.2
Layers palette view.

Option-click between two layers in the layers palette.

Choose Group with Previous from the Layer Menu.

Type Command-G.

Changing the Stacking Order

When changing the stacking order of the layers, you'll want to be careful; otherwise, you might accidentally ungroup some layers. If you move one of the grouped layers above a layer that is not part of the group, you'll be ungrouping that layer. Or if you move an ungrouped layer between two layers that are grouped, then it will become part of that group. If you move the bottom layer of a group above or below a layer that is not part of the group, all the layers in the group will move with it.

Now that you know how to group your layers, let's take a look at a few of the things you can accomplish by grouping layers.

Photographic Edges

To create a rippled-edge effect, try this out. First, open the photograph you want to apply the effect to, then create a new layer. Now, make a selection by using the Marquee tool. You are going to have to crop the image a bit in order to achieve a rippled-edge effect, so make sure your selection is a little inside the edge of the photograph. Then fill the selection by choosing Fill from the Edit menu. It doesn't matter what color you fill the selection with. I usually choose a bright color so that I can easily see it (see Figure 11.3). Next, you'll need to change the stacking order of the layers so the layer that contains the box you just made is underneath the photograph. You can do this by clicking on the name of the layer and dragging it below the name of the photograph's layer in the Layers palette.

To get the photograph to show up only where the rectangular box is, click on the top-most layer and then type Command-G to group the layers (see Figure 11.4).

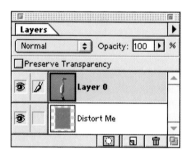

Figure 11.3
Bright-colored rectangle directly below the photograph.

Figure 11.4
Photograph grouped to red box.
(© 1998 Adobe Systems, Inc.)

Now click on the layer that contains the box. You can distort this box by using any filter you'd like (see Figures 11.5 to 11.7). For now, just use one of the filters under the **Filter> Distort** menu, such as, Ripple, Twirl, or Polar Coordinates. By doing this, you will distort the box you created earlier and because it is grouped to the photograph above it, the edge of the photo will become distorted as well.

Once you're happy with how the edge looks, you might want to add some other effects, such as a black border around its edge. There's a trick for that, too. Click on the layer that contains the distorted rectangle and choose **Layer>Layer Effects>Inner Glow** (see Figures 11.8 and 11.9). Now click on the color swatch to pick the color you would like to use and set the Mode pop-up menu to Normal. To get the color to appear around the edge of the image only, be sure Edge is chosen at the bottom of the dialog box. Now you can experiment with the Opacity, Blur, and Intensity settings to fine-tune the result. If you are having trouble getting the edge to completely show up, try bringing the Opacity and Intensity settings all the way up to 100%. You don't have to restrict yourself to the Inner Glow effect, so experiment with the other layer effects until you find your favorite.

Figure 11.5
Result of distorting bright-colored rectangle.

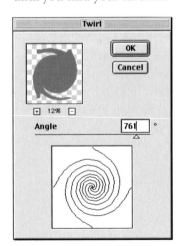

Figure 11.6
First apply the Twirl filter.

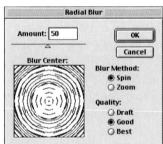

Figure 11.7
Then apply the Radial Blur filter.

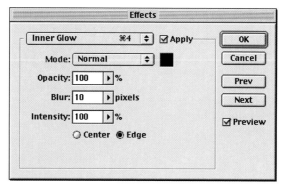

Figure 11.8
Adding an Inner Glow layer effect.

Figure 11.9
Inner Glow settings used to create border.

Grouping Adjustment Layers

Grouping layers can also be helpful when using adjustment layers. An adjustment layer usually affects all the layers that are below it. By grouping an adjustment layer, you can force it to affect only the layers that are within the group. This can be extremely helpful when you want to brighten or darken a single layer and you don't want to make the change permanent. See Figures 11.10 to 11.13.

Limiting Shadows

I use Grouping all the time when I'm creating shadows. Let's say you have some text, and underneath the text is an image of a piece of string, and you want the text to cast a shadow on the string. Once you create a layer that contains a shadow, all you need to do is group it with the string, and then the shadow will show up only where the string is. See Figures 11.14 to 11.16.

Stacking Order Tricks

I occasionally use the grouping feature when I really don't want to restrict where a layer appears. That way I can fool Photoshop into doing some tricks. Here's an example: Ordinarily, you can only move one layer at a time up or down in the stack; that is, unless you group some layers together. By grouping multiple layers, you can drag the bottom layer of the group (the one that is underlined) up

NOTE

In the Layers palette, the background image is always stuck at the bottom of the palette; you can't move another layer below it in the layers stack. But you can always double-click on the background image and change its name, which will convert it into a normal layer. Once it's a layer, you can change its stacking order, or drag a layer below it.

Figure 11.10
Original image. (Courtesy of Chris Klimek)

NOTE

To quickly group multiple layers together, link the layers by clicking and dragging in the column just to the left of their preview icons in the Layers palette, then choose Group Linked from the Layers palette. After you have grouped the layers, you can drag across the link symbols to turn them off.

or down in the stack; and all the layers within the group will also move (see Figures 11.17 and 11.18). This can be immensely helpful when you are working on complicated images that contain dozens of layers.

Once you have changed the stacking order, you'll probably need to ungroup the layers; that is, unless you really want to restrict where they are visible. To quickly ungroup a series of layers, click on the bottom-most layer of the group and choose **Layer>Ungroup**.

Figure 11.11
Adding an adjustment layer at the top of the layers stack affects the entire image.

Figure 11.12
Grouping the adjustment layer makes it apply only to the layers within the group.

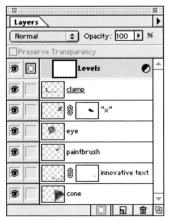

Figure 11.13
Layers palette view.

Figure 11.14
Original image.

Figure 11.15
Grouping the shadow to the string.

Figure 11.16
Layers palette view.

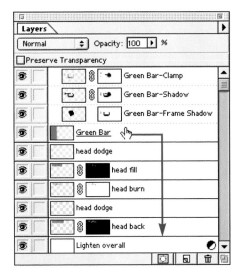

Figure 11.17
Drag the bottom layer of a group to change the stacking order of all the layers within the group.

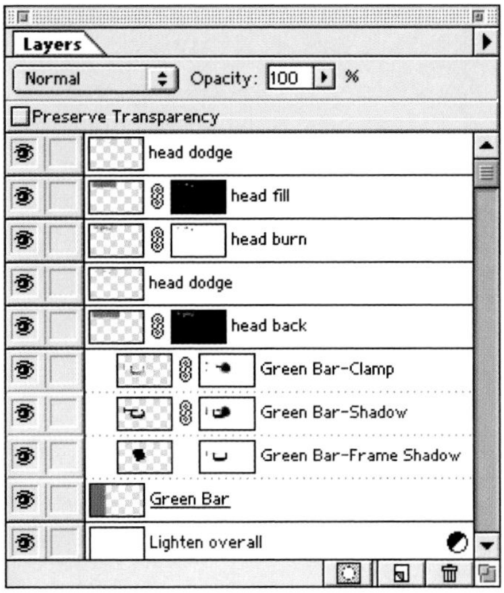

Figure 11.18
Result.

Blending Sliders

The blending sliders will allow you to quickly make areas of a layer transparent based on how bright or dark the image appears. You'll find the blending sliders by double-clicking a layer. If you are working on a Type or Adjustment layer, choose Layer Options from the side menu of the Layers palette instead. The blending sliders are at the bottom of the Layer Options dialog box, shown in Figure 11.19. The first thing you'll notice is that there are two sets of sliders. One is labeled "This Layer" and the other is labeled "Underlying." The slider called This Layer will make areas of the active layer disappear. The slider labeled Underlying deals with all the layers underneath the layer that was double-clicked. This slider will make parts of the underlying image show up as if a hole was punched through the layer you are working on.

This Layer Sliders

First, let's take a look at the topmost sliders. If you move the left slider towards the middle, the dark areas of the

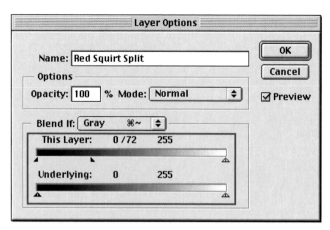

Figure 11.19
The blending sliders.

image will start to disappear (all the shades that are to the left of the slider will disappear). This slider can be a great help when trying to remove the background from fireworks or lightning. The only problem is, once you get the background to disappear, the edges of the fireworks will have hard, jagged edges. See Figures 11.20 to 11.22.

To remedy this situation, all you have to do is split the slider into two pieces by Option-dragging on its right edge. When this slider is split into two parts, the shades of gray that are between the halves will become partially transparent and blend into the underlying image (see Figures 11.23 and 11.24). The shades close to the left half of the slider will be almost completely transparent, and the shades near the right half will be almost completely opaque.

When you move the right slider, you will be making the bright areas of the image disappear (all the shades of gray to the right of the slider will disappear). This slider can be useful when you come across a multi-colored logo that needs to be removed from its white background. Just like the upper left slider, you can split this slider into two halves by Option-dragging its left edge. See Figures 11.25 to 11.27.

Figure 11.20
Original unblended image. (Fireworks image © 1998 Corel Corporation; Lake image © 1998 Adobe Systems, Inc.)

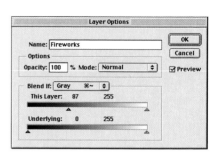

Figure 11.22
Moving the upper left slider makes the dark areas of the current layer disappear.

Figure 11.21
Removing the black sky from the fireworks image.

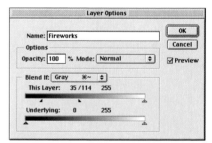

Figure 11.24
Splitting a triangle into halves allows the image to smoothly blend into the underlying image.

Figure 11.23
The edges of the fireworks blend into the underlying image.

Underlying Sliders

By moving these two sliders, you'll be able to make areas of the underlying image show up as if they were creating a hole in the layer you double-clicked. These sliders are useful when you don't want a layer to completely obstruct the view of the underlying image. I might use this to reveal some of the texture in the underlying image. And, just like the top sliders, you can Option-click to separate the sliders into two parts. See Figures 11.28 to 11.30.

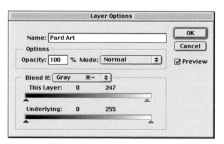

Figure 11.27
Moving the upper right sliders makes the bright areas of this layer disappear.

Figure 11.25
Original image. (Courtesy of Nik Willmore)

Figure 11.26
The result of removing all white areas by using the blending sliders.

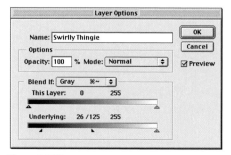

Figure 11.28
Original image.

Figure 11.29
Result of blending in the dark parts of the underlying image.

Figure 11.30
Moving the lower left slider makes the dark areas of the underlying image show up as if they are poking a hole in the active layer.

Understanding the Numbers

The numbers that appear above the sliders indicate the exact location of each slider. If you haven't split any of the sliders, then there should be a total of four numbers (one for each slider). When you split one of the sliders into two parts, you'll see one number for each half of the slider. These numbers use the same numbering system that is used in the Levels dialog box (see Chapter 6, "Optimizing Grayscale Images," for more information about the Levels dialog box).

If you move the upper left slider until its number changes to 166, for example, you'll have made all the shades darker than 35% gray on that layer disappear. It would be much easier if Adobe would allow us to switch between percentages and the 0-255 numbering system like you can when using the Curves dialog box.

Using Color Channels

If you leave the pop-up menu at the top of the blending slider area set to gray, then Photoshop will ignore the colors in your document and just analyze the brightness of the image (it will be as if the image were in Grayscale mode). By changing this menu, you will be telling Photoshop to look at the information in the individual color channels to determine which areas should be visible (see Figure 11.31). If you have a document that is in CMYK mode and you change the pop-up menu to cyan and move the upper right slider to 26, for example, you'll make all areas of the layer that contain 10% or less cyan disappear. This can be useful when you want to remove a background that contains one dominant color.

Choosing the best channel from this pop-up menu usually involves a lot of trial and error. Because of that, I'll show you how I usually figure out which color would be most effective for different images.

First of all, if the color you would like to work with is one of the components of your image (red, green, or blue in RGB mode), then the choice is pretty straightforward—to work on someone's blue eyes, just work on the blue channel. But what if you want to work on an area that is yellow and your image is in RGB mode? Well, to find out, I usually hold down the Command key and press the number keys on my keyboard (1-3 for RGB mode, 1-4 for CMYK mode); this will display the different color channels. You'll want to look for the channel that separates the area you're interested in from the areas surrounding it (see Figures 11.32 to 11.34). Once you've found the best channel, glance up at the top of your document and you'll see the name of the channel you are viewing right next to the name of the document. The name of the channel that looks best will be the choice you'll want to choose from the pop-up menu in the Layer Options dialog box.

NOTE

To convert between percentages and the 0-255 numbering system, open the Color palette and choose Grayscale slider from its side menu and enter the percentage you would like to use. Then to convert to the 0-255 numbering system, just choose RGB sliders from the side menu of the palette.

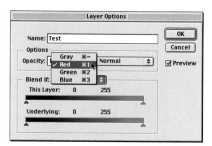

Figure 11.31
The Color Channel pop-up menu determines which channels will be analyzed.

Figure 11.32
Red channel. (© 1998 PhotoDisc)

Figure 11.33
Green channel.

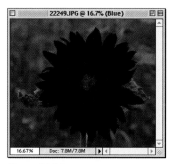

Figure 11.34
Blue channel.

WARNING

If you've chosen a color from the pop-up menu before applying the blending sliders, be sure to flatten your image when converting it to another color mode (RGB to CMYK, for example). The appearance of unflattened layers will change because the blending settings will no longer affect the same color channels. If you apply the sliders to the red channel (first choice in the menu), then convert the image to CMYK mode, the same slider settings will now be applied to the cyan channel (because it is the first choice in the menu). The image will not look the same because the cyan channel does not contain the same information that was in the red channel.

Now that you have a general feeling for how the blending sliders work, let's take a look at some of the things we can do with them.

Enhancing Clouds

When you choose **Filter>Render>Clouds**, you'll get great-looking clouds, but there is one problem—you can't see through them. You'll probably want to see through the dark parts of the clouds, so double-click the name of the clouds layer. By moving the upper left slider in, you're going to make the dark parts of the clouds disappear so you can see the underlying image. To make the edges of the clouds blend into the underlying image, hold down the Option key and split the upper left slider into two parts. Now by experimenting with the halves of the slider, you'll be able to create the look of fog, faint clouds, or dense clouds. See Figures 11.35 to 11.38.

Figure 11.35
Original image.

Figure 11.36
After creating a new layer and applying the Clouds and Twirl filters.

Figure 11.37
Result of discarding the dark area of the clouds by using the blending sliders.

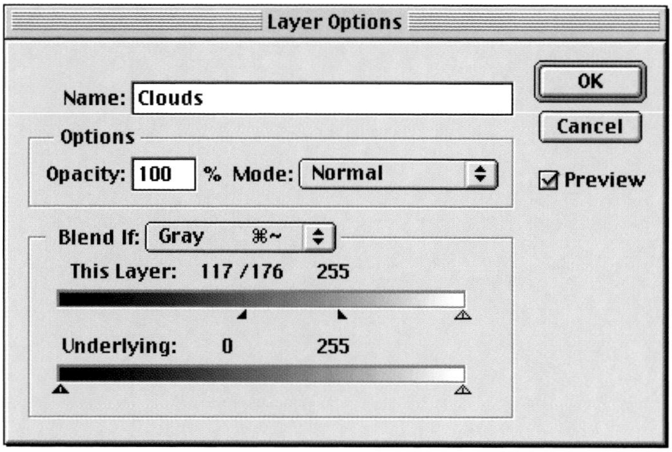

Figure 11.38
Settings used on preceding image.

Homemade Lightning

If you want to play Zeus and create your own lightning, you'll need to start with some clouds; so first create a new layer, then reset your foreground and background colors to their default colors. Next, go up to the Filter menu and choose **Render>Clouds**. This will give you clouds, but it won't look anything like lightning, as Figure 11.39 reveals.

To get closer to something that resembles lightning, go back up to the filter menu, and choose **Render>Difference Clouds**. Then go to the Image menu and choose **Adjust> Invert**. This should get you a little bit closer to lightning, but we still have a few steps before it looks electric (see Figure 11.40).

If you remove all the dark information from this image, it might resemble lightning. So, double-click the layer and pull in the upper left slider. You'll want to hold down the Option key and split the slider into two pieces. Move the right half of the slider all the way to the right edge, as far as you can move it. Then grab the left edge of the slider and start moving it to the right until the lightning looks appropriate for the image, as in Figure 11.41. You'll have to move it almost all the way across.

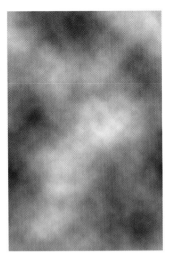

Figure 11.39
The Clouds filter is the starting point for creating artificial lightning.

Figure 11.40
Result of applying Difference Clouds, then choosing **Image>Adjust>Invert**.

Figure 11.41
Result of removing all the dark information. (© 1998 PhotoDisc)

Making the Changes Permanent

The problem with the blending sliders is that they are just settings attached to a layer, and Photoshop does not provide an obvious way to permanently apply the changes. Well, if you've used only the top sliders, then there is an easy way to get Photoshop to permanently delete the hidden areas. To do this, create a brand-new empty layer, and then move that empty layer underneath the layer that is using the blending sliders. Then all you have to do is merge those two layers. To do that, click on the layer that is using the blending sliders, go to the side menu on the Layers palette, and choose Merge Down. By doing this, Photoshop will permanently delete the areas that were transparent. This can be nice if your client requested the layered file, but you don't want them to know how you did it! See Figures 11.42 and 11.43.

Layer Masks

Now let's take a look at my favorite method for blending images together, layer masks. By adding a layer mask to a layer, you can control exactly where that layer is transparent and where it's opaque. You'll find that layer masks are used to create most high-end images. It's one of the features that really separate the beginners from the pros. But there's no

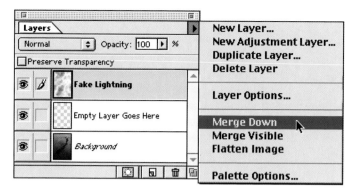

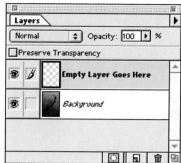

Figure 11.42
To permanently apply blending slider settings, merge the layer with an empty one.

Figure 11.43
Result.

reason why you can't be as adept at layer masks as the most seasoned veteran. It just takes a little time and sweat.

Creating A Layer Mask

You can add a layer mask to the active layer by clicking on the leftmost icon at the bottom of the Layers palette (the icon that looks like a rectangle with a circle inside it). Once you click this icon, you'll notice that the layer you're working on contains two thumbnail images. The one on the left is its normal preview thumbnail, the one to the right is the layer mask thumbnail. After adding a layer mask, you can edit it by painting across the image window with any painting tool. Even though this would usually change the image, you're really just editing the layer mask; it just isn't visible on the main screen. The color you paint with (really, shades of gray) determines what happens to the image. Painting with black will make areas disappear and painting with white will bring back the areas again. And remember, because you are using a painting tool, you can choose a hard- or soft-edged brush to control what the edge looks like. See Figures 11.44 and 11.45.

What's nice about this is that it doesn't permanently delete areas, instead it just makes them temporarily disappear. If you paint with white, you'll be able to bring back areas that are transparent. This can be helpful if you're doing a very quick job for a client who wants to see a general concept. You can do just a very crude job of getting rid of the backgrounds of images, then later on go back in and refine that layer mask to get it to look just right.

Figure 11.44
The softness of your brush determines how soft the edge of the image will appear.

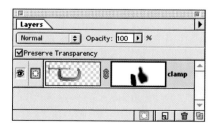

Figure 11.45
Layers palette view.

Hiding Selected Areas

If a selection is present when adding a layer mask, Photoshop will automatically fill the nonselected areas of the layer mask with black so the image is visible in the selected area only (see Figures 11.46 and 11.47). You can see exactly what Photoshop has done by glancing at the layer mask thumbnail in the Layers palette (see Figure 11.48).

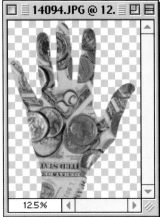

Figure 11.48
Layers palette view.

Figure 11.46
Make a selection before adding a layer mask. (© 1998 PhotoDisc)

Figure 11.47
Result of adding a layer mask.

NOTE

If you are working on an adjustment layer, the thumbnail that shows up in the Layers palette is a layer mask. This layer mask is automatically added when you create the layer. Adjustment layers don't contain a normal image thumbnail because there is no photographic information in the layer (it just contains adjustment settings).

NOTE

When a selection is present, you can Option-click the layer mask icon in the Layers palette to add a layer mask and hide the selected areas. If no selection is present, Option-clicking the icon will hide the entire image.

If you choose Add layer mask from the Layer menu, you will be offered some choices:

Reveal Selection—Hides the nonselected areas giving you the same result as using the layer mask icon in the Layers palette.

Hide Selection—Hides only the areas that are currently selected, leaving the non-selected areas visible.

Reveal All—Does not hide any areas of the layer.

Hide All—Hides the entire layer.

Paste Into

If there is a selection present when pasting an image into your document, you can choose **Edit>Paste Into** (instead of **Edit>Paste**) to automatically create a layer mask. This layer mask will make the image show up only in the area that was selected. You can also hold down the Option key and choose **Edit>Paste Into** to hide the selected areas. If you choose **Select>All** before choosing Paste Into, Photoshop will create a layer mask and reveal the entire image. You can also hold down the Option key and choose Paste Into to hide the entire image.

Disabling a Layer Mask

After you've created a layer mask, you can temporarily disable it by Shift-clicking its thumbnail in the Layers palette (see Figures 11.49 to 11.51). With each click you will toggle the layer mask on or off. This is a great help when you want to see what the layer would look like if you didn't have a layer mask restricting where it shows up.

NOTE

To quickly switch between editing the layer mask and editing the main image, use the following keyboard commands. Type Command-~ to work on the image, or type Command-\ to work on the layer mask.

Figure 11.49
Layer mask active.

Figure 11.50
Layer mask disabled.

Figure 11.51
Layers palette view.

Switching Between the Layer Mask and the Image

Now that you have two thumbnails attached to a layer, you have to be able to determine if you are working on the layer mask or the main image. If you look at the layer mask icon right after you've created one, you'll notice a bold border around its edge (see Figures 11.52 and 11.53). That border indicates what you're working on. If you want to work on the main image instead of the layer mask, click the image thumbnail in the Layers palette. The bold border will appear around the image thumbnail indicating that you are editing the main image instead of the layer mask. To work on the layer mask again, just click its icon and the bold border will move.

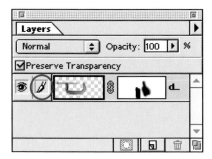

Figure 11.52
Editing the main image.

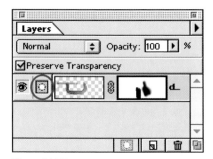

Figure 11.53
Editing the layer mask.

There is another way to get a visual indication of whether you're working on the main image or the layer mask. If you look just to the left of the image thumbnail, you'll see a Paintbrush icon if you are working on the main image, or the layer mask icon if you're working on a layer mask.

Viewing a Layer Mask

You can also view the layer mask so it fills the main image window. To view the layer mask, hold down the Option key and click on the layer mask thumbnail (see Figure 11.54). Then you'll see it looks just like a grayscale image, and you can actually paint right on this image. I use this a lot when I get someone else's document, or I open an old document I worked on months ago and I can't remember exactly what I did in the layer mask. To stop viewing the layer mask, just Option-click its icon a second time.

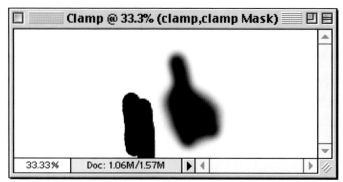

Figure 11.54
Viewing the layer mask in the main image window.

Shades of Gray

Photoshop treats a layer mask as if it were a grayscale document. That means that you can use any editing tool that is available to a grayscale image. Areas that are full of pure black will become transparent, pure white areas will be completely opaque, and areas that contain shades of gray will become partially transparent. Painting with 20% gray in a layer mask will lower the opacity of that area to 80%. So, using a painting tool with an opacity setting of 80% will produce the same result as painting with 100% opacity, then adding a layer mask that is full of 20% gray.

Filling Areas

Because Photoshop treats layer masks as if they are grayscale documents, you can create selections and fill those areas with white or black to hide or show the contents of a layer. To fill a selected area with the current foreground color (which is usually black), press Option-Delete. To fill a selected area with the current background color (usually white), or press Command-Delete. This is nice because it frees you from having to use the painting tools.

Using Gradients

The most common way to make one image fade into another is to add a layer mask and then use the Gradient tool. In a layer mask, areas that are pure black become completely transparent and areas that are pure white are completely opaque. Shades of gray in a layer mask will make the image become partially transparent. So, if you would like one image to fade into another, use the Gradient tool set to "black,white." See Figures 11.55 to 11.57.

If you try to apply the gradient a second time, you might run into a few problems. If you apply the gradient from right to left one time, and then right after that you apply it in the other direction, the second gradient will completely obstruct the first one. To combine two gradients, set the Gradient tool to Foreground to Transparent and make sure the foreground color is set to black. Then you should be able to apply the Gradient tool as many times as you want within a layer mask, and it simply adds to what was already in the layer mask. See Figures 11.58 to 11.61.

Figure 11.55
Ruler layer before adding a layer mask.

Figure 11.56
Result of applying a gradient to a layer mask.

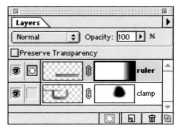

Figure 11.57
Layers palette view.

Figure 11.58
First gradient.

Figure 11.59
Second gradient using Foreground to Background setting.

Figure 11.60
Second gradient using Foreground to Transparent setting.

Figure 11.61
Both ends of the ruler image blend into the underlying image because two gradients were used.

Applying Filters

After painting in a layer mask, you can enhance the result by applying filters to it (see Figures 11.62 to 11.65). Go up to the Filter menu, choose Distort, and choose something like Ripple. Then, instead of having a really smooth transition, you will have some texture in it.

If you want the edge of an image to slowly fade out, you can choose **Filter>Blur>Gaussian Blur.** You can blur a layer mask as many times as you'd like; each time you blur it, the edge will become softer. See Figures 11.66 to 11.68.

You can also expand or contract the areas that are transparent by choosing Minimum or Maximum from the **Filter>Other** menu (see Figures 11.69 to 11.71). The Minimum filter will make more areas transparent, while the Maximum filter will make fewer areas transparent.

Figure 11.62
Original image.

Figure 11.63
Original layer mask.

Figure 11.64
Result of applying the Ripple filter to the layer mask.

Figure 11.65
Modified layer mask.

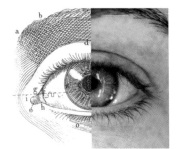

Figure 11.66
Color eye image contains a pure black and pure white layer mask. (Photo © 1998 PhotoDisc)

Figure 11.67
Apply the Gaussian Blur filter to a layer mask to give it softer edges.

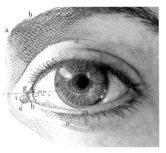

Figure 11.68
Result of blurring the layer mask.

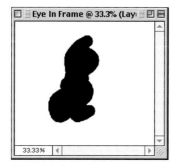

Figure 11.69
Original image.

Figure 11.70
Result of applying the Minimum filter.

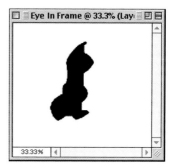

Figure 11.71
Result of applying the Maximum filter.

Adjusting with Levels

You can also adjust the appearance of a layer mask by choosing **Image>Adjust Levels**. The sliders in the Levels dialog (see Figure 11.72) will do the following to your image:

Upper left slider—Forces the darkest shades of gray to black, which will make more areas transparent.

Upper right slider—Forces the brightest shades of gray to white, which will make more areas opaque.

Middle slider—Changes the transition from black to white and, therefore, changes the transition from opaque to transparent.

Lower left slider—Lightens the dark shades of gray, which will make transparent areas appear more opaque.

Lower right slider—Darkens the bright shades of gray, which will make opaque areas appear more transparent.

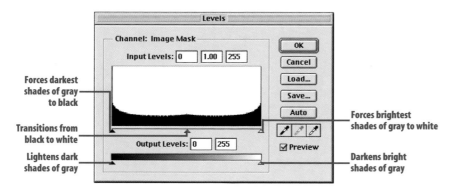

Figure 11.72
The Levels dialog box.

Figure 11.73
Scanned image to be used as a layer mask.

Figure 11.74
Two images blended together using scanned image as layer mask. (© 1998 PhotoDisc)

Image as Layer Mask

You can achieve interesting transition effects by pasting scanned images into a layer mask (see Figures 11.73 and 11.74). I like to run off to the art supply store and purchase interesting handmade papers and spatter a bunch of ink on them using paintbrushes. Then, to get the image into a layer mask, I scan the paper on my desktop scanner, select the entire image by choosing **Select>Select All**, and then copy the image by choosing **Edit>Copy**. After I've done that, I can close the scanned image and switch over to the image I would like to use it in. Next, I click on the layer I would like to work on and add a layer mask. There is one little problem: In order to paste something into a layer mask, you must be viewing the layer mask. That means you must Option-click the layer mask before pasting something into it. To stop viewing the layer mask, just Option-click its thumbnail again.

Using the Move Tool

After you have created the perfect layer mask, you might want to start rearranging your document by using the Move tool. You have three choices; you can move just the layer, just the layer mask, or both at the same time. The link symbol between the layer mask and image thumbnails determines what will move when using the Move tool. If the link symbol is present (the default), the layer and layer mask will move together. See Figures 11.75 to 11.77.

Figure 11.75
Original image.

Figure 11.76
Eye layer and layer mask moved together.

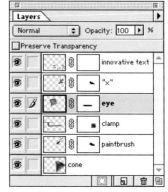

Figure 11.77
Layer and layer mask thumbnails linked together.

If you turn the link symbol off (by clicking it), then you'll only be moving what has the bold border around it. That means if the layer mask has a bold border, you'll just be moving that around the screen. And if the main image has the bold border, you'll move the main image around the screen, leaving the layer mask in its original position. See Figures 11.78 and 11.79. You'll want to move just the layer and not the layer mask if part of the layer mask lines up with another part of the image. (See Figures 11.80 and 11.81.)

NOTE

To quickly paste something into a layer mask, press the \ key to view the layer mask, then choose type Command-V to paste the image, and finally type \ again to stop viewing the layer mask. This technique does not view the layer mask as it would normally appear, instead it shows up as a color overlay.

Figure 11.78
Moving just the layer mask, leaving the main image stationary.

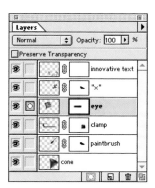

Figure 11.79
When the link symbol is missing, the bold border (layer mask) determines what will get moved.

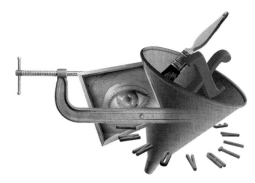

Figure 11.80
Moving just the layer, leaving the layer mask stationary.

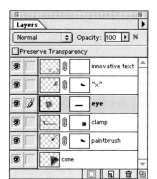

Figure 11.81
When the link symbol is missing, the bold border (layer) determines what will get moved.

Load as Selection

Once you have perfected a layer mask, you might need to select the areas that are visible in order to add a border or perform another effect. You can do this in many ways. The fastest method is to Command-click the layer mask thumbnail, as demonstrated in Figures 11.82 and 11.83. If there is already a selection present, you can Shift-Command-click to add to the selection, Option-Command-click to subtract, or Shift-Option-Command-click to intersect the selection. Or, if you are not very good at remembering a bunch of keyboard commands, you can Control-click (or right-click in Windows) the layer mask thumbnail to get a menu of options.

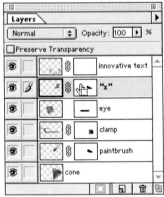

Figure 11.82
Command-click the layer mask thumbnail to select the areas that are visible.

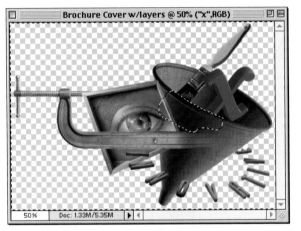

Figure 11.83
Result of Command-clicking on the "x" layer's layer mask thumbnail.

Converting the Blending Sliders into a Layer Mask

Earlier in this chapter we talked about making areas of a layer transparent using the blending sliders. Occasionally, you might need to turn off the sliders and create a layer mask that produces the same result. Then you'll be able to edit the layer mask using painting tools and filters instead of the blending sliders. To accomplish this, you'll need to go through a multi-step process.

First, create a new empty layer below the layer that is using the blending sliders. Next, click the layer above it (the one that uses the blending sliders) and type Option-Command-E. This deposits information into the new layer that does not use the blending sliders, but produces the same results (permanently deleting the transparent areas).

Now you can double-click the layer that uses the blending sliders and set all the sliders back to default positions so they are no longer affecting the layer. Then, to add a layer mask that produces the same result, Command-click the layer directly below the one that was using the sliders (to select its shape), and finally click the layer mask icon on the layer that used the sliders. See Figures 11.84 and 11.85.

Figure 11.84
Result of Option-merging the clouds layer with an empty layer.

Figure 11.85
Layer mask added after Command-clicking the merged layer.

Remove Layer Mask

If you know you will no longer need to edit a layer mask and would like to permanently delete the areas that are transparent, you can choose **Layer>Remove Layer Mask** (see Figures 11.86 and 11.87). When you do this, you will be presented with three choices.

Cancel—Leaves the layer mask intact.

Apply—Removes the layer mask and deletes all transparent areas.

Discard—Removes the layer mask and brings the image back into full view.

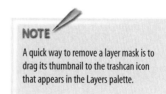

NOTE

A quick way to remove a layer mask is to drag its thumbnail to the trashcan icon that appears in the Layers palette.

Figure 11.86
Final "Dog & Cat" image. (Original image courtesy of Robert Bowen Studio, Sony Electronics, Inc., and Lowe & Partners/SMS. Photography by Howard Berman.

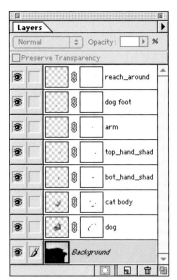

Figure 11.87
Simplified version of the "Dog & Cat" image shown at the beginning of this chapter. I removed over a dozen adjustment layers, all of which had layer masks attached to them.

Closing Thoughts

I hope that you get as much of a kick out of blending images as I do. It's one of those things that never gets old; I can always count on another surprise waiting for me around the corner. We always have bets going on in our office about whether or not certain images have been "Photoshopped." That's how Robert Bowen's dog/cat piece for Sony found its way into this book. We saw the Sony ad in a magazine and had a day-long debate about whether or not you could actually get a dog and a cat to embrace like that. I lost the bet. Photoshop won.

I also hope that you'll devote some serious time to playing around with the three methods of blending (grouping layers, blending sliders, and layer masks). Both separately and together, they will give you enormous amounts of freedom to do wondrous and strange things with your images. And besides all that, it can impress the heck out of your boss or next client.

Ask Adobe

Q: When I use the blending sliders on individual channels of the image, and then convert to another mode (RGB to CMYK), why does the image change?

A: Because the blending sliders are directly tied to particular color components. When you change image modes, those components are replaced with different components with different values. Once again: You almost always want to flatten before doing mode conversions.

Q: Why is a layer mask automatically added when you create an adjustment layer? And why does the adjustment layer only have one thumbnail in the Layers palette?

A: An adjustment layer has one channel for controlling where it applies. This is essentially the same role as a layer mask plays for a normal layer.

Courtesy of Robert Bowen Studio, Sony Electronics, Inc., and Lowe & Partners/SMS. Photography by Howard Berman. Art Director: Maria Kostyk-Petro. Copywriter: Steve Doppelt.

The image of the dog and cat together on the sofa was created as an ad for a Sony video camera that has the capability of actually seeing in the dark. This picture is a composite created from several photographs that Howard Berman made of each animal (shown on the following page). There were various heads, paws, tails, and body positions, which we brought together in Photoshop layers. These layers were then distorted and merged. The Shear filter was used to wrap many of the elements. We studied the viewfinder of the actual video display and emulated the shadowing effect produced by the camera. We wanted the final image to appear both humorous and accurate to the technology it was representing.

–Robert Bowen

Photography by Howard Berman.

Courtesy of Albert Sanchez (photographer), Ani DiFranco, and Righteous Babe Records.

Courtesy of Albert Sanchez (photographer), Ani DiFranco, and Righteous Babe Records.

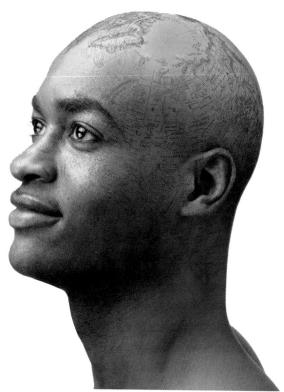

Courtesy of Jeff Schewe.

Courtesy of Jeff Schewe.

Courtesy of Jeff Schewe

12 Enhancement

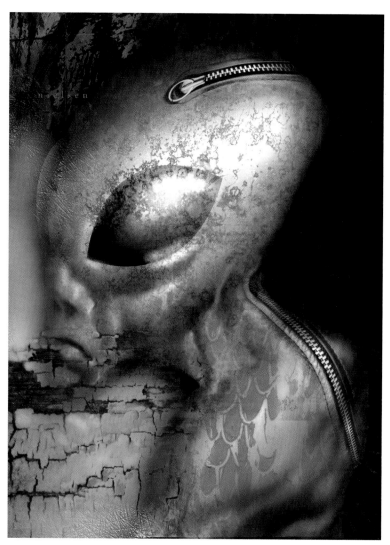

Elwood: It's 106 miles to Chicago, we've got a full tank of gas, half a pack of cigarettes, it's dark and we're wearing sunglasses. Jake: Hit it!
—The Blues Brothers

© 1998 Cliff Nielsen for the "X-Files."

To claim that I can teach you everything you need to know about enhancement is pure insanity. The potential is so vast that there really is no road map, only past experience, to guide us. So use this chapter as your fueling stop, and then break loose and go looking for your own orbit. We'll fill up on a mixed bag of methods and techniques for enhancement, sort of a cookbook of digital recipes that takes what you've already learned from previous chapters and adds some interesting twists and embellishments (in this case, a lot of the twists have to do with blending modes). And if anyone tries to slow you down, just remember what Elwood Blues said to the policeman, "The light was yellow, sir."

Cooking With Pixels

As we get into each recipe, I will oftentimes show you multiple ways of accomplishing the same result. I do that on purpose. Sometimes you need the quick and easy method, and at other times you will want to use the slow and more precise method, which gives you more control and flexibility. Instead of being limited to just one technique, you can glance through the different approaches and choose what you think might be best for your particular situation.

First, a little bit about how this chapter is organized. Since a large number of the techniques I'm going to cover involve blending modes, the chapter has been organized using blending modes as the underlying structure. I'll start with the top of the list and slowly work my way down (see Figure 12.1).

Dissolving Glows

Sometimes I find inspiration in the weirdest of places. A friend of mine wanted to stop by a local StarBucks, and I obliged, even though I can't stand the taste of coffee (and you don't want to see what happens to me when I have caffeine). I was sitting there right next to the checkout register when I spotted a bottled coffee drink called

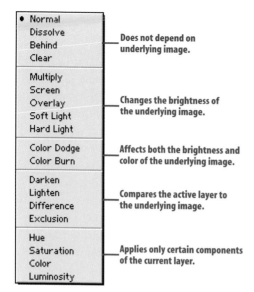

Figure 12.1
The Blending Modes menu is organized into five sections.

Frappuccino®. And right at that moment I figured out a use for two unusual features in Photoshop. This might not sound all that exciting to you; but the more uses I can find for these things, the more I really understand them. So, I'll share with you what I came up with. The Frappuccino® logo had an interesting two-color noisy glow behind the text and I thought it might be fun to make it (see Figure 12.2). So let's give it a try.

Figure 12.2
Example of Diffused Glow effect.

Create Glow Behind Text

First, scan in some black text and then let's remove the white background that always comes along for the ride (or you can skip removing the background and just use the Type tool in the first place). So, press Option-Command-~ to load the image as if it were a channel. (That will produce a selection that is the same shape as the text. It will even contain any shades of gray that were in the edge of the text. Thus, if there was 30% gray at the edge, now you have an area that is 30% selected.)

Now you want to fill this selection, so first create a new layer, then reset your Foreground color to black by pressing D, and finally pressing Option-Delete to fill it with black. You should have a layer containing the text, sans the white background. Now it's safe to get rid of the layer that contains the original scan. One word of caution at this point: When you typed the first keyboard command, Photoshop might have selected the exact opposite of what you were expecting (the background instead of the text). This can happen if you've messed with the settings in the Channels palette. But that's no problem, all you have to do is choose **Select>Inverse** to fix things up.

Okay, now we want to add an interesting glow behind the text, but we know that Layer Effects won't give us what we want, so let's go the manual route instead.

First, we need to get the text selected again, so choose **Select>Reselect** to get your last selection back. (If that doesn't do it for you, just Command-click the name of the text layer and you'll get the same result.) Then, you want to make sure the glow will be easy to see, so choose **Select>Modify>Expand** and use a low number like 6. This will pull out the edges of the selection to make it larger. Next, you'll want to create a red glow, so create a new layer below the layer that contains the text, change your Foreground color to red, and press Option-Delete to fill the selection (see Figure 12.3).

Next, get rid of your selection by choosing **Select>Deselect**, and set the blending mode of the layer to Dissolve. The Dissolve blending mode does not allow any pixels to become partially transparent. Instead, it uses a pattern of noise to allow an area to blend into the underlying image. Now all you need to do is to get the red information to blend into the underlying image. So, choose **Filter>Blur Gaussian Blur** and experiment until you get just the right amount of glow. For this example I used a Radius of 5 (see Figure 12.4).

Figure 12.3
The beginnings of a red glow.

Figure 12.4
Result of blurring a layer that is set to Dissolve.

This looks good; but the glow on the Frappuccino® bottle contains two colors, so we still have some work to do. So, create a new layer directly above your red glow and set its mode to Dissolve as well. We want this second color to appear only where the original red glow was, so I choose **Layer>Group with Previous**. (Grouping two layers forces the top layer of the group to show up only where the bottom layer contains information.) After you get all that put together, use the Lasso tool to select the bottom half of the red glow, choose **Select>Feather**, and use the same setting you used when you blurred the original glow. Then to fill the selected area, change your foreground color to green, and then press <Option-Delete (see Figure 12.5).

Figure 12.5
Filling the bottom of the glow with green.

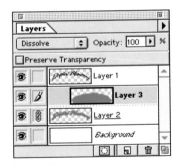

Figure 12.6
Link the glow layers and drag them to the new document.

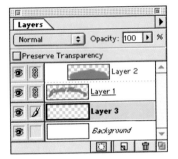

Figure 12.7
Create a new layer, then link the glow layers to it.

Figure 12.8
After choosing Merge Linked from the Layer menu, the glow will no longer use the Dissolve blending mode.

Chunkify the Glow

After doing all that, I decided the glow didn't look chunky enough; the pixels were just too darn small. I decided to try something a little different. So, if you're still along for the ride, we will need to create a new document that is the same size as the one you were working on. Choose **File>New** and then choose the name of your document from the Window menu (that enters the width, height, and resolution of the document). Next, you need to copy the two glow layers into that new document, so link the layers together and drag them to the second document with the Move tool (see Figure 12.6); hold down Shift to keep them in the same position.

Now we need to get the pixels to change size. To do this, we're going to scale the document down, mess with it, and then scale it back up again. First, choose **Image>Image Size**, make sure the Resample Image and Constrain Proportions checkboxes are checked, and set its menu to Bicubic (the default settings). Then change the Width pop-up menu to percent, use 50%, and click OK.

Now we want to lock in the pixels of the glow at their current size, which means that we don't want to use the Dissolve blending mode anymore. When you use Dissolve, you cannot vary the size of the pixels. So to keep the same look and lock in the size of the pixels, create a new layer and position it below the two layers that make up the glow (see Figure 12.7). Next, link the new layer to the two glow layers, then choose **Layer>Merge Linked**. This should cause the two glow layers to lose their blending mode setting (but keep the visual look), combine together, and appear on the new layer (see Figure 12.8).

Now we just need to enlarge the pixels into squares and get them back into the original document. So, choose **Image>Image Size** and again make sure Resample Image is turned on; but this time set its pop-up menu to Nearest Neighbor. Most people think of this mode as almost useless because it just turns pixels into big squares; but in this case, it will be a big help. Now, when we scaled down the image, we used 50%; so to get it back to its original dimensions, we'll have to use 200%.

To finish the effect, we'll need to get our modified glow back into the original document, so use the Move tool and drag the image back into the original document while presssing the Shift key. Now you will have two glows, so just throw away the two layers that made up the original glow and move the new glow so it is centered below the text (see Figure 12.9).

Figure 12.9
After replacing the original glow, you should have the finished effect.

Colorizing Line Art

My brother is an artist in New York City. He does sketches with a fine ink pen, and his pieces always have lots of very intricate and involved detail, the kind of detail that you have to do a double or triple take on before you realize what's going on in the image. He likes to experiment with colors before he starts turning these images into paintings or other types of finished art. So he scans in these black and white sketches and uses Photoshop to add color between all the black lines.

Well, you can do that very quickly in Photoshop as long as you know about the blending mode called Multiply (we've already used it once in Chapter 10, "Shadows"). Multiply is very similar to sandwiching two transparencies (slides) on top of each other while viewing them on top of a light table. For instance, if you had a slide that contained a black and white sketch and you laid it on top of another slide that contained solid colors, the black lines of the sketch would completely obstruct your view of the colors, and the white areas of the slide would virtually disappear, revealing the colors below. Using Multiply, you should be able to fill white areas in an image without having to worry about messing up the black lines of a sketch. All I'd do is set the Paint Bucket tool's blending mode to Multiply and use a medium Tolerance setting (so it can get into any grays that are on the edge of the sketch).

With each click of the Paint Bucket tool, you will be filling in another area of the sketch (see Figure 12.10). Then, after making your way across the entire image, you'll have a fully colorized image.

If you really want to see what Multiply does to an image, just open your favorite photo and create a new layer that is set to Multiply. Then use the Gradient tool set to Black, White and drag across the entire width of the document. You should notice that white areas don't change the image at all, and shades of gray darker than white, darken the image. You can also try placing two photographs, one on top of each other, and setting the top one to Multiply. See Figures 12.13 to 12.14.

Figure 12.10
You can quickly colorize a line art image using the Paint Bucket and the Multiply blending mode. (Courtesy of Nik Willmore)

Figure 12.11
Original image. (© 1998 Adobe Systems, Inc.)

Figure 12.12
Gradient set to Multiply.

Adding Density to Areas

Many of the images I'm asked to work with are less than ideal. Whenever the images don't originate from a professional photographer, I can always count on having to do a lot more color correction and making up for areas that are not properly exposed. But as long as there is still some detail in the under and over exposed areas, I can usually fix them. However, if I go the traditional route of adjusting the image with Curves, I often end up with a posterized image, such as the one in Figure 12.15.

But if you are crafty with blending modes, you can often perform miracles on these problematic images. There are two modes that will help you out, Multiply and Screen. I've already talked about Multiply in the chapter on Shadows and in the technique previous to this one; so before we start repairing images, let's talk about Screen. If Multiply is like sandwiching two 35mm slides together, then Screen is the exact opposite. You might be thinking, "What could possibly be the opposite of that?" Well, think of taking those 35mm slides and placing them in two slide projectors. Now point both of the slide projectors at one screen, and bingo, you have Screen mode. The main thing to get out of this is that Multiply can only darken areas, and Screen can only brighten them.

Figure 12.13
This image contains two layers. (© 1998 PhotoSpin)

Figure 12.14
The top layer of this document is set to Multiply.

Figure 12.15
Posterization due to an overaggressive Curves adjustment.

Try this simple experiment: Open an image that contains some overly bright areas, but make sure they still contain some detail. Now select the area that is overly bright, then choose **Layer>New>Via Copy** to duplicate that area onto a new layer. Next, set the blending mode of that layer to Multiply (see Figure 12.16). You should end up with an area that is about twice as dark as it used to be. If that is too dark, just lower the opacity of that layer.

This technique might sound nice, but it has a few problems. First of all, what if you find a defect in the original image and need to retouch it? If that's the case, you'd have to retouch both layers; otherwise, you'd still see a hint of the defect. Also, what if you have to increase the area that is affected by the layer? Well, you'd have to select another part of the original image, get it onto a new layer, merge that layer with the original duplicate, and so forth. Thank goodness there is a much more efficient method that also uses a whole lot less memory.

Figure 12.16
The man's outfit was darkened using Multiply.

Instead of copying the image into a new layer, select the area and then choose **Layer>New>Adjustment Layer**. Then choose any type of adjustment layer (I usually use

Curves), set the blending mode of the layer to Multiply and click the OK button. Once the Curves dialog box appears, just click the OK button without making any changes to the Curve.

This should give you the same result you achieved earlier, but the adjustment layer does not actually contain any image data. That makes the layer take up much less memory than if you had used the original technique. And if you retouch the original image, the darkening effect also changes. But that's not all you can do. You can also change the adjustment layer to fine tune the result. Just double-click the layer and adjust it using Curves.

This same technique can be used to fix areas that appear overly dark (but still contain detail). All you have to do is use the Screen blending mode instead of Multiply (see Figure 12.17).

Figure 12.17
The dark areas of this image were brightened using the Screen blending mode.

Each adjustment layer contains a layer mask, which determines which areas of the image will be affected by the adjustment. So, at any time, you can add or take away from the areas that are being adjusted by painting on the layer mask. If you don't feel comfortable using layer masks yet, be sure to refer to Chapter 11, "Image Blending."

Using One Image to Ghost Another

On occasion, I've needed to ghost (lighten) a photograph, using a second image to determine which areas will be lightened (see Figures 12.18 and 12.19). I usually use the Screen blending mode to accomplish this (see Figure 12.20). It works best when the underlying image is dark so it doesn't look too washed out. But when you use blending modes on color images, they sometimes produce unusual and unwanted results (especially in CMYK mode). This problem occurs because the modes act on the individual channels of the image independently. This means that the information in the red channel only affects the red channel of the underlying image, which can cause the colors of an image to shift in an undesirable way.

In order to get an effect that applies evenly to all the channels (and therefore does not shift the colors), you'll have to desaturate the image before using a blending mode. By desaturating the image, you are turning it into a grayscale image that contains only neutral grays. And, if you remember from Chapter 8, "Color Correction," you create a neutral gray by using equal amounts of red, green, and blue. By using equal amounts of red, green, and blue, you won't drastically shift the colors of the underlying image. So, now that we have that out of the way, let's figure out how to ghost an image based on the content of a second image.

Figure 12.18
Underlying image. (© 1998 PhotoSpin)

Figure 12.19
Active layer. (© 1998 PhotoSpin)

Figure 12.20
The topmost layer is using the Screen blending mode.

First, open the two images you would like to use. Next, combine the images into a single document by dragging between documents using the Move tool. Be sure to place the image you want to ghost below the image you want to ghost it with. Then, click on the top image and choose **Image>Adjust>Desaturate** to turn that layer into a grayscale image, as seen in Figure 12.21.

Next, set the blending modes of the top layer to Screen. This should lighten the underlying image, but will most likely look overly complicated because all of the detail in the top layer is being used.

In Screen mode, areas that are filled with black do not affect the underlying image (see Figure 12.22). That means you can simplify the image by adjusting it with Levels until the majority of the image becomes black and therefore disappears. So, choose **Image>Adjust>Levels** and move the upper left slider to force areas to black. You can also adjust the middle slider to brighten or darken the shades that remain (see Figure 12.23).

Figure 12.21
To convert an image to shades of gray, choose **Image>Adjust>Desaturate**.

Figure 12.22
Grayscale images will not shift the color of the underlying image.

If you really want to see what Screen does to an image, just open your favorite photo and create a new layer that is set to Screen. Now use the Gradient tool set to Black, White and drag across the entire width of the document. You should notice that black areas don't change the image at all, and shades of gray (brighter than black) brighten the image.

Figure 12.23
Adjust the image with Levels to fine tune the result.

Fixing the Emboss Filter

I have a love/hate relationship with the Emboss filter. I love what it can do, but I hate the grays it leaves behind. If you want to see what I mean, just create a new layer, choose a soft-edged brush and paint a few strokes across the image (use black paint). Now choose **Filter>Stylize>Emboss** and mess with the settings. Sure you'll get an embossed effect (highlight and shadow), but you probably didn't want the filter to replace your original image with gray, as shown in Figure 12.24!

There is a pretty easy fix for this problem, and guess what, it involves the blending modes (aren't they great). But before we get on to the fix, let's find out a little about the blending modes that will help us. Start out by opening any color photograph and creating a new layer. Next use the Gradient tool set to Black, White and drag across the full length of the image. Now, set that layer to Overlay and see what happens. Areas that are 50% gray simply don't show up, areas that are brighter than 50% gray brighten the underlying image, and areas that are darker than 50% will darken the image (see Figure 12.25). Hard Light is really a combination of the Multiply and Screen blending modes.

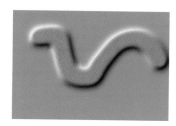

Figure 12.24
The Emboss filter always replaces the original image with 50% gray.

Figure 12.25
In Hard Light mode, 50% gray areas disappear. (© 1998 PhotoDisc)

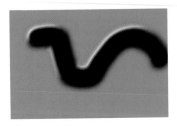

Figure 12.26
Hard Light can eliminate the 50% gray areas the Emboss filter always introduces.

Now, let's figure out how this can help us. First of all, the grays that I so hate are always 50% gray, and Hard Light mode makes areas that are 50% gray disappear, as seen in Figure 12.26! So, why not duplicate the layer you want to emboss, set the duplicate layer to Hard Light, and then apply the Emboss filter? Go ahead, try it!

That works great, but there is still one little problem. When you apply the Emboss filter to a color image, you don't just end up with grays; you often get some unwanted color remnants (see Figure 12.27). You can solve that by choosing **Image>Adjust>Desaturate** before applying the Emboss filter. That way the layer will contain only grays and you will avoid the color remnants (see Figure 12.28).

Figure 12.27
Embossing a color image always produces an unwanted color residue. (Original Image © 1998 Adobe Systems, Inc.)

Figure 12.28
Embossing a grayscale image prevents color residue.

Fixing the Lens Flare Filter

These are two filters that I have an interesting relationship with, lens flare and lightning effects. In real life, lens flares are created when the sun interacts with the optics in a lens and produces an annoying flare. Most photographers go out of their way to avoid them. But I guess if you work for the *National Enquirer* or the *Weekly World News*, you might want your image of an Elvis/Alien/Frog baby to look more realistic, so you slap a lens flare on top of it. So, I guess having the filter is okay, but what I don't like is that I'm forced to apply the filter directly to a single layer. That means I can't apply a lens flare and continue retouching the original image because if I do, I'll mess up the lens flare. Instead, try this out: Create a new layer, then choose **Filter>Render>Lens Flare**. Then, low and behold, you get the pesky "Could not complete the Lens Flare command because the selected area is empty" error.

Well, the only thing this filter is capable of doing is brightening or darkening the information in a layer. And since the layer you were working on was empty, you pretty much crippled the filter. But, Hard Light can come to the rescue! Just think about it. Hard Light ignores areas that are 50% gray, while areas that are brighter than 50% brighten the underlying image, and areas that are darker than 50% darken it. So, what if we created a new layer and filled it with 50% gray! Give it a try. Choose **Layer>New** and set the blending modes to Hard Light (see Figure 12.29). Did you notice the checkbox that showed up? By turning on that checkbox, Photoshop will automatically fill the layer with 50% gray! So, do it.

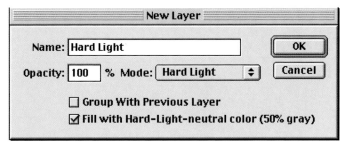

Figure 12.29
Turning on the checkbox at the bottom of the New Layer dialog box will fill the layer with 50% gray.

Because the layer is set to Hard Light and it is full of 50% gray, it shouldn't affect the underlying image at all. But, now try choosing **Filter>Render>Lens Flare**—it works! You've placed a lens flare on its own layer (see Figure 12.30). By the way, you can also use the same trick to apply the Lighting Effects filter on an empty layer.

But now there are still a few problems. First of all, when you applied the filter, did you notice that the preview image was just full of gray? That made it so you couldn't see where the flare would appear relative to the image. To fix that, just apply the filter directly to the image first, then choose **Edit>Undo** to remove it. Next, create your 50% gray layer and run the filter again; it will remember where you applied it the last time!

Figure 12.30
Lens Flare applied to a layer that contains 50% gray.

The other problem I have with this filter is that it's really hard to precisely position the lens flare; the preview is just too darned small. Well, that's easy to fix as well. Before you apply the filter, move your cursor over the exact area where you would like the center of the flare to appear. Then write down the X and Y numbers (measured in pixels) out of the lower left corner of the Info Palette, as shown in Figure 12.31. Now choose **Filter>Render>Lens Flare** and Option-click on the little crosshair that determines where the flare is positioned. A dialog box will appear, allowing you to type in the exact position of the flare, using the numbers you wrote down (see Figure 12.32).

Figure 12.31
Use the Info palette to record the exact position where the Lens Flare should appear. (© 1998 Adobe Systems, Inc.)

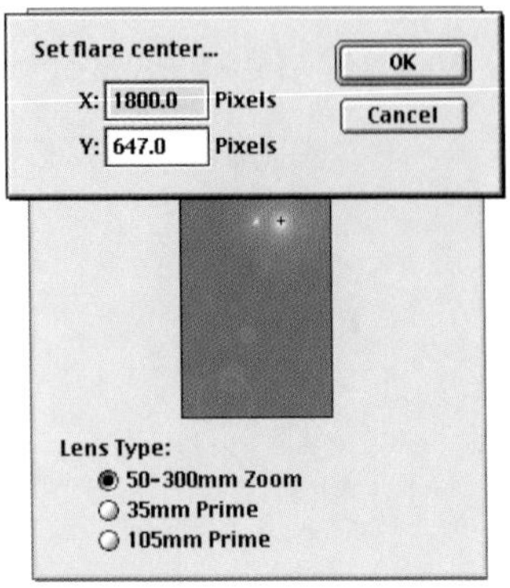

Figure 12.32
Option-click the crosshair to specify an exact position.

Adding Contrast to an Image

If you ever run across a really flat looking image such as the one in Figure 12.33, it can be next to impossible to pull out detail without causing posterization. Curves just doesn't seem to do the job, that is, unless you couple Curves and Overlay together! Why not create a new

Curves adjustment layer and set its blending modes to Hard Light (see Figure 12.34)? That will automatically give you more contrast. Then you can fine tune the result by tweaking the settings in the Curves dialog box. This is just like the technique I showed you earlier in this chapter where we added density to a washed-out image.

Figure 12.33
Low contrast original image. (© 1998 PhotoSpin)

Creating Reflections

Once upon a time, I was planning on building a house out here in Boulder, Colorado. I went as far as hiring an architect and getting some plans drawn up. My architect (hi, Tim, I know you are going to read this) even took hours (if not days) to create an incredible-looking wooden model. We thought it would be fun to scan a photo of the model and place it in a photograph of the land where it would be built. If you've ever attempted to do this, you'd know that it usually doesn't look very realistic, especially without reflections in the windows (compare Figures 12.35 and 12.36). But, as I learned with my house project, you can easily add your own reflections as long as you know about blending modes. The first thing you have to do is place the reflection image onto a layer above the object you would like to reflect it onto. Next, you'll want that reflection to be backwards. After all, when you look at text in a mirror, isn't it backwards? So, click on that layer, then choose **Edit>Transform>Flip Horizontal**.

Figure 12.34
Result of applying a Curves adjustment layer using the Hard Light blending mode.

Next, you will probably want to distort the image to match the perspective of the window, so choose **Edit>Transform> Distort**. Now you should be able to pull on the corners of the image to distort it to match the corners of the window you are reflecting it onto.

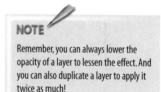

NOTE

Remember, you can always lower the opacity of a layer to lessen the effect. And you can also duplicate a layer to apply it twice as much!

When you get it looking just right, press Return to finalize the transformation. Now, to turn it into a reflection, change the blending modes of the reflection layer to Overlay, Soft Light, or Hard Light. One of those modes should do the trick. If you want to lessen the effect, just lower the opacity of the layer. If you need to intensify it, duplicate the layer.

Figure 12.35
Windows without reflections appear flat and lifeless. (Courtesy of Tim Bjella)

Figure 12.36
Reflections add more realism to architectural models.

You can use this same technique (minus the distortions) to apply textures to an image. But if you want to try that out, you should be reading Chapter 14, "Type and Effects Background," now shouldn't you?

I always think of Overlay, Soft Light, and Hard Light as a group. I've already described exactly what Hard Light does (back in the Emboss section of this chapter), so let's take a quick look at Soft Light and Overlay. They work like Hard Light, in that they ignore 50% gray; but Overlay is the exact opposite of Hard Light, and you can think of Soft Light as being somewhere in between the other two. So, if

Overlay is the opposite of Hard Light, that means that it looks at the underlying image and appears to brighten and darken the active layer. But that's not how I think of it when I'm actually applying these modes. When I'm using them, Hard Light always seems to make the *active* layer dominant, Overlay seems to make the *underlying* layer dominant, and Soft Light mixes them almost equally.

Better Blending

In Chapter 12, "Image Blending," we talked about image blending. Now you can refine your blending techniques by supplementing them with blending modes. I'm sure you have run into those occasions when you apply clouds, or create fake lightning, and the result doesn't look quite right (see Figure 12.37). Maybe the lightning you created looked perfect; but when you placed it on top of another photo, it appeared to be surrounded by a bunch of fog. This can happen because the lightning is not just brightening the underlying image, it might also be darkening it in certain areas. To prevent this, all you have to do is set the blending modes of the lightning layer to Screen (see Figure 12.38). That way it won't be able to darken the underlying image.

Or, let's say you wanted to blur the background of an image (see Figure 12.39). Most of the time I think the blur filters produce very unnatural-looking results. They make it look like you smeared a thick coat of petroleum jelly on the surface of a camera lens.

To improve the look of the Gaussian Blur filter, you can choose **Filter>Fade Gaussian Blur** after applying the filter. By lowering the opacity setting, you will be able to blend the blurry version of the image into the original and bring back some real detail (see Figures 12.40 and 12.41). I think this looks much more natural.

You can further enhance the result by changing the blending modes. Use Lighten if you want to brighten the photo, and Darken to darken it (see Figures 12.42 and 12.43). These modes aren't quite as simple as they sound though. Because a color image is made out of red, green, and blue channels, Photoshop applies these modes to the individual channels independently of each other. That

NOTE

If you are reading this chapter from start to finish, you've probably noticed that I've been pretty much going down the list of blending modes one at a time, in order. Well, now you might notice that I'm going to skip two modes, Color Dodge and Color Burn. I'm doing that because they are used extensively in the last two chapters of this book.

NOTE

If you would like the blurred area to slowly fade into the image, you can create a feathered selection using Quick Mask mode (see Chapter 9) before applying the Blur filter.

means the red channel of one layer will affect only the red channel of the underlying image, and the same goes for the green and blue channels. So, you can't always predict what your result will look like unless you are working in grayscale mode, where there is only one channel for Photoshop to work with.

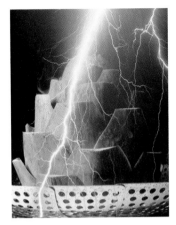

Figure 12.37
Lightning layer set to normal. (© 1998 PhotoDisc)

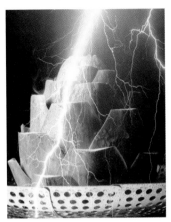

Figure 12.38
Setting a layer to Screen prevents it from darkening the underlying image.

Figure 12.39
The Gaussian Blur filter usually produces a very unnatural look.

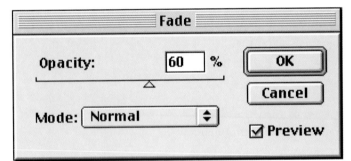

Figure 12.40
Choose **Filter>Fade Gaussian Blur** to blend the blurred image with the original sharp image.

Figure 12.41
Fading the Gaussian Blur filter produces a more natural-looking blur effect.

Figure 12.42
Fade using Lighten.

Figure 12.43
Fade using Darken.

NOTE

You can also refer to Chapter 6,
"Optimizing Grayscale Images," for more
uses of Lighten and Darken. There they are
used to get more control over the sharpening process.

Changing the Color of Objects

So you land a big project from a major toy manufacturer. Your mission: to produce their very expensive-looking annual report. You're feeling a little impish so you decide, why not make all the pie charts out of yo-yo's? After all, it is a toy company. But there is just one minor problem; you have no idea how to do it! Well, all you have to know about is, guess what, another blending mode.

To start the project, you create a new layer and make a wedge-shape selection. Now, hoping to change the color of the yo-yo, you fill the selection with blue (see Figure 12.44).

But the yo-yo is completely obstructed by the color. That's because Photoshop divides a color into three components, hue, saturation and brightness (also known as lightness or luminosity). Hue is the basic color (red, green, orange, purple, and so on), Saturation is how vibrant the color appears (intense red, or light pink), and Brightness is how bright or dark the color appears. First, you have to think about what you want to accomplish. Do you want to brighten or darken the yo-yo?—No. Do you want to change how vibrant the color is—No. Do you want to change the basic color of the yo-yo—Yes! That's it. All you have to do is change the blending mode of the layer to Hue (see Figure 12.45). That way Photoshop will ignore how saturated and how bright the color is and just change the basic color of the underlying image.

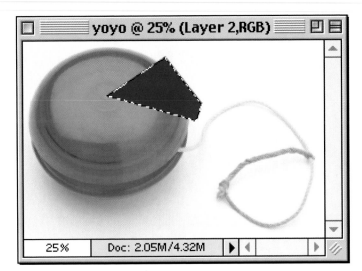

Figure 12.44
When a layer is set to Normal, Photoshop applies all three components of the color (Hue, Saturation, and Brightness). (© 1998 PhotoDisc)

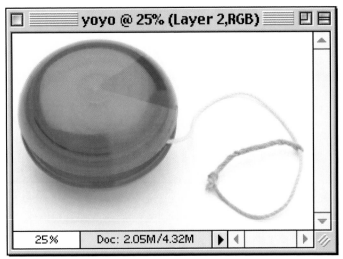

Figure 12.45
By setting the blending mode to Hue, only the basic color of the yo-yo is changed.

After you have finished adding colors to the yo-yo (see Figure 12.45), you decide you'd rather have a more interesting transition between the colors. So you decide to start playing with filters. Your first choice turns out to be great; it's **Filter>Distort>Ripple**. Now you've got your interesting edge (see Figure 12.46).

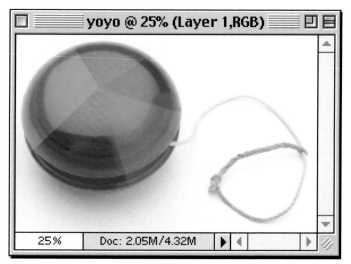

Figure 12.46
Result of applying multiple-colored wedges of color.

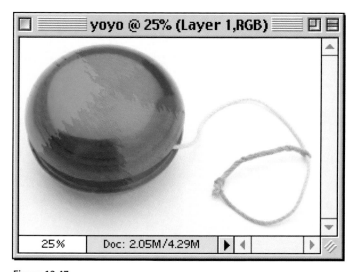

Figure 12.47
The edges of the color were modified by applying the Ripple filter.

But now you notice that the shadow under the yo-yo does-n't look right. For your first attempt to fix the shadow, you try to remove any color from above the shadow. So you use the Elliptical Marquee tool to select the basic shape of the yo-yo, then choose **Select>Inverse** to get the background. But after pressing Delete, you notice that the shadow appears to be red (see Figure 12.48). Remember-ing that the original yo-yo was red, you figured that every-thing was normal, but just not natural looking.

With the background still selected, you decide to remove any hint of color from the underlying image. To accomplish this, you click on the layer that contains the yo-yo and choose **Image>Adjust>Desaturate**, and bingo! You're done. See Figure 12.49.

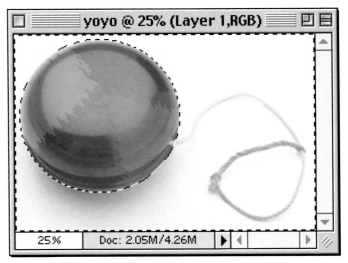

Figure 12.48
Deleting the excess color reveals the image's original reddish shadow.

Figure 12.49
After desaturating the shadow, the image looks more natural.

For your next chart you decide to change the color of half of the yo-yo. But you don't really want a crisp edge, so you decide to create a new layer and again set it to Hue. But instead of selecting an area, you decide to grab the Gradient tool and change its setting to Foreground to Transparent. Finally, you change your foreground color to blue and drag across the yo-yo—great job! See Figure 12.50. (You even get visions of next year's report—a yo-yo with a flame job! No problem, all you need is a fancy selection and the Gradient tool.)

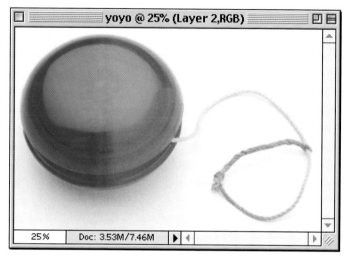

Figure 12.50
Result of applying the Gradient tool using the Foreground to Transparent setting.

Adding a Background

Now you're ready to finish the cover of the report, so you hire an artist to make a painterly background using brightly colored pastels (see Figure 12.51). But after a week on the assignment, you get back something that you are a little disappointed with. The colors are all wrong! The company color is blue, and there is hardly any blue in the whole image.

So you decide to roll up your sleeves and fix it yourself. You choose **Image>Adjust>Hue/Saturation** and start tweaking the Hue setting, knowing that Hue means basic color (see Figure 12.52). After a few minutes of tinkering, you end up with some nice blues, as shown in Figure 12.53.

Figure 12.51
The original image does not contain enough blue. (© 1998 PhotoSpin)

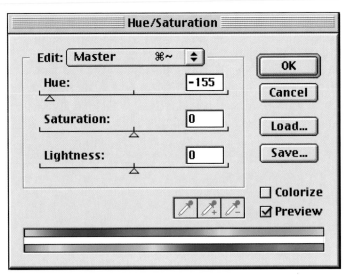

Figure 12.52
The Hue/Saturation dialog box allows you to change the Hue of all colors in a document.

Figure 12.53
Result of shifting the Hue to produce an overall blue theme.

But now you don't like a few of the other colors in the image. Maybe there is too much green, so once again you're off to the Hue/Saturation dialog box. But this time you must figure out all the intricacies of this fine tool, so you take a little crash course on the Hue/Saturation dialog box. First you discover that you can change the pop-up menu at the top of the dialog box to work on a preset range of colors (see Figure 12.54). At the bottom of the dialog box, you found two gradients. The top gradient represents the colors as they would appear before making an adjustment, and the bottom gradient shows you the result of your adjustment.

Since the choices under the pop-up menu are rather limited, you figured that you might want to customize them. When you do this, a bunch of controls show up between the gradients at the bottom of the dialog box. These controls determine exactly which colors will be changed. The colors above the dark gray bar indicate which colors you are changing. The light gray bars determine how much the changes will blend into the surrounding colors. You know that you can change these settings at any time and quickly review the options:

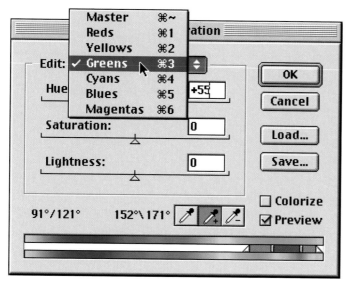

Figure 12.54
Choosing a color from the pop-up menu at the top of the Hue>Saturation dialog box allows you to adjust a narrow range of colors.

Drag the dark gray bar to move all the sliders as a group.

Drag one of the light gray bars to move the sliders that appear on both sides of it.

Drag the individual controls to move them independently.

Click on the main image window to center the dark gray bar on a specific color from the image.

Shift-click on the image to expand the dark gray bar to include more colors.

Command-drag the gradient to reposition the gradient and all the sliders at the same time.

After finishing your crash course on the controls in the Hue/Saturation dialog box, you find out that the client absolutely detests the color green, but loves blue. With a quick trip back to the dialog box, you choose Greens from the pop-up menu and then click on the particular shade that is present in your image. Then, to make sure you're going to get all the greens, you hold down the Shift key and drag across all the greens while you watch the controls at the bottom of the dialog box following your every command. Once you have isolated the greens, a simple move of the Hue slider changes all those greens to the client's favorite color, blue (see Figure 12.55).

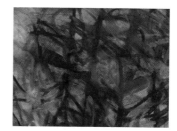

Figure 12.55
The greens have shifted to cyan.

Selective Black and White

Your next assignment is from a hat designer who brings you a nice image of one of their hats sitting on the beach. But your client is not happy. She thinks the hat does not stand out enough. So, you get the idea of making the background behind the hat grayscale; that way the hat will pop right out from it. Remembering back to how Photoshop deals with color (Hue, Saturation, and Brightness), you decide that you don't want to change the color of the beach (that's Hue), and you think the brightness looks just fine. So, what's left over? Saturation! So you set a new layer to Saturation and start to experiment, first painting with a really bright green color (see Figure 12.56).

But Photoshop seems to ignore the fact that you're painting with green; instead, it just changes the saturation of the sand to match the saturation of the color you're painting with. So you think about it for a moment. What color should I paint with to take away all the color from the underlying image? Why not a shade of gray? After all, grays don't contain a hint of color (see Figure 12.57).

Figure 12.56
Using the Saturation blending mode causes the underlying image to match the saturation of the color that is being applied. (© 1998 PhotoSpin)

Figure 12.57
Painting with a shade of gray will completely desaturate the image.

To quickly finish up the job, you decide to select the background, then type Option-Delete to fill the area with black (your Foreground color). But then you decide you want just a hint of color in the beach, so why not lower the opacity of the layer that contains the gray? Aaah...looks great (see Figures 12.57 and 12.58).

NOTE
You can also force an area to black and white by selecting an area and choosing **Image>Adjust>Desaturate**.

Figure 12.58
You can also select areas and fill them with gray.

Figure 12.59
Lowering the Opacity of the layer will allow some of the underlying color to show through.

You don't have to limit yourself to the technique that was just described. It will always change the saturation of an area to match the saturation of the color you are painting with. What if you just wanted to slightly increase the saturation of an object? Well, that's where the Sponge tool comes in. By painting across an area with this tool you can increase or decrease the saturation by large or small amounts. All you have to do is adjust the pressure setting.

Colorizing Grayscale Images

If you are going to colorize grayscale images in Photoshop, you're in luck. Photoshop is a godsend when it comes to colorizing and offers what might seem like an overabundance of colorizing features. Let's start off with a few blending modes, then we'll progress into more advanced methods. The first thing you'll have to do is change the mode of your grayscale image to RGB mode. Then, to colorize the image, you want to apply the Hue and Saturation of a color while leaving the brightness of the image unchanged (see Figure 12.60). Photoshop offers you a mode that does exactly that; it's called Color. So, give it a try, create a new layer, set the layer to Color and start painting away.

If you like the color you are using, but feel you're changing the image a little too much, then lower the opacity of the painting tool (see Figure 12.61). You can change the opacity of your painting tool using the number keys on your keyboard (0=100%, 1=1%, 3=30%, 48=48%, and so on).

If you create a new layer for each area of the photo that you are colorizing (flesh tone, hair, clothes, and the like), then you can quickly adjust those colors by clicking on the layer you want to change and choosing **Image>Adjust>Hue/Saturation**. In this dialog box, you can change the Hue to change the basic color, or mess with the Saturation to adjust the vibrancy of the color.

When you paint using the Color blending mode, you might find that in certain areas, the color just seems to sit on top of the image and does not look integrated or natural. In those cases, you should switch over to the Color Burn blending mode. It will push the color into the image much more aggressively than Color ever would (see Figure 12.62). Most of the time you'll need to lower the Opacity setting so Color Burn doesn't overdo it.

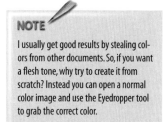

NOTE

I usually get good results by stealing colors from other documents. So, if you want a flesh tone, why try to create it from scratch? Instead you can open a normal color image and use the Eyedropper tool to grab the correct color.

Figure 12.60
Painting with the Color blending mode applies the Hue and Saturation without changing the brightness of the image. (Original image © 1998 PhotoDisc)

Figure 12.61
Left: 100% Opacity; Middle: 70% Opacity; Right: 30% Opacity.

Figure 12.62
Color Burn mode will more aggressively apply color to the image.

NOTE

Photoshop 5's default settings for the Colorize checkbox are different from older versions. In earlier versions the Saturation setting would be at an unreasonable 100%; but in Photoshop 5, Adobe changed the default to 25%, which is much more sensible.

Colorizing Selected Areas

You'll probably find that you don't always feel like painting to colorize an area, so I'll show you another method. You can select an area and then choose **Image>Adjust>Hue/Saturation** (or use an adjustment layer) and turn on the Colorize checkbox in the lower right to get things started (see Figure 12.63). Now you can change the Hue and Saturation settings until you get just the right color, as in Figure 12.64.

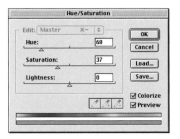

Figure 12.63
The Colorize checkbox allows you to apply color to a grayscale image.

Figure 12.64
Background colorized using the Hue/Saturation dialog box.

Two-Tone Colorizing

Now let's look at some more methods of colorizing that are a little more out of the ordinary. First create a new layer, fill it with the color you desire, and then set the blending modes of the layer to Difference. This will give you a two-tone effect (see Figure 12.65).

Another option is to convert a grayscale image directly to Indexed Color mode and then choose **Image>Mode>Color Table** to edit each shade of gray individually (see Figures 12.66 and 12.67). When you get to the Color Table dialog box, you have two methods for converting the grays to color: First, you can click on the individual shades one at a time and choose replacement colors. Second, you can drag across a range of shades to change them using a gradient between two colors.

Figure 12.65
The Difference blending mode will produce a two-tone effect.

After you drag across a range of grays, the Color Picker will open asking you for the first color to be used in the gradient. Immediately after you click the OK button, the Color Picker will open again asking you for the color to end the gradient with.

I use this technique whenever I'm presented with a grayscale logo that needs to be colorized or when I'm given scientific data (like weather maps or satellite images) that contains only shades of gray.

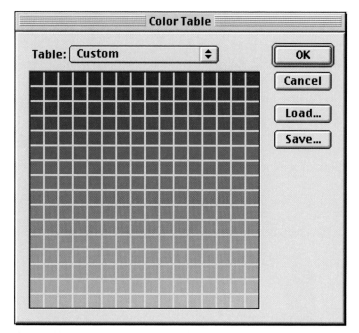

Figure 12.67
Result of applying the Color Table shown above.

Figure 12.66
Editing the Color Table of an Indexed Color image allows you to replace shades of gray with colors.

Using Lab Mode to Colorize

Now let's look at one more method of colorizing. This one will allow you to get a little more variation in your image without having to spend a lot of time painting. To get started, convert your image to Lab mode by choosing **Image>Mode>Lab Color**. Next, select one of the areas you would like to colorize and then choose **Edit>Copy**. Now open the Channels palette and click on the "a" channel if you would like that area to appear cyan or magenta, or click on the "b" channel for blue or yellow. Now, to get some color, choose **Edit>Paste** (see Figure 12.68).

If you don't like the color you've ended up with, you can choose **Image>Adjust>Levels** and change the Channel pop-up menu to the name of the channel you pasted the image into. Now you can adjust the top sliders to intensify the colors or change the overall look, or use the bottom sliders to lower the intensity of the colors (see Figures 12.69 and 12.70).

If you would like to use colors other than cyan, magenta, blue, and yellow, then you'll need to paste the image into both the "a" and "b" channels. Then, when adjusting the result with Levels, work on the "a" channel to shift the overall look towards cyan or magenta, and work on the "b" channel to shift it towards blue or yellow. I use this technique only when the others I've already mentioned don't give me the results I've been looking for; you can think of it as your last resort.

Figure 12.68
Result of pasting a portion of the image into the "a" channel. (© 1998 PhotoDisc)

Figure 12.69
Result of applying Levels to the "a" channel.

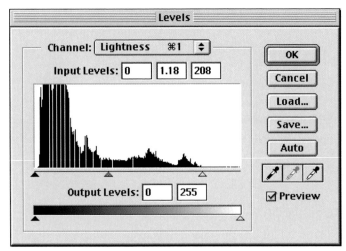

Figure 12.70
Use Levels to fine tune the colors.

Adjusting Brightness without Shifting Colors

Back in Chapter 7 we talked about brightening, darkening, and pulling out detail using the Curves dialog box. Although I really like using Curves, I run into a big problem when it comes to color images. Oftentimes, I'll just want to brighten up an image, but when I start to make the adjustment the colors also start to shift, as demonstrated in Figures 12.71 and 12.72. This happens because Curves makes adjustments to all the color channels (RGB) in equal amounts.

You can fix this problem pretty quickly. If you are working with an adjustment layer, just set the blending modes of that layer to Luminosity (see Figure 12.73). Or, if you applied Curves directly to the image, you can choose **Filter>Fade Curves** immediately after applying Curves.

There is one more time when I find Luminosity helpful, and that's when I'm performing color correction. Occasionally, I'll have an image that has perfect brightness, but the colors aren't so hot. When I adjust the colors, I seem to screw up the brightness. Well, I can fix that quickly by duplicating the layer and setting it to Luminosity, then adjusting the colors of the layer directly under it. That way I can adjust the colors to my heart's content and, no matter what I do, I can't screw up the brightness of the image.

Figure 12.71
Original image. (© 1998 PhotoSpin)

Figure 12.72
The colors of an image shift when applying a Curves adjustment.

Figure 12.73
Using the Luminosity blending mode will prevent adjustments from shifting the colors in an image.

Figure 12.74
Applying filters to a color image often adds unwanted color variations. (© 1998 PhotoDisc)

Figure 12.75
Blending the filter into the image using the Luminosity blending mode.

Adding Grain to an Image

Sometimes you get sick of normal crisp images and might want to create something different. I'll show you how to add noise to your images without changing the colors present in the image. If you attempt to do this by simply applying filters to the image, you'll find that the colors will shift (see Figure 12.74). But if you first duplicate the layer and set the duplicate to Luminosity, the colors will not be able to change (see Figure 12.75). Then you can experiment to your heart's content until you come up with a satisfactory result.

Special Filter Effects

Now we've made it through all the blending modes and are ready to move on to other nifty Photoshop features. To be honest, you can never really be "done" with blending modes. I learn something new about them almost every time I play with them. The more you use them, the more comfortable you'll get. So, keep playing and let me know when you come up with a new use for one of these modes. You can also find out what I've been doing with blending modes by checking out my Web site at **www.digi-talmastery.com**. Whenever someone gives me a new idea, or I've got a new technique, that's the first place it goes.

You'll find the blending modes menu in so many places in Photoshop it's often difficult to know which menu to use. An easy way of approaching this is to ask yourself if you want to affect *all* the underlying layers, or just the *active* layer? If the answer is all the layers, then you'll have to use the menu attached to a layer. If the answer is just the active layer, then you can grab the blending modes menu from anywhere in Photoshop.

Wrapping One Image Around Another

Let's say you've got a client who wants to have wood bent into the shape of someone's face. How much would you charge, and how long would it take? Well, if you knew how to use one of Photoshop's less-traveled filters, you could probably finish it up in about five minutes and charge the client as much as you'd like. The filter that will do the job is called Displace, and in order to use it you need to do some unusual things to your image. I find the results to be simply amazing. So let's give it a whirl.

To start out, I'm going to use a simple checkerboard image to show you what happens when you run the Displace filter; then I'll substitute some wood to get the effect we're looking for. The Displace filter is going to need some information to determine exactly how it should bend your image. What it really needs is a grayscale image where the dark areas will dictate where the image should be bent down and to the right, and bright areas will dictate where the image should be bent up and to the left. The good news is that you don't have to come up with a wild document to do this; a blurry grayscale version of your image will do just fine. So, choose **Image>Duplicate** to create an exact copy of your image (see Figure 12.76).

Now choose **Image>Mode>Grayscale** to discard all the color info, and flatten the image while you're at it. This filter does not seem to like crisp edges, so choose **Filter>Blur Gaussian Blur** and use a setting just high enough to soften the edges of any crispy areas (see Figure 12.77).

Figure 12.76
Original. (Courtesy of Albert Sanchez, Ani Difranco, and Righteous Babe Records)

Figure 12.77
Blurred grayscale version of the file to be used with the Displace filter. (Courtesy of Albert Sanchez (photographer), Ani Difranco, and Righteous Babe Records)

Next, you'll need to save this image in the Photoshop file format; so choose **File>Save As**, then close the grayscale image. Before you apply the filter, you'll want to place the image you would like to blend on top of the image you've been working on. The Displace filter gets messed up if your image contains any "Big Data," so choose **Select>All**, then choose **Image>Crop** to get rid of any part of the image that is extending beyond the boundaries of your document. Now you can choose **Filter>Distort>Displace**. The setting at the bottom of the dialog box doesn't apply to our image because the grayscale document you created was exactly the same size as the image you are currently using. The only settings that matter are the Horizontal and Vertical Scale settings. You'll have to experiment with these settings. They determine how much bending or wrapping will occur; the higher the resolution of your document, the higher the setting you'll have to use. I usually start with the default settings, then try another setting if the image doesn't look right. See Figures 12.78 and 12.79.

After you have bent your image, you can use a blending mode to apply it to the underlying image. Because the image I used was so basic, Multiply should do the job (see Figure 12.80). Now if you want the bent information to show up in certain areas only, you can either group it to the layer below or use a layer mask to hide areas.

Figure 12.78
Layer to be distorted.

Figure 12.79
Result of applying the Displace filter.

Figure 12.80
Checkerboard applied using the Multiply blending mode.

Once you know how to apply the filter, you are free to experiment with different images, settings, and blending modes (see Figures 12.81 and 12.82). Go have fun.

Figure 12.81
Original wood texture after applying the Displace filter. (© 1998 PhotoSpin)

Figure 12.82
This wood texture was applied using the Color Burn blending mode.

Converting Photos into Drawings

All right, so you want to change a photo into a drawing; let's find out how it's done. We're going to need to use a layer mask to accomplish this, but you can't add a layer mask to the background image. So, if you are working on the background image, give it a quick double-click and change its name. Now you need to get a grayscale version of your image into the layer mask. I'll give you an odd, but quick technique to do that. First press Option-Command-~7 to load a grayscale version of the image as if it were a channel. Now choose **Layer>Add Layer Mask> Reveal Selection**. You should see a grayscale version of your image sitting in the layer mask, and the main image should look pretty strange (see Figure 12.83).

To get just the edges to show up, choose **Filter>Stylize>Find Edges** and then choose **Image>Adjust>Invert** (see Figure 12.84). Now you should be looking at the edges of your image. If the rest of your screen is full of a checkerboard pattern, then you'll want to add another layer underneath this one by choosing **Layer>New>Background**.

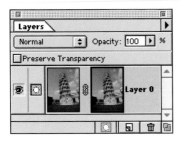

Figure 12.83
Start with a grayscale image pasted into a layer mask.

Figure 12.84
Use the Find Edges filter to eliminate all but the edges from the image. (Original image © 1998 PhotoSpin)

You can fine-tune the result by choosing **Image>Adjust>Levels** and playing with the top three sliders. Or, if you want to fill the lines with a solid color, click the image thumbnail (as opposed to the layer mask), change your foreground color, and then press Option-Delete to fill the layer.

Painting with Filters

By utilizing the History palette, you can turn any filter into a painting tool. The History palette is a new and very welcome addition to Photoshop. Just briefly, it keeps track of all the changes you make to your image, then with a simple click in the History palette you can get back to any previous version. It takes a lot of the worry out of your work in Photoshop and gives you more freedom to experiment. In this section, we're going to be using the palette in conjunction with filters, but first let's take a quick look at how it works (see Figure 12.85).

Here are the History palette features:

Every time you make a modification to a document, your steps show up in the History palette.

The steps are named after the tools and dialog boxes you use to modify your image.

Only document-specific changes are recorded; program-wide changes are ignored.

With default settings, the palette will store the last 20 steps you performed (can be increased to a maximum of 100 steps).

The steps in the History palette are not saved with your file.

To revert to a previous step, just click the name of the step.

If you change the image after clicking a step, all steps after that one will be deleted.

So, the History palette is really multiple undo's on steroids. To get back to a previous version of your image, all you have to do is click one of the steps listed in the palette. You can even increase the total number of steps stored in the palette (maximum=100) by choosing History Options from the side menu of the History palette (see

Figure 12.86). But if you perform more steps on your image than the setting you used for Maximum History *States*, Photoshop will start discarding the oldest steps to make room for the ones you are currently performing.

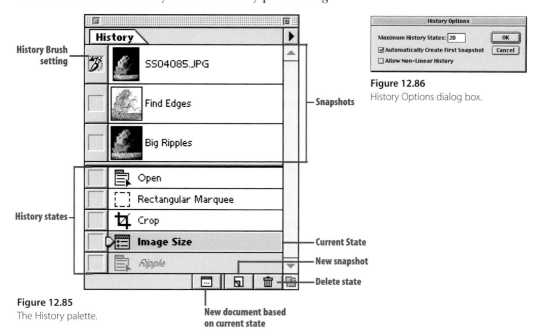

Figure 12.85
The History palette.

New document based on current state

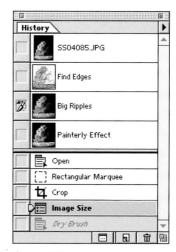

Figure 12.86
History Options dialog box.

Because the steps are named after the tools and dialog boxes you used to modify the image, it can sometimes be a little less than straightforward. If you really want to use this palette effectively, you can create snapshots of different document states. You can do this by choosing New Snapshot from the side menu of the palette or by clicking on the center icon in the palette (Option-click the icon to name the snapshot as you create it). Snapshots work just like the normal steps in the History palette; but they are stored at the top of the palette, have user-defined names, and display a preview thumbnail (see Figure 12.87). And unlike normal steps, they will not be removed when Photoshop runs out of space for steps (20 steps is the default).

When you create a Snapshot, the options you specify will determine what you'll be able to do when reverting to the snapshot. Entire Document will record the current state of all layers in the document and takes up the most

Figure 12.87
Snapshots appear at the top of the History palette.

memory. Current Layer will record only the state of the currently active layer and takes up a lot less memory than the Entire Document setting. Merged Layers will record the visual look of the document as if all the layers were merged together—this can be useful if you want to use the History Brush on a different layer than the one that originally contained the information.

The History Brush

The History palette by itself is a great addition to Photoshop, but it becomes even more useful when you couple it with the History Brush. The History Brush will allow you to paint across a layer and bring it back to what it looked like in any previous state. All you have to do is specify which step in the History palette the brush should use as its guide. You do this by clicking just to the left of the name of one of the steps in the palette. Then, any time you use the History brush, it will paint using information from that step.

I use this all the time to trick Photoshop into converting a filter into a painting tool. Try this out: Open a color image and apply any filter to it. Now to get back to the unmodified image, open the History palette and click the snapshot that appears at the top of the palette. This snapshot is automatically added and represents the original, unchanged document.

Figure 12.88
Using the History Brush to paint with a filter.

Now click just to the left of the bottom step in the History palette (it should be named after the filter you applied) to tell the History Brush which step to paint from. Then paint across your image. It should look like you're painting with a filter (see Figure 12.88). If you want to paint with multiple filters, you'll want to create a snapshot after applying each filter, then choose **Edit>Undo** to get back to the original image before applying the next filter. That way you can have a whole pile of filter effects sitting at the top of the History palette, and all you have to do is set the History Brush to the one you want to use.

I use this technique to add the Motion Blur filter to the edge of objects (it usually applies across the entire image), or to add distortion to text (remember to render the layer before you apply a filter).

Closing Thoughts

If someone were to actually publish all of the great enhancement techniques out there, you'd be wading through a book ten times the size of *War and Peace*. With this chapter, I tried to give you some nice, tasty samples that would inspire you to go forth and try some more on your own. I hope you enjoyed it. This part of Photoshop is always a pure pleasure for me—I could do this stuff every day. The more you work with Photoshop, the more you'll be able to add to your own personal cookbook of enhancement recipes. The trick is to find the time to play. I used to stay at work until rush-hour traffic died down just so I could have more time to play with Photoshop. When I went to college, there weren't any Photoshop classes; so I'm self taught thanks to a lot of midnight jam sessions with the tunes cranked up and Photoshop glowing on my computer screen. And look at me, I got to write this book!

> **NOTE**
>
> On the CD-ROM accompanying this book, you'll find a PDF file that supplements this chapter. The file, called extras.pdf, contains the following topics:
> Creating a slide show
> Punching holes in a layer
> Inverted photo foolery
> Intertwined text
> Blending for better grays
> Creating distorted features
> Utilizing other programs
> Clipping paths

Ask Adobe

Q: What the heck do you use the Exclusion Blending mode for? What is it good for? Can you give me an example?

A: It can be useful for some solarization-like effects. At one point in its development, it was actually called "Solarize," but that name didn't stick out of concern that it would cause confusion with the filter of the same name.

Q: How do the Color Dodge and Color Burn Blending modes relate to the Dodge and Burn tools?

A: They don't particularly have any relationship other than both lightening or both darkening.

Q: How'd you come up with the History palette? How does the History palette affect memory usage?

A: The History palette doesn't particularly affect memory usage. It affects scratch disk usage in proportion to the number of pixels changed. Hence, localized painting operations incur a small scratch disk hit. Running a filter on an entire image incurs a big hit. RAM is used as a cache for the scratch disk; that is, Photoshop will keep copies of the scratch disk data in RAM to avoid spending the time reading and writing the scratch files. So, obviously, with a bigger scratch disk file, you may want more RAM if you jump around a lot in History and don't want to wait for your disk drives. Another way in which the History palette may appear to increase RAM pressure is because of history scratch disk space, and hence RAM space cannot be recycled as rapidly as in previous versions (since the space is still in use). As a result, operations that ran entirely within RAM in previous versions may now start hitting the scratch disk to save older history out which would have gotten thrown away previously. If you pause much between operations, you shouldn't see much effect because Photoshop will update the scratch disk during idle periods.

Ben's Techno-Babble Decoder Ring

Blending Modes—A function in Photoshop that alters the behavior of a layer or tool, allowing it to interact with the underlying image.

Snapshot—A user-created record of the current state of a document (content and order of layers, adjustment settings, and so forth).

Scratch Disk—The virtual memory scheme used by Photoshop. This allows Photoshop to create an invisible file on your hard drive that is used as a substitute for actual physical memory (RAM). That way Photoshop can manipulate files larger than could be opened in RAM.

RAM—Random Access Memory. The physical memory chips that are installed in your computer. If your machine contains 64MB of memory, that is known as 64MB of RAM.

Keyboard Shortcuts

The following keyboard commands change the blending mode of the current tool (if it supports blending modes); otherwise, they will change the blending mode of the currently active layer.

Previous blending mode	Shift -
Next blending mode	Shift +
Normal	Shift-Option-N
Dissolve	Shift-Option-I
Behind	Shift-Option-Q
Clear	Shift-Option-R
Multiply	Shift-Option-M

Screen	Shift-Option-S
Overlay	Shift-Option-O
Soft Light	Shift-Option-F
Hard Light	Shift-Option-H
Color Dodge	Shift-Option-D
Color Burn	Shift-Option-B
Darken	Shift-Option-K
Lighten	Shift-Option-G
Difference	Shift-Option-E
Exclusion	Shift-Option-X
Hue	Shift-Option-U
Saturation	Shift-Option-T
Color	Shift-Option-C
Luminosity	Shift-Option-Y

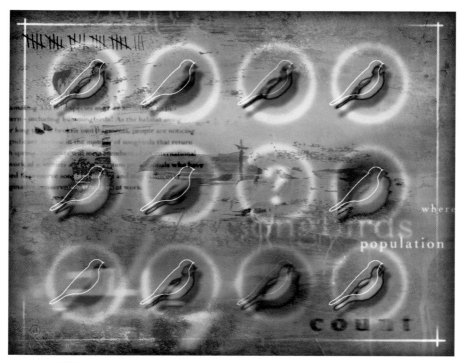

Courtesy of Alicia Buelow.

Courtesy of Russell Sparkman.

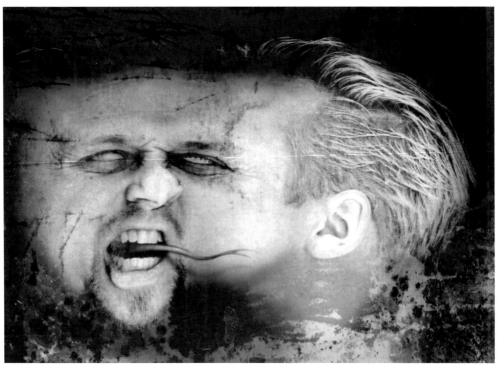

© 1998 Cliff Nielsen

© 1998 Cliff Nielsen for the "X-Files"

© 1998 Cliff Nielsen for the "X-Files"

13 Retouching

A doctor can bury his mistakes, but an architect can only advise his clients to plant vines.
—Frank Lloyd Wright

© 1997 Adam Woolfitt, adampix@dircon.co.uk.

The doctoring of photographs didn't begin with the advent of computers in magazine production departments. One of history's most notorious photograph "doctors" was Joseph Stalin, who used photo retouching as a way to control public perception and opinion. People who vanished in real life, whether banished to the farthest reaches of the Soviet Union or eliminated by the secret police, vanished from photos as well, and even paintings. In many cases, they were airbrushed out completely; in others their faces were clumsily blacked out with ink.

Then there were the Hollywood photo doctors. They didn't want to get rid of anyone; they just wanted to make them look better. I think they actually coined the term "too good to be true." Think about it—did you ever see a photograph of a starlet with a blemish, or a wart, or bags under her eyes, or even the slightest indication that her skin actually had pores? Of course not!

If you look at it from these two extremes, you can appreciate why the subject of retouching is something of a touchy subject. If you're brave enough to bring it up at a photographer's convention, you're likely to spark a pretty lively debate. A purist might tell you that every aspect of a photograph (including the flaws) is a perfect reflection of reality and should never be tampered with. Then again, a graphic artist, who makes a living from altering images, might tell you that an original photograph is just the *foundation* of an image, and that the so-called "tampering" is, in fact, a means of enhancing and improving upon it. Either way you look at it, you can't deny the fact that retouching photographs has become an everyday necessity for almost anyone who deals with graphic images. And when it comes to retouching, hands down, nothing does it better than Photoshop.

Photoshop packs an awesome arsenal of retouching tools. These include the Dodge and Burn tools, Blur and Sharpen tools, and the Rubber Stamp tool. We'll get to play with all of them, and for each one I'll also give you a little bag of tricks to play with. You'll learn how to do all sorts of neat things like retouching old ripped photos, getting rid of those shiny spots on foreheads, and adding highlights to hair. Or, you can put yourself in the doctor's seat and give someone instant plastic surgery. Remove a few wrinkles, perform an eye-lift, reduce those dark rings around the eyes, and poof!—you've taken off ten years. So, let's look at these tools one at a time, starting with what I consider to be the most important one.

Rubber Stamp Tool

The Rubber Stamp tool is also known as the clone tool because that's what it does. It copies from one area of your image and applies it somewhere else. Before applying the Rubber Stamp tool, there is one thing you should know. All retouching tools use the Brushes palette, shown in Figure 13.1. So you have to decide if you want what you're about to apply to fade into the image or to have a distinct edge. For most applications it helps to have a soft edge on your brush so you can't see the exact edge of where you've stopped.

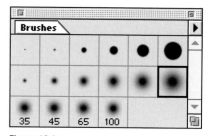

Figure 13.1
The brush you choose determines how much your retouching work will blend into the underlying image.

Cloning Around

After you've chosen your brush, you'll need to tell Photoshop exactly where you'd like to copy from. Do this by holding down the Option key and clicking the mouse button. Then move to a different part of the image and click and drag the mouse. When you do, you'll notice two cursors (see Figure 13.2). The first one will be in the shape of a crosshair; that shows you the source of Photoshop's cloning. Then when you apply the Rubber Stamp tool, there will be a second cursor, a circle showing you exactly where it's being applied (if the Caps Lock key is pressed, you may get a crosshair cursor). When you move your mouse around you'll notice both of the cursors moving in the same direction. As you drag, Photoshop is constantly copying from the crosshair and pasting it into the circle.

Figure 13.2
The Rubber Stamp tool copies from under the crosshair and pastes into the circle. (© 1998 PhotoDisc)

Figure 13.3
You can release the mouse button as many times as you want with the align checkbox turned on because the pieces of the cloned image will line up to create a continuous image. (© 1998 PhotoSpin)

Figure 13.4
When the Aligned checkbox is turned off, the Rubber Stamp tool resets itself to the original starting point each time you release the mouse button.

Clone-Aligned

The Rubber Stamp tool operates in two different modes; aligned and non-aligned. In aligned mode, when you apply the Rubber Stamp tool, it doesn't matter if you let go of the mouse button and click again. Each time you let go and click again, let go and click again, the pieces that you're applying line up (see Figure 13.3). It's as if you're putting together a puzzle, where once you have all of the pieces together, it looks like a complete image.

Clone-Non-Aligned

But if you turn off the Aligned checkbox, it's a different story. Then if you apply the tool and let go of the mouse button, the next time you click the mouse button it will reset itself, starting back at the original point from where it was cloning (see Figure 13.4). So if you click in the middle of someone's nose, go up to the forehead, click and drag, you'll be planting a nose in the middle of the forehead. Then if you let go, move over a little bit, and click again, you'll add a second nose. But that would happen only if you have the Aligned checkbox off. For most retouching, leave the checkbox on. That way you don't have to be careful with letting go of the mouse button.

Opacity Settings

Sometimes you don't want to completely cover something up; you may just want to lessen the impact (see Figure 13.5). To do that, lower the opacity on the Rubber Stamp tool (see Figure 13.6). You can also press the number keys on your keyboard; pressing the 1 key will give you 10%, the 2 key will give you 20%, and so on. To get it all the way up to 100%, just type 0 (zero). This will allow you to paint over an area and partially replace it, so that the area you're applying blends with what used to be in that area.

Straight Lines

Have you ever seen a carpenter "snap a chalk line" to get a straight line over an area? There are occasions in Photoshop when I've been grateful to know how to do something similar. Let's say you've got a few people walking on a sidewalk. You're going to remove the people because you only need the sidewalk. That means you're going to have to replace them with a new chunk of sidewalk. In order to look realistic, the new chunk of sidewalk will have to align perfectly with the rest of the sidewalk. When you get into this kind of situation, try this: Move your cursor until it's touching the original line (or sidewalk in my case). When it's perfectly touching it, you'll want to Option-click (see Figure 13.7). Then go to the area where you want the new piece of sidewalk to appear and click right where you think it would naturally line up with the other part of the sidewalk. Then when you drag, your two cursors will line up just right, making the line look continuous and straight, as in Figure 13.8. Other examples would be stairs, or a lightpost, or any object with straight lines that has been obstructed by another object.

Figure 13.5
Some features might be recognizable and therefore should not be completely removed.

Figure 13.6
By lowering the Opacity of the Rubber Stamp Tool, you can reduce the impact of undesirable features.

Figure 13.7
When retouching straight lines, Option-click when your cursor touches the line, then click in another area that also touches the line. (© 1998 PhotoSpin)

Figure 13.8
If the cursors align, straight lines will remain nice and straight.

Layers

If you are using layers in your document, the Rubber Stamp tool will work on one layer at a time unless you turn on the Use All Layers checkbox located in the Options palette. With this option turned on, Photoshop will act as if your document has no layers at all. In other words, it will be able to take from any layer that is below your cursor, as if they were all combined together.

However, it will only apply, or deposit, the information you are cloning onto the layer you are working on. That way, you can create a new empty layer, turn on the Use All Layers checkbox, and retouch your image (see Figure 13.9). Don't worry if you mess up because the information is sitting on its own layer, while the unretouched image is directly below it (see Figures 13.10 and 13.11). This allows you to switch over to the Eraser tool and erase small areas of that layer, or do other things such as lowering the opacity of the layer.

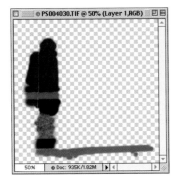

Figure 13.9
You can place your retouching on a new layer so it is isolated from the underlying image.

Figure 13.10
The underlying image will be untouched under the retouching layer.

Figure 13.11
When the layers are viewed at the same time, you can see the complete retouched image.

Patch Work

Sampling from one area and applying it all over the place will make it look pretty obvious that you've cloned something. You'll start seeing repeated shapes. For instance, if there happened to be a little dark area in the image you were cloning from, you will see that same dark area in the image you've applied it to. And, if you look at it close enough, you will see the shape repeat itself, which can start to look like a pattern. (You've just been busted cloning!) Sometimes, though, you might want to do this just to fill in an area, but then go back and fix up the places that appear patterned. You can do this by Option-clicking a random area around the place you've retouched, and then applying it on top of one of the patterned areas. This will cover up those areas that look as if they've obviously been cloned.

Let's see how this works in action. I'll show you how I reconstructed a forehead using the Rubber Stamp tool. Figure 13.12 displays a photo of a man's face. I copied one side of his face, and chose **Edit>Transform>Horizontal** to make it appear as a mirror image (see Figure 13.13). However, the top of his head was cut off in the photograph, so I decided to put in a new one (forehead, that is). The first thing I did was clone the area directly below the part of his forehead that was missing (see Figure 13.14). With the cloned forehead material, I filled in the missing part of his forehead, doing my best to make it as even as possible. After I applied several doses of forehead, it was obvious to me that I had cloned from one large area. So, I went in and touched up any repeated shapes to make it look more natural (see Figure 13.15).

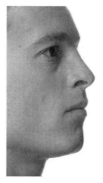

Figure 13.12
Original image. (© 1998 PhotoDisc)

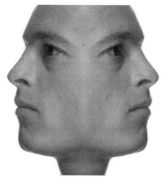

Figure 13.13
Two sides blended together, but missing a forehead.

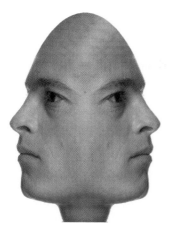

Figure 13.14
Generic cloning to reconstruct forehead.

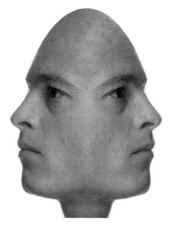

Figure 13.15
Repeated patterns retouched.

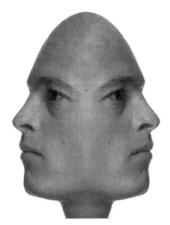

Figure 13.16
Highlight added to edge of forehead.

Figure 13.17
Original image.

Figure 13.18
Scratch retouched by using the Rubber Stamp tool set to Darken.

Now, however, if you look at the top of his head, there is a highlight on each edge that suddenly stops in the area I retouched. When I was filling up his forehead by clicking back and forth, I didn't get any of the highlights. So to add the highlight on the edge of his head, I grabbed from very small areas on other highlighted parts of his forehead and applied it right on the new edge (see Figure 13.16).

Lighten/Darken

When you are retouching small scratches or little imperfections in the image that are much brighter or much darker than the image that surrounds it, they can be easy to get rid of if you know a few little tricks. Let's say you have a background that has a scratch that is much brighter than the area around it. Naturally, you'll want to clone from the area around it; but before you do, you'll need to mess with the choices in the Options palette. The pop-up menu in the upper left of the palette is known as the blending mode (we talk about the different blending modes in Chapter 12, "Enhancement," but for now we'll just look at what we need for the Cloning tool). There will be a choice called Lighten, and one called Darken, both very useful when retouching. If you set that menu to Lighten, it will compare what you're about to apply to what the image looks like underneath. And, it will only allow you to lighten things. So let's say you had a light-colored scratch in the background of your image (see Figure 13.17). You could clone from an area directly around it, that is the correct brightness. But *before* you apply it on the scratch, you might want to set the blending mode to Darken (see Figure 13.18). (In Darken, all Photoshop can do is darken your picture. Under no circumstances will it be able to lighten it.)

The Blending Mode menu can also be useful when you have a background with little bitty dark specks in it (see Figure 13.19). To remove them, choose the Rubber Stamp tool and set the blending mode to Lighten (see Figure 13.20). Then clone from the areas around the specks and cover up the dark specks. This will allow the retouched areas to blend into the image more so you don't see a big gob where you retouched the image.

Figure 13.19
Image contains dark blotches in the background.

Figure 13.20
Blotches removed by using the Rubber Stamp tool set to Lighten.

Automatic Sharpening

The automatic sharpening built into some scanners makes retouching much more difficult. If possible, turn off any sharpening settings in your scanning software (see Figures 13.21 and 13.22).

Cloning Between Documents

With the Rubber Stamp tool, you're not limited to just cloning from what's in the active document. You can open a second image and clone from that image as well (see Figure 13.23). All you have to do is move your cursor outside the current image window and on top of another document that is open. Now you can Option-click anywhere in that second document and apply it within the document you are working on. It will copy from one document and paste it into another.

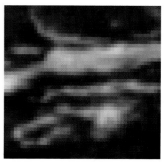

Figure 13.21
Unsharpened image.

The Dodge and Burn Tools

Now that we've had some fun with the Rubber Stamp tool, let's take a look at the Dodge and Burn tools. The words "Dodge" and "Burn" are taken from a photographic darkroom. In a darkroom, an enlarger projects an image onto a sheet of photographic paper. While the image is being projected, you could put something in the way of the light source, which would obstruct the light in such a way that it would hit certain areas more than others, otherwise known as dodging the light. Or you could

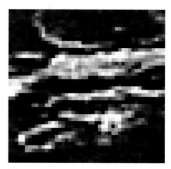

Figure 13.22
Image sharpened during scan.

WARNING

In order to clone between two documents, both documents need to be in the same color mode. If one of the documents is in RGB and the other is in CMYK, Photoshop won't allow you to do this.

intensify the light by cupping your hands together, creating just a small hole in between them, and allowing the light to concentrate on a certain area more than others, otherwise known as burning. Using a combination of these two methods, you can brighten or darken your image. Photoshop reproduces these techniques with two tools: Dodge and Burn. If you look at the icons for these tools, you'll see that one of them looks like a hand; that would be for burning, allowing the light to go through the opening of your hand. The other one looks like (at least I think it looks like) a popsicle, which you can use for obstructing, or dodging, the light.

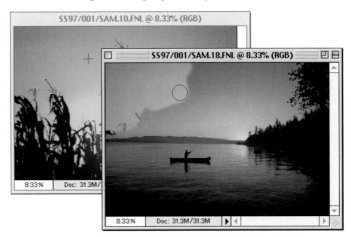

Figure 13.23
Cloning between two documents. (© 1998 Adobe Systems, Inc.)

The Dodge Tool

Now let's take a closer look at the Dodge tool. The Dodge tool comes in handy when you are working on people with dark shadows under their eyes because it can lighten your image. But before we get into that, there is a very important pop-up menu that is associated with this tool, which you can find in the upper left corner of the Options palette (see Figure 13.24). The pop-up menu has three choices: Shadows, Midtones, and Highlights. This menu tells Photoshop which shades of gray it should change when you pan across your image.

If you use the Shadows setting, you will change mainly the dark part of your image (see Figure 13.25). As you paint

NOTE

The spacing setting of your brush will also affect how much the image is changed when using the Dodge and Burn tools. Higher spacing settings will affect the image less.

across your image, your brush will brighten the areas it touches. But as you get into the midtones of the image, it will apply it less and less. And if you paint over the light parts of the image, it won't change them much, if at all. The second choice is Midtones. If you use this setting, you will affect mainly the middle shades of gray in your image, or those areas that are about 25%–75% gray (see Figure 13.25). It shouldn't change the shadows or highlights very much. They may change a little bit, but only so they can blend into those areas. The third choice is Highlights. Highlights will mainly affect the lightest parts of your image and slowly blend into the middle tones of your image (see Figure 13.25).

So you'll need to decide exactly which setting would work best for your situation. If you don't make this decision before using the Dodge tool, you might cause yourself some grief. You might be trying to fix dark areas around someone's eyes, for example, but the Dodge tool doesn't seem to be doing the job (see Figure 13.26). Then, after dozens of tries, you finally realize that the pop-up menu is set to Highlights instead of Midtones (look at the eyes in Figures 13.27 and 13.28).

You also have an exposure setting that controls how much brighter the image will become. And as with most Photoshop tools, you can use the number keys on your keyboard to change this setting.

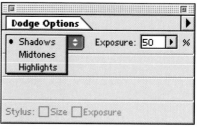

Figure 13.24
Dodge tool Options palette.

Figure 13.25
Top: Shadows, Middle: Midtones, Bottom: Highlights

Figure 13.26
Original image. (© 1998 PhotoDisc)

Figure 13.27
Dodge tool set to Highlights.

Figure 13.28
Dodge tool set to Midtones.

Color Images

The Dodge tool works exceptionally well on grayscale images. All you have to do is choose which part of the image you want to work on—Shadows, Midtones, or Highlights—and paint across an area. Unfortunately, it's not as slick with color images. If you use the Dodge tool on color, you'll find that it tends to wash out some of the colors and in some cases even change them (see Figures 13.29 and 13.30).

So, for color I would forgo the Dodge tool and just use the Paintbrush tool. You can set your Paintbrush tool's blending mode to Color Dodge and choose white to paint with (see Figure 13.31). Go ahead and try painting across an image. It should look rather ridiculous because all it's doing is blowing out the detail.

To get it to work correctly, just lower the opacity setting on the tool to about 20% (see Figure 13.32). This will allow you to create highlights or to brighten up areas. Sometimes this works a little bit better than the Dodge tool. So, you have two choices; either use the Dodge tool itself, or use a normal painting tool set to Color Dodge.

Figure 13.29
Original image. (© 1998 PhotoDisc)

Figure 13.30
Eyes lightened by using the Dodge tool.

Figure 13.31
Painting with white by using the Color Dodge mode.

Figure 13.32
Eyes lightened by painting with white by using the Color Dodge blending mode and a low Opacity setting.

The Burn Tool

The Burn tool is designed for darkening areas of an image. And just like the Dodge tool, it has the same options in its palette (Highlights, Midtones, Shadows) and an exposure setting. It too works great with grayscale images. So if you are ever dealing with a shiny spot on someone's forehead or nose because the light is reflecting off of it, you can go ahead and try to fix it with the Burn tool (compare Figures 13.33 and 13.34).

Color Fixes

Just like the Dodge tool, you'll start having problems when you use the tool with a color image. Flesh tones are the worst, they just seem to look sunburned or turn black (see Figures 13.35 and 13.36).

Figure 13.33
Original image. (© 1998 PhotoDisc)

Figure 13.34
Forehead darkened by using the Burn tool.

Figure 13.35
Face darkened by using the Burn tool set to Midtones.

Figure 13.36
Face darkened by using the Burn tool set to Highlights.

Let's say you're in CMYK mode. When you use the Burn tool, it's going to darken all of the different channels in your image (see Figure 13.37). Remember, a CMYK image is made out of cyan, magenta, yellow, and black. Think about a face. Do you want very much black on somebody's face? Probably not. Do you want very much cyan? Maybe only a tiny bit. For the most part, faces are mainly made up of magenta and yellow. (Black, Asian, and Hispanic people might need a wee bit extra Cyan; it makes the skin look tan.) By using this tool, if you try to get rid of a bright spot on somebody's forehead and you're in CMYK mode, it's just going to make that forehead get darker and darker and, of course, look terrible. To overcome this, start out by setting the pop-up menu in the Options palette to Highlights because you want to work on the light part of the image. Then you'll want to isolate just the magenta and yellow channels by opening the Channels palette and clicking the magenta channel, then Shift-clicking on the yellow channel (see Figures 13.38 and 13.39).

Now, there's one more thing you need to do for the sake of convenience. If you look at the main image window, it will appear as if your entire image is made from just magenta and yellow. That makes it a little difficult to work with. Ideally, you could view the image in full color, but still only work on magenta and yellow. To do this, turn on the eyeball on the topmost channel, which is the Composite channel (see Figure 13.40). That will make it so you see all four channels of the image, but you're still editing magenta and yellow only.

Figure 13.37
Burning all the color channels.

Figure 13.38
Magenta and Yellow channels visible.

Figure 13.39
Editing the Magenta and Yellow channels.

Now you can go in and try to get rid of those bright spots on foreheads and noses (see Figure 13.41). This should work quite nicely. If you are working in RGB mode, you can accomplish the same thing. You just want to work on the green and blue channels.

One Last Step

Okay, you've retouched your image; now you have one very important bit of housekeeping to take care of. Remember when you clicked on the specific channels to isolate the colors? Well, if you leave the Channels palette as is, everything you do from now on will affect only those two channels. To remedy this, click the topmost channel in the Channels palette so that all the channels are highlighted and all the channels are visible for editing, as shown in Figure 13.42. Now you're ready to go.

The Sharpen and Blur Tools

When you need to blur or sharpen an area, you have two choices: Select an area and apply a filter, or use the Blur and Sharpen tools. Using filters to blur and sharpen your image has a few advantages over using the tools. These include getting a preview of the image before you commit to the settings being used, and having the ability to apply the filter effect evenly to the area you are changing. But, occasionally, the Blur and Sharpen tools can really help when working on small areas; so let's take a look at how they work and when to use them.

The Blur Tool

The Blur tool is pretty straightforward. You can paint across any part of your image and blur everything that your cursor passes over. In the Blur tool options palette, you will find a pressure setting that determines how much you will blur the image; higher settings blur the image more. This can be useful if there are little, itty bitty areas of detail obstructing your image. I prefer to use the Gaussian Blur filter instead of this Blur tool because it does a better job of evenly blurring an area.

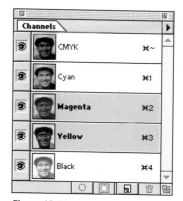

Figure 13.40
Editing the Magenta and Yellow channels while viewing all the color channels.

Figure 13.41
Eyes darkened by using the Burn tool on the Magenta and Yellow channels.

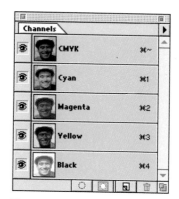

Figure 13.42
When finished, be sure to click the topmost channel to make all channels active for editing.

I like to use the Blur tool instead for reducing, not removing, wrinkles (see Figure 13.43). If you take the tool and turn the pressure way up and paint across a wrinkle a few times, you'll see it begin to disappear. But you'll also notice that it doesn't look very realistic. It might look as if you had smeared some Vaseline on the face. To really do a wrinkle justice, you have to take a closer look. Wrinkles are made out of two parts, a highlight and a shadow (light part and dark part). If you paint across that with the Blur tool, the darker part of the wrinkle will be lightened, while the lightest part will be darkened, so that they become more similar in shade (see Figure 13.44).

To reduce the impact of a wrinkle without completely getting rid of it (if I wanted to get rid of it, I would use the Rubber Stamp tool), turn the pressure setting all the way up. Then change the blending mode menu to either Darken or Lighten. If the part that makes that wrinkle most prominent is the dark area, then you want to set the blending mode menu to Lighten (see Figure 13.45). Then when you paint across the area, the only thing it will be able to do is lighten that wrinkle. But because you are using the Blur tool, it's not going to completely lighten it and make it disappear. Instead, it will reduce the impact of it. You really have to try this to see how it looks.

WARNING

Don't go over the image once with it set to Lighten and then switch it over to Darken and go over it again. That would be the same as leaving it set to normal, and you would have Vaseline face all over again. So use it just once, with it set to either Lighten or Darken. You just think about what is most prominent in a wrinkle. Is it the light area of the wrinkle, or the dark area? That will indicate which setting you should use.

Figure 13.43
Original image. (© 1998 PhotoSpin)

Figure 13.44
Forehead wrinkles blurred.

Figure 13.45
Forehead wrinkles lessened by using the Blur tool with a blending mode of Lighten.

Layers

When I'm retouching wrinkles, I usually create a brand-new, empty layer (see Figure 13.46). Then, in order to be able to use the Blur tool, I have to turn on the Use All Layers checkbox in the Options palette (see Figure 13.47). Otherwise, Photoshop can look at only one layer at a time, and it won't have any information to blur. By creating a brand new empty layer, turning on the Use All Layers checkbox, and blurring the image on that empty layer, I can easily delete areas or redo them without having to worry about permanently changing the original image.

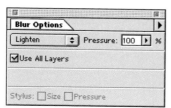

Figure 13.46
By creating a new layer before using the Blur tool, you can isolate the unretouched image.

Figure 13.47
The Blur tool will not be able to use information on other layers without turning on the Use All Layers checkbox.

The Sharpen Tool

The Sharpen tool works in a fashion similar to the Sharpen filter. But with the tool you have to adjust the pressure setting in the Options palette to determine how much you want to sharpen the image. With this tool, you have to be careful. If you turn the pressure setting up too high or paint across an area too many times, you're going to get some really weird effects (see Figures 13.48 to 13.50).

Figure 13.48
Original image. (© 1998 PhotoDisc)

Figure 13.49
Sharpened using the Sharpen Tool with a medium Pressure setting.

Figure 13.50
Sharpened using the Sharpen Tool with a high Pressure setting.

Reflected Highlights

When you run across an image that contains glass, metal, or other shiny objects, it usually contains extremely bright highlights. This usually happens when light reflects off one of those very shiny areas, such as the edge of a glass. These extra bright highlights often look rather flat and lifeless after being adjusted. This happens because whenever we adjust an image to perform color correction, or prepare it for printing or multimedia, the brightest areas of the image usually become 3% or 4% gray (instead of white). But if you sharpen those areas, you're going to brighten them up and make them pure white. This will make them jump off the page and look more like they do in real life. So this means any time you have jewelry, glassware, or reflected light in people's eyes, you'll want to use the Sharpen tool and bring down the pressure to about 30%, and go over those areas once. That will make them so that they are almost pure white; and when you print them, they will almost jump off of the page, as they should (see Figures 13.51 and 13.52).

Figure 13.51
Original image. (© 1998 PhotoSpin)

Figure 13.52
Metallic highlights sharpened.

Closing Thoughts

Okay, we've covered all the tools you'll need to become a bonafide "Photo Doctor." Bear in mind that you don't need to limit yourself to just photographs; the tools and techniques we covered in this chapter can be used for non-photographic images as well. And, as with everything else in Photoshop, once you've gone around the block with these tools a few times, you'll probably think of a dozen other things you can do with them.

So, whether you're giving someone a facelift, removing your ex-boy/girlfriend from a photograph, or clear cutting telephone poles from an otherwise perfect Kodak moment, just promise me that you won't do anything underhanded for some ethically challenged, third-world dictator.

Ask Adobe

Q: Why does the Spacing setting of my brush change how the retouching tools affect my image? Lower spacing settings seem to produce a more pronounced change.

A: Lower spacing values mean that the tools are applied more densely, which results in a stronger effect.

Q: Why don't the Dodge and Burn tools work well on color images? When I burn someone's forehead, it turns either bright red or dark black, depending on which choice I'm using (highlights, midtones, shadows).

A: The tools are adjusting the values in each channel independently. This changes the saturation and can cause some hue shifting.

Ben's Techno-Babble Decoder Ring

Specular Highlight—An area that shines light directly into the camera lens, usually caused by a light source reflecting off the reflective surface of glass, metal, or other shiny objects. Specular Highlights do not contain any detail and should be reproduced as solid white to maintain realism.

Keyboard Shortcuts

Next Brush	]
Previous Brush	[
First Brush	Shift-[
Last Brush	Shift-]
Tool Opacity	0 through 9
Dodge Tool	O
Cycle Toning Tools	Shift-O
Use Shadows	Option-Shift-W
Use Midtones	Option-Shift-V
Use Highlights	Option- Shift-Z

Courtesy of Derek Brigham, www.visi.com/~dbrigham/noctago.home.html.

14 Type and Background Effects

What everybody in this car needs is some good ol' worthwhile visceral experience. -Mike in "Dazed and Confused"

Courtesy of Derek Brigham, www.visi.com/~dbrigham/noctago.home.html.

Typography has taken some titanic-sized strides since the days when newspaper printers used hand-carved wood blocks to print their headlines. The old dependables like Helvetica and Times have been left gasping in the dust, while the young daredevils of typography break all the rules in their rush to create the ultimate, wild type effect.

But let's not forget, type fads are just like fashion. They've got short fuses and are completely at the mercy of a fickle public. Twenty years ago if you designed a headline that looked like it was made from scratched and eroded type, you might get an award. Today you're lucky if anyone even notices. Let's face it, we're jaded. Pick up any newspaper or magazine and you'll see a staggering profusion of type effects. That means you've got a tough job; you've got to come up with a type style that not only grabs the reader, but also does the best possible job of enhancing your message and organizing its content. And if you're using a background, you want to make sure that you've got one that perfectly complements your text. I can't help you with your design, but I can help you master the tools you'll need to create some awesome type and background effects.

But before we set sail on our typographical adventure, a word of caution: Throw caution to the wind. No matter how many type effects you see out there, there are still a million more yet to be imagined. With text, there are no boundaries.

The New & Improved Type Tool

Given Photoshop's past limitations with text, the new Type tool is nothing short of amazing. The previous version was so limited that there were very few circumstances under which I would recommend using it. Instead, I would tell people to produce text in Adobe Illustrator (where you'd have much more control over your text), and then copy and paste it into Photoshop. But thanks to Photoshop 5, you now have almost the same degree of control and ease of editing that you would if you were using Illustrator.

But (but!) even though the new version is light years ahead of its predecessor, Photoshop still creates text characters in the same way it did in the past—out of pixels. These pixels have a certain size. And if the pixels are too large, the text will appear jagged when it is printed. Remember, the resolution of a document determines how large the pixels will appear when they are printed (see Figures 14.1 to 14.3).

Figure 14.1
30 Pixels Per Inch (ppi).

On the other hand, text created in illustration and page layout programs are not made out of pixels, they are created from *objects*. As objects, they can be printed without jaggies on almost all printers (see Figure 14.4).

So, even though the Type tools have become much more user friendly and productive, I would still create text in Photoshop only if I was not able to create the desired effect in other programs (such as 3D chrome or liquid type), or if I were going to use it for on-screen display (such as multimedia, video, or the Web). If I just wanted some solid text on top of a photo, I would save the Photoshop image as a TIFF or EPS file, load it into my page layout program, and add the text in that program.

Figure 14.2
100 Pixels Per Inch (ppi).

With version 5 of Photoshop, Adobe has completely rethought the way text is created and manipulated in Photoshop. With the newly designed tools, you can mix multiple typefaces, fine tune tracking, kerning, leading, and baseline shift almost like a page layout application. And best of all, you can now do it with special type layers that retain their formatting characteristics and can be edited at any time. So, let's jump in and take a look at the new, improved text support in Photoshop 5.

Figure 14.3
300 Pixels Per Inch (ppi).

Entering Text

To add text to your document, choose the Type tool (the one that looks like a solid "T") and click anywhere on the image. Photoshop will present you with the text entry dialog box, as shown in Figure 14.5. The bottom of this dialog box is where you can enter and edit the text you want to add to your image. If you enter a long passage of text, unfortunately, Photoshop will not automatically break in into multiple lines. Instead, you have to act as if you are using an old-style typewriter and hit the return key to

Figure 14.4
Text in Illustrator is resolution independent—it will always appear as smooth as possible when printed on a Postscript printer.

NOTE

Photoshop offers you two text tools, vertical and horizontal; but you don't have to limit yourself to text at 90° increments. After you have created a type layer, you can choose Edit>Transform>Numeric to rotate your text to any angle. No matter which angle you choose, the text will still be fully editable. In fact, you can even choose Edit>Transform>Skew without losing the editable quality of the text.

force information to the next line. But with the new version of the Type tool, you actually get an on-screen preview of your text in the main image window, which makes it much easier to work with than it was with previous versions.

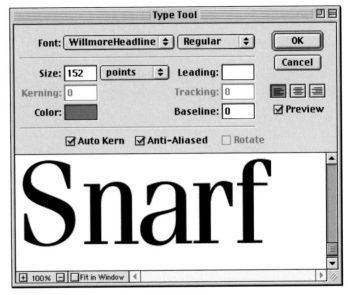

Figure 14.5
Text Entry dialog box.

Editing Text

The top of the type dialog box offers a wide range of choices for editing text. But, before you start messing with these settings, you'll need to highlight the text you would like to edit. You can do this by dragging across a range of text, or typing Command-A to select all the text.

Size—There are two ways to measure how large the text will become, in pixels or in points. The pixels option is resolution dependent, meaning that the height of the text in pixels will depend on the resolution of your image. More often than not, I prefer to measure text in points because I can use the same setting in multiple documents and know that the text will appear the same size when printed regardless of the resolution of the file it is used in. The only time I use the pixels option is when I need to match the height of some existing text that I have measured in pixels. To be honest, it isn't very often that I pay attention to the actual size settings; instead, I glance at the document to see how large the text is compared to the rest of my document. To quickly adjust the size of the text in increments of two, highlight the text and type **Shift-Command->** or **Shift-Command-<**. To change the size in increments of ten, just add the Option key to these keyboard commands.

Kerning—If you need to tighten up or loosen the space between two letters, click between the letters, then turn off the Auto Kern checkbox. Now you can change the Kerning setting to increase or decrease the amount of space between those letters (see Figures 14.6 and 14.7). To quickly change the Kerning setting in increments of 20, type **Option-Right Arrow** and **Option-Left Arrow**. You can also add the Command key to these keyboard commands to increase the kerning setting in increments of 100.

DAVE DAVE

Figure 14.6
Text entered with Auto Kern turned on.

Figure 14.7
Manually kerned text.

Color—To change the color of the text, click on the color swatch to bring up the standard Color Picker. This setting controls the color of all the text in the dialog box so you don't have to highlight a range of text before changing the setting. If you want a letter or word to have a different color, you'd have to create a separate Type layer. Each Type layer can contain only one color; so for every color you want to use, you'd have to create another Type layer.

Leading—To change the vertical space between lines of text, you'll need to change the Leading setting. If you leave this setting empty, Photoshop will automatically calculate its own setting and keep it hidden from you (see Figure 14.8). It does this by multiplying the size of the text by 120%; so, 100pt text, for example, would have an automatic leading setting of 120. If you don't like the auto setting (leaving it blank), you can type in your own setting (see Figure 14.9). To quickly change the leading in increments of two, highlight the text, then type **Option-Up Arrow** or **Option-Down Arrow**.

Graphic Savage

Figure 14.8
Leading setting determined by Photoshop (left blank).

Graphic Savage

Figure 14.9
Leading setting adjusted manually.

Figure 14.10
Tracking: 0.

Figure 14.11
Tracking: 260.

$$E=MC_2$$

Figure 14.12
No Baseline shift.

$$E=MC^2$$

Figure 14.13
Equal sign and small 2 baseline shifted.

Tracking—To add or remove space between all the letters in a range of text, highlight the text, then change the tracking setting (compare Figures 14.10 and 14.11). Or type **Option->** or **Option-<** to change the Tracking in increments of 20. To change the Tracking setting in increments of 100, just add the Command key to these keyboard commands.

Baseline—To shift one or more letters up or down, highlight the letters, then change the Baseline settings (see Figures 14.12 and Figure 14.13). To change this setting in increments of two, type **Shift-Option-Up Arrow** or **Shift-Option-Down Arrow**.

Anti-Aliased—This checkbox will cause the pixels on the edge of the text to blend into the image and create a non-jagged edge. I usually leave this option turned on unless I have a specific reason to turn it off (see Figures 14.14 and 14.15).

Type Layers

The addition of Type layers in Photoshop 5 is one of the most welcome changes Adobe has ever made. After you add text to your image, the text will appear on a special Type layer. This layer is special because you can double-click its name to re-edit the text. Photoshop will not permanently convert the text to pixels until you choose **Layer>Text>Render Layer**. Not only that, but Photoshop allows you to do a whole bunch of stuff to the Type layers without having to permanently convert them to pixels. Let's take a quick look at your choices.

Apply most of the Edit>Transform functions

Add Layer Effects

Add a Layer Mask

But before you can apply a filter or perform adjustments to the text, you have to convert the Type layer into a normal layer by choosing Render Layer from the **Layer>Text** menu. You just have to keep in mind that after you have used this option, you will no longer be able to edit the text. Photoshop will no longer think of it as text, in fact, and will treat it as if it were a regular scanned image.

Figure 14.14
Anti-Aliased off.

Type Mask Tool

The Type Mask tool (which looks like a dashed-outline of the letter "T") is used for creating selections in the shape of text. This tool works just like the normal Text tool except that it does not give you an on-screen preview and it does not create a Type layer; you get a *selection* instead. I can honestly say that I never use this tool. I don't really like it because I can't see what I'm doing on screen when I'm creating the text. Instead of using the Type Mask tool, I usually use the normal Type tool (so I can get an on-screen preview); then I Command-click the name of the Type layer and drag its name to the Trash icon. This gives me the same result as the Type Mask tool, but provides me an on-screen preview. That's much better than fumbling around blindfolded.

Figure 14.15
Anti-Aliased on.

Now that you've seen the options that are available when creating text, let's get into the fun stuff and start creating type effects. I'll break the effects into three sections: The first section will cover effects that use Layer Effects. It is important to know that the effects in this section are the *only* ones that allow the text to still be edited. The second section, "Basic Filter Effects," uses filters and basic effects by enhancing a Layer Effect or by distorting the text itself. The third section, "Photo-realistic Filter Effects," will use filters to their full advantage and create photo-realistic type effects. So without further ado, let's get started.

Layer Effects

Let's start off with text effects that are attached to a Type layer. First and foremost, it's very important to remember that with the Type layer you get the added benefit of being able to edit the text after you have applied the effect. And because the effects are made by using the Layer Effects, they don't require much memory and should not increase the file size of your image too much. Layer Effects allow you to create some great effects such as edge embossing, extruded or indented type, inner shadows, and beveled type. To add a Layer Effect to the currently active layer, choose one of the options from the **Layer>Effects** menu.

Inner Shadow

An Inner Shadow will make it look as if you poked a hole in the image and put a sheet of colored paper behind the hole. To apply this effect, be sure a Type layer is active; then choose **Layer>Effects>Inner Shadow**. In the dialog box that appears, you can specify the mode, opacity, angle, distance, blur, and intensity of the shadow.

After adding this effect, you might need to change the Opacity setting to lighten the shadow. I usually set the angle to the upper left (somewhere between 120° and 135°), then play with the Distance and Blur settings until the shadow looks appropriate for the text I've chosen (see Figure 14.16).

Bevel and Emboss Effects

The Bevel and Emboss Effects all use the same set of options. The default settings for highlight and shadow usually produce acceptable results. As with most type effects, I usually set the angle to the upper left (between 120° and 135°); this determines where the light source is coming from. The Depth and Blur settings determine how strong the effect will be and the Up and Down radio buttons determine if the text will appear above or below the surface of the image. The Style menu at the bottom of the dialog box determines what type of effect you'll end up with (see Figure 14.17).

An Outer Bevel will add a highlight and shadow under the text. This will make the text appear as if it is raised above the surface of your image (see Figures 14.18 and Figure 14.19).

NOTE

You can also move a shadow (or other effect) by dragging anywhere within the main image window. As you're dragging, watch the Layer Effects dialog box to see exactly what's happening to the angle and distance settings.

Figure 14.16
Inner Shadow Layer Effect. (© 1998 Adobe Systems, Inc.)

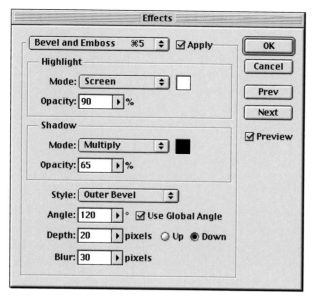

Figure 14.17
Bevel and Emboss Effects dialog box.

Figure 14.18
Outer Bevel using In setting.

Figure 14.19
Outer Bevel using Out setting.

The Inner Bevel effect can produce a simple 3D effect. Out of all the controls, the Blur setting is the most critical to achieving a satisfactory result (see Figure 14.20).

The Emboss Effect looks similar to applying both the Inner and Outer Bevel Layer Effects at the same time. This will give you 3D type that appears to be extruding from the surface of your image (see Figure 14.21).

Those are the basic Layer Effects that I use to create simple type effects. At first, they might seem limited. But, you can do much, much more with these effects if you trick Photoshop into *not* displaying the solid text that is in the Type layer. Let's take a look at the possibilities.

Figure 14.20
Inner Bevel Type Effect.

Figure 14.21
Emboss Type Effect.

TV Type

What the devil is TV type? Well, you know when you flick on the TV set and the networks have their ever-present logo embossed into the lower right corner of the screen (like when you're recording old reruns of *Gilligan's Island* and you're constantly reminded of which network you stole it from?)—that's TV type. Whether you love it or hate it, most people want to know how to create it. We're going to use a Layer Effect to create the edges of the text, but we don't want the middle of the text to be a solid color; we want it to be transparent, instead. To achieve this, you'll need to choose 50% gray before entering the text (or you can change the color within the text dialog box itself). To make sure it really is 50% gray, click on your foreground color and set the HSB settings to 0, 0, and 50. Next, open the Layers palette and set the blending mode of the text layer to Hard Light. This should make the text disappear (only shades brighter or darker than 50% will show up). Next, add a Layer Effect by choosing **Layer>Effects>Bevel and Emboss**. You should only need to mess with the bottom set of controls (that is, unless you've already screwed up the top ones). I like to set the Style pop-up menu to Outer Bevel, set the Angle to 135, then play with the Depth and Blur settings until the image looks good (see Figure 14.22).

Figure 14.22
TV type effect.

Indented Type

With this effect we'll get the text to darken the image and have an inner shadow that makes it appear to be slightly below the surface of the image. To create this effect, change your foreground color to white before entering the text, then set the blending mode of the Type layer to Multiply. Now, choose **Layer>Effects>Inner Shadow** to create the shadow edge (see Figure 14.23).

Figure 14.23
Indented type effect.

To make the text appear as if it is truly pushed into the image, you'll need to darken the inside of the text. You can do this by changing the pop-up menu at the top of the Layer Effects dialog box to Inner Glow and turning on the Apply checkbox. To darken the area, you will need to change the color swatch to black and set the Mode to

Multiply. Then, to get an even fill, set the Blur setting to 0 and choose Center from the bottom of the dialog box. Now you should be able to change the darkness of the text by adjusting the Opacity setting (see Figure 14.24).

Soft-Edged Indented Type

As in the previous effect, this one will make the text appear as if it is slightly below the surface of the image but with a soft edge. To create this effect, change your foreground color to 50% gray before entering the text, then set the blending mode of the Type layer to Hard Light. Now, choose **Layer>Effects>Bevel and Emboss**, and set the Style menu to Outer Bevel to create the soft edge (see Figure 14.25).

To make the text appear as if it is truly pushed into the image, you'll need to darken the inside of the text. You can accomplish this by changing the pop-up menu at the top of the Layer Effects dialog box to Inner Glow and turning on the Apply checkbox. To darken the area, you will need to change the color swatch to black and set the Mode to Multiply. Then, to get an even fill, set the Blur setting to 0 and choose Center from the bottom of the dialog box. Now you should be able to change the darkness of the text by adjusting the Opacity setting (see Figure 14.26).

Extruded Type

To create this effect, you'll need to change your foreground color to black before entering the text, then set the blending mode of the Type layer to Multiply. Next, choose **Layer>Effects>Bevel and Emboss**, and set the Style menu to Outer Bevel. Now adjust the Depth setting until the text has the desired depth, and then change the Blur setting until the text no longer has a flat-topped look (see Figure 14.27).

Edge Emboss

With this effect, we'll add a shadow and highlight to the inner edge of the text. To create this effect, you'll need to change your foreground color to white before entering the text; then set the blending mode of the Type layer to

Figure 14.24
Finished indented type effect.

Figure 14.25
After applying the first step of the Soft-Edged Indented Type effect.

Figure 14.26
Finished Soft-Edged Indented Type effect.

Figure 14.27
Result of Extruded Type effect.

Figure 14.28
After first step of Edge Emboss effect.

Figure 14.29
Result of Edge Emboss effect.

Screen. Next, choose **Layer>Effects>Bevel and Emboss**, and set the Style menu to Emboss. Turn the Depth setting all the way to 20 and use a low Blur setting so the edge does not look too blurry (see Figure 14.28).

To add a shadow to the upper left edge of the text, change the pop-up menu at the top of the Layer Effects dialog box to Inner Shadow and turn on the Apply checkbox. Set the Blur setting to a low number like three, then experiment with the Distance setting until the shadow you are adding appears only near the edge of the text (see Figure 14.29).

With all the effects we just created, you can double-click the name of the Type layer to edit the text, and the effect will also update. The rest of the effects in this chapter will be a little more involved; and, therefore, will either not update when you edit the text, or will require you to convert the Type into a normal layer.

Basic Filter Effects

There are so many filters in Photoshop (about 100) that you can create an infinite variety of type effects. The best way to familiarize yourself with the filters is to just dive in and experiment to your heart's content. Here are a few to get you started. The effects in this section involve filters and therefore cannot be applied directly to a Type layer. That means you'll have to enter the text, edit as necessary, and then render the layer by choosing **Layer>Text>Render Layer**. After rendering a Type layer, we'll no longer be limited to Layer Effects; so we'll be able to achieve more radical results such as better glows, curved type, and type wrapped around a circle.

Glows

You can create a simple glow around the edge of some text by choosing **Layer>Effects>Outer Glow** and messing with the settings that are presented to you. But, you'll find this is rather limited because if you want a bright, intense glow, you have to turn the Opacity and Intensity settings all the way up to 100%. That would be okay as is; but then if you try to make the glow larger, your only option is to increase the Blur setting. After a certain point, the glow just gets too blurry. Well, there is a solution.

Adjust the settings for the outer glow until the glow is about as blurry as you'd want it to be, then choose **Layer> Effects>Create Layer**. This will create a new layer below the text that contains the glow you just created (see Figure 14.30). To make the glow larger, click on the name of the layer that contains the glow, then choose **Filter>Other> Minimum** and play with the Radius setting. You should be able to make the glow just about any size you want (see Figure 14.31).

If you want the glow to become smaller instead of larger, choose **Filter>Other>Maximum** and mess with the Radius setting (see Figures 14.32 and 14.33).

If you'd like to create a two-tone glow, you'll need to duplicate the glow layer by dragging it onto the New Layer icon (folded paper icon). Next, change your foreground color to the second color you would like to use; then type Shift-Option-Delete to fill the glow with your new color. If you would like the edge to fade out more, choose **Filter>Blur>Gaussian Blur**. Finally, choose **Filter>Other> Minimum** to make the glow larger (see Figure 14.34).

You can make things a little more interesting by applying one of the filters found under the **Filter>Distort** menu (see Figure 14.35). I also occasionally choose **Filter>Stylize> Diffuse** to create a slightly noisy look.

Figure 14.30
Text with Outer Glow layer effect applied.

Figure 14.31
After layer effect is converted into layers, then Minimum filter applied.

Figure 14.32
Original glow effect.

Figure 14.33
After applying the **Filter>Maximum** filter.

Figure 14.34
Two-color glow effect.

Figure 14.35
Ripple filter applied to layer that contains the red portion of glow effect.

Figure 14.36
Created in RGB mode and converted to CMYK without flattening.

Figure 14.37
Created in RGB mode and flattened when converting to CMYK.

Any time you create a bright-colored glow on a black background, the result will look much better if it is created in RGB mode. If you need to convert an image that contains a glow into CMYK mode, be sure to flatten the image when prompted, otherwise, the glow will look rather washed out (see Figures 14.36 and 14.37).

Type on a Curve

I have found that most people use Adobe Illustrator to bend text along a curve. Well, I don't always find it convenient to have to switch between programs to achieve such a simple effect, so I'll show you how to do the same thing in Photoshop. The Shear filter will do the job for us, but there is one little problem—this filter is able to bend things only vertically (see Figures 14.38 and 14.39).

All you have to do to make the filter bend things horizontally is to rotate the layer you are working on. You can do this by choosing **Image>Transform>Rotate 90° CW** (see Figure 14.40). But before applying the filter, you'll need to choose **Layer>Text>Render Layer** to turn the text into pixels; otherwise, you won't be able to apply a filter to it. (See Figure 14.41.)

Figure 14.38
Original image. (© 1998 Adobe Systems Inc.)

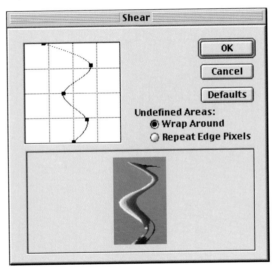

Figure 14.39
Shear filter.

After you have bent the text, all you need to do is rotate the layer back to its original position by choosing **Image>Transform>Rotate 90° CCW**. (See Figure 14.42.)

Figure 14.42
End Result.

Figure 14.40
After rotating.

Figure 14.41
After rendering and applying Shear filter.

> **NOTE**
> To produce type on an oval, start with a rectangular document instead of a square.

Type on a Circle

With this technique, we'll bend some text around a circle. If you want to bend your text around a perfect circle, you'll need to start with a document that is perfectly square. Enter the text at the bottom of the document, then choose **Layer>Text>Render Layer** (see Figure 14.43). To bend the text, choose **Filter>Distort>Polar Coordinates** and use the Rectangular to Polar setting (see Figure 14.44).

If you really want to know what this filter is attempting to do, open a normal photo and add a different-colored dot to each corner of the image, as depicted in Figure 14.45. Now run the Polar Coordinates filter and see what happens to the colors in each corner (see Figure 14.46).

> **NOTE**
> You can change the size of the circle the text is wrapped around by placing the text higher in the document. Also, remember you can change the spacing between the letters of the text by using different tracking settings (in the text dialog box).

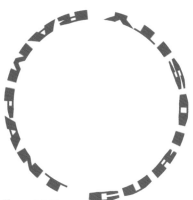

Figure 14.44
After applying Polar Coordinates.

RAMPANT CURIOSITY

Figure 14.43
Original Image.

Figure 14.45
Original image. (© 1998 Adobe Systems, Inc.)

Figure 14.46
After applying Polar Coordinates.

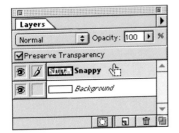

Figure 14.47
Command-click the layer that
contains the text.

Photo-realistic Filter Effects

The steps used to create these effects may not always seem logical, but just stick with me until you see the result. I came up with them after many hours of experimentation. If you would like to create your own type effects, I suggest you start by getting a basic understanding of what each of the filters in Photoshop does. Each one applies its own unique brand of magic and there's no end to the possibilities. Once you're on familiar terms with the filters, and you create something interesting, you might be able to think of the perfect filter to enhance the end result. The way I got used to the filters was to commit to experimenting with one side menu each day (distort, pixelate, and so on). I did this day after day until I could actually predict the result I'd get from most of the filters. Now I can create some interesting effects without having to go through the time-consuming task of randomly applying filters.

3D Type

Before we jump in and create some great 3D effects, I'm going to explain why you need to be careful when creating them. To create 3D type, you're going to need to use the Emboss filter. Since the Emboss filter gives you weird color artifacts when you work on color originals, we'll just use shades of gray, then colorize them later.

The first thing you need to do is use the Type tool to create some black text. Then, because we're going to distort this text in ways that aren't possible with a Type layer, you'll need to choose **Layer>Text>Render Layer**. Next, open the Layers palette and turn on the Preserve Transparency checkbox to make sure we don't end up with any residue around the edges (see Figure 14.47). Preserve Transparency will prevent you from modifying the empty (transparent) areas of the layer. Now, Command-click the name of the layer to select everything that is on the layer (see Figure 14.48).

Next, we need to add a light-gray rim around the edge of the text. To accomplish this, change your foreground color to a light gray. You don't have to be too particular when picking the gray, just make sure it's not really dark. We need to have the gray rim slowly blend into the text, so choose **Select>Feather** and use a setting of three (any number between one and ten will work, I'm just picking a number off the top of my head). Now, to add the gray rim, choose **Edit>Stroke**, set the Width to the same setting you used when feathering the selection (three in my case), and set the Location to Inside. This should add a nice light-gray, soft-edged line around the edge of the text, as in Figure 14.49.

Now, to get the 3D look, all we have to do is choose **Filter>Stylize>Emboss** and mess with some settings. When the Emboss dialog box appears, I like to type **Command-H** to hide the edges of the selection so you get a clear view of the result. The angle setting determines which direction the light source is coming from, so click and drag the line until it matches the angle of the light that is hitting the image you are placing the text on top of. If creating the image from scratch, I'd choose an angle of 135 because most light sources are above the objects they illuminate. The Amount settings determine how much space the 3D edge takes up. This setting is dependent on the previous steps, so set the Amount to one number higher than what was used when you feathered the selection (3+1=4 in my case). The Amount setting determines how much contrast you'll end up with. I usually move this slider around until I have as much contrast as I can get without making the brightest areas pure white (see Figure 14.50).

Once you are done embossing the image, you can choose **Select>None** because you shouldn't need the selection anymore. Now you should have some nice-looking, grayscale 3D type. In Figure 14.50, I used a setting of three for most of the steps. You can use any number between one and ten to create different 3D looks (the Emboss filter maxes out at ten).

Figure 14.48
Result of Command-clicking.

Figure 14.49
Result of adding gray rim to the text.

WARNING

All type and background effects that use the Emboss filter should be applied when the image is in RGB mode. You'll end up with a brown result if you work in CMYK mode because the Emboss filter is not smart enough to add the proper amount of cyan to the image.

Snappy

Figure 14.50
After applying the Emboss filter.

Coloring 3D Type

Now that you have some 3D type, you might want to add a bit of color. Let's explore a couple of options. The easiest way to colorize the text is to choose **Image>Adjust>Hue/Saturation** and turn on the Colorize checkbox (see Figure 14.51). By moving the Hue slider, you can change the basic color of the text. Moving the Saturation slider will change how intense the color appears (from gray to a very vibrant color). You'll also need to adjust the Lightness slider a wee bit, occasionally, to tweak the brightness of the text (see Figure 14.52).

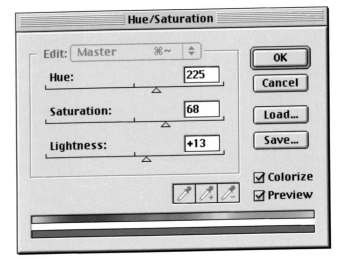

Figure 14.51
Hue/Saturation dialog box.

Figure 14.52
Result of colorizing.

If you would rather have some two-tone, 3D type, change your foreground color to one of your desired colors, then choose **Edit>Fill**. In the dialog box that appears, choose Foreground Color from the Contents pop-up menu, change the blending mode to Difference, and turn on the Preserve Transparency checkbox. The result will include the color you chose and its exact opposite, just as if you chose **Image>Adjust>Invert** (see Figure 14.53).

Okay, one more method for colorizing your text. We could go on for days (literally), but I'll just throw in an interesting technique that gives you multicolored text. First, make sure you are working on the layer that contains the text and the Preserve Transparency checkbox is turned on (that will make sure you don't color outside the lines). Next, double-click the Paintbrush tool and set its blending mode to Difference. Now, choose a really bright, intense color and paint across the text. Repeat this process using different bright, intense colors until you get an interesting result (see Figure 14.54).

Figure 14.53
Two-tone colorizing effect.

Figure 14.54
Wild colorizing effect.

Chroming Your 3D Type

Before creating chrome, you'll need to create some 3D type by using the technique we just went over. After you've created 3D type, be sure to choose **Select>None** to make sure you're working on the entire layer, then choose **Image>Adjust> Curves**. We're going to want to create a pretty weird curve, so click on the Pencil icon at the bottom of the Curves dialog box, then start scribbling in the grid area. By drawing different shapes, you'll end up with different types of metal (aluminum, chrome, pewter, and so on) or plastic-looking type. To create chrome, you usually need to create either a big "W" or a big "M" (see Figures 14.55 to 14.58).

After you have a result that's looking pretty good, you can click the Smooth button to smooth out the shape you drew, then click the Curve icon (right next to the Pencil icon) to convert your curve into a normal curve. To fine tune the curve, move your cursor out of the Curves dialog box (but don't click OK yet), and click any area of the image that you don't like. A circle should appear in the Curves dialog box indicating which area of the curve would need to be changed to affect that area (see Figure 14.59). Once you've got the shape to your liking, be sure to click the Save button and give that setting a name. That way the next time you create 3D type, you'll be able to turn it into chrome in no time by choosing **Image>Adjust> Curves**, then clicking on the Load button.

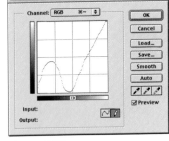

Figure 14.55
Result.

Figure 14.56
Experimenting with the curve.

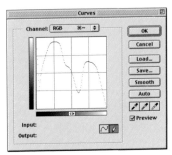

Figure 14.57
Result.

Figure 14.58
Creating a large "M" shape.

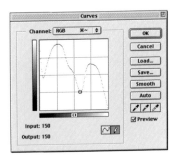

Figure 14.59
Click anywhere in the image window to find out which area of the curve is affecting that area.

After applying Curves, you should end up with something that resembles chrome. To add even more realism, you might want to add a little bit of color to the type. To accomplish this, choose **Image>Adjust>Hue/Saturation** and turn on the Colorize checkbox. Adjust the Hue slider until the text appears light blue; then move the Saturation slider to the left until you can barely see the blue because you just want a hint of color (see Figure 14.60).

Figure 14.60
Chrome type colorized to add a little blue to the image.

Liquid Type

To create liquid type, you'll need to start with 3D type. After you've created your 3D type (using the technique shown in the previous section), apply the Emboss filter a second time using the same settings used to create the 3D type. Then, to get a liquid look, choose **Filter>Artistic>Plastic Wrap**. You can experiment with the settings, but I usually set the Highlight Strength to 18, the Detail to 11, and the Smoothness to 11 (see Figure 14.61).

If you want the liquid to look a little more ripply, just apply the Plastic Wrap filter multiple times (see Figure 14.62). After you've achieved the look you want, you can add some color by choosing **Image>Adjust>Hue/Saturation** and turning on the Colorize checkbox (see Figure 14.63).

Figure 14.61
Liquid type effect.

Figure 14.62
Apply the Plastic Wrap filter a second time for an extra ripply liquid type effect.

Figure 14.63
Result of colorizing by using Hue/Saturation dialog box.

Figure 14.64
Start by creating black circles on a new layer.

Figure 14.65
Result of applying 3D type effect.

Figure 14.66
After applying the Plastic Wrap filter.

Figure 14.67
The Clouds filter will supply the "raw material" needed to create stone.

Figure 14.68
Final stone effect.

Water Droplets

Now let's find out how to create some water droplets to go with our liquid type effect. First, create a new layer, then change your foreground color to black. Next, choose the Paintbrush tool, then choose a hard-edged brush from the Brushes palette. Click around the image wherever you would like your water droplets to appear. You should end up with a layer that contains a bunch of black circles (see Figure 14.64).

To turn them into water droplets, just go through the exact same steps you used to create 3D type earlier in this chapter (and use really low settings, such as two) as shown in figure 14.65, and then apply the Emboss filter a second time (see Figure 14.66). You can also choose **Filter> Artistic>Plastic Wrap** to create a softer look.

Backgrounds & Textures

In this section I'll show you how to create interesting background effects. The first ones will be simple black and white textures that can be applied to photographs or colorized using the techniques described in Chapter 13, "Enhancement." I want to give you a general sense of how these backgrounds are created, then you can experiment with similar filters to create an infinite variety of effects.

Stone

To create a simple stone background, create a new layer, then reset your foreground and background colors to their default colors by pressing D. Next, choose **Filter> Render>Clouds** to add some texture to your image, then choose **Filter>Render>Difference Clouds** to get more variation in the texture (see Figure 14.67).

Now, choose **Filter>Stylize>Emboss** and mess with all the settings until you like the result. I used Angle: 135, Height: 3 pixels, and Amount: 500% (see Figure 14.68). As with the other textures that use the Emboss filter, you can colorize the result using any of the techniques described in the Enhancement chapter.

Cloth

To create cloth, you'll first need to get some random information to distort. One way to fill your screen with random dots is to choose **Filter>Noise>Add Noise**. This filter will not be able to work if an empty layer is active, so most of the time I fill the layer with white by typing D (to reset the foreground and background colors), then Command-Delete (to fill with the background color). If you know you are going to use the Emboss filter (we are), then you'll want to turn on the Monochromatic checkbox when applying the Add Noise filter (see Figure 14.69). If you Emboss a color image, you'll get unpleasant color residue after applying the filter.

Now that you have some raw material, you'll need to stretch it into some thread. So, choose **Filter>Blur>Motion Blur**, set the angle to 0° and use a Distance setting that still shows a little bit of variation in the image (see Figure 14.70).

Now to weave the cloth, apply the Motion blur filter again using an angle of -90°. The result should look like a blurry blob of gray junk (see Figure 14.71).

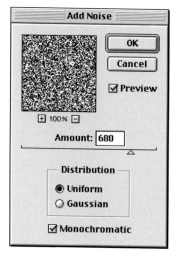

Figure 14.69
Turn on the Monochromatic checkbox when applying the Add Noise filter.

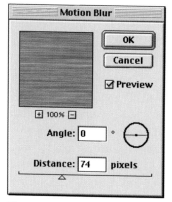

Figure 14.70
Be sure to turn on the Monochromatic checkbox when applying the Add Noise filter.

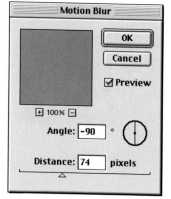

Figure 14.71
Apply the Motion Blur filter a second time with a different angle.

To add some dimension to your pixel soup, choose **Filter>Stylize>Emboss**. A Height setting between 1 and 3 and an Amount of 500% usually produce the best result (see Figure 14.72). The result should appear dark with little contrast. Before we brighten this up, you'll want to crop off the edges of the image because they contain areas that do not look woven. To do this, select the areas you would like to keep, using the Marquee tool, then choose **Image>Crop** (see Figure 14.73). To brighten the image, choose **Image>Adjust>Levels** and move in the upper right and upper left sliders until they touch the edge of the histogram (see Figures 14.74 and 14.75).

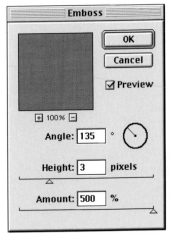

Figure 14.72
Apply the Emboss filter with a low Height setting.

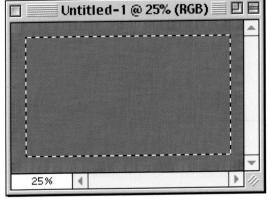

Figure 14.73
Crop off the non-woven area.

Figure 14.74
End result.

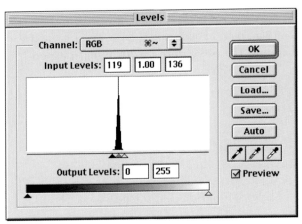

Figure 14.75
Apply Levels and pull in the upper left and upper right sliders.

Simulated Leather

Now let's try to create the texture that is applied to the plastic dashboard of most cars (do they really think you'll be fooled into thinking you have a real leather dash?). We'll need to start with some random info, so reset your foreground and background colors (by typing D) and choose **Filter>Render>Clouds** (see Figure 14.76). To turn these clouds into something a little more interesting, choose **Filter>Stylize>Find Edges** (see Figure 14.77).

To add a little dimension to the result, choose **Filter>Stylize>Emboss**, set the angle to −48, use a low Height setting, and move the Amount slider all the way to the right (see Figure 14.78). If you would rather end up with a more fiber-like result, use an angle of 135°.

Finally, to brighten up the result, choose **Image>Adjust> Levels** and move the upper right and upper left sliders until they touch the histogram.

Now I'd like to show you how I create color backgrounds. By varying the filters used in these effects, you should be able to create a wide variety of color backgrounds.

Painted Backgrounds

Here is the technique I use to simulate a painted background. First create a new layer, then change your foreground and background colors to two bright, intense colors. Next, choose **Filter>Render>Clouds**, then choose **Filter> Blur>Motion Blur**, pick an angle at random, and set the distance to around 100 (see Figure 14.79). You can experiment with different distance settings to get different results.

Now create another new layer and pick two more bright, intense colors. And repeat the steps you did earlier but use different angle settings (**Filter>Render>Clouds**, then **Filter>Blur>Motion Blur**); and once you're finished, set the blending mode of the layer to Difference (see Figure 14.80). Now you'll want to repeat this process multiple times until you have an interesting collection of colors. You don't have to worry about the specific colors; you just want to get a good distribution of colors. After you have

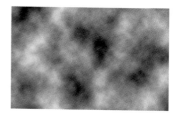

Figure 14.76
Result of applying the Clouds filter.

Figure 14.77
Result of applying the Find Edges filter.

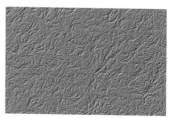

Figure 14.78
Result of applying the Emboss filter.

Figure 14.79
Result of applying Clouds and Motion Blur filters.

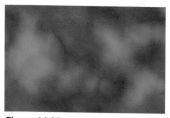

Figure 14.80
Result of applying Clouds and Motion Blur multiple times.

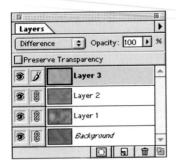

Figure 14.81
Once you have a good distribution of colors, merge the layers together.

Figure 14.82
Result of applying Polar Coordinates and Ripple.

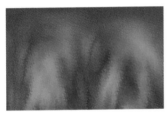

Figure 14.83
Result of applying the Emboss filter.

achieved that, link all the cloud layers together by dragging down the column just to the left of the preview thumbnails in the Layers palette, then choose Merge Linked from the side menu of the Layers palette, as shown in Figure 14.81. If you don't like the overall color scheme, you can choose **Image>Adjust>Hue/Saturation** and move the Hue slider around until you get a pleasing result.

To vary the distribution of the colors, choose **Filter>Distort> Polar Coordinates** and use the Polar to Rectangular setting. This should give the image more of a vertical emphasis. Choose **Filter>Distort>Ripple** and use an Amount of 200 and a Size of Medium (see Figure 14.82). Now apply the filter a second time by pressing Command-F.

To bring out some more texture in the image, choose **Filter> Stylize>Emboss**, set the Angle to 135, the Height to 2, and the Amount to 275 (see Figure 14.83). Then choose **Filter> Fade Emboss** and set the blending mode to Hard Light.

To add a brushed look, choose the Eyedropper tool and Option-click one of the brighter colors in the image (this will change your background color). Then choose **Filter>Artistic>Colored Pencil**; set the Pencil Width to 4, the Stroke Brightness to 8, and the Paper Brightness to 25 (different settings will result in different painterly effects), as shown in Figure 14.84. Now blend this into the image by choosing **Filter>Fade Colored Pencil** and set the blending mode to Luminosity.

Finally, to add a little dimension to the image, duplicate the layer you've been working on and choose **Image> Adjust>Desaturate** to remove any hint of color. Next, set the blending mode of the duplicate layer to Hard Light in the Layers palette, then choose **Filter>Stylize>Emboss** (see Figure 14.85). I usually set the Height to 1 or 2, then I just play around with the Amount and Angle settings until the image looks good. To finalize the effect, choose Merge Down from the side menu of the Layers palette.

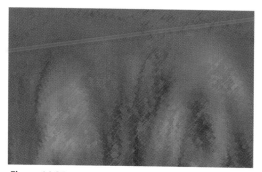

Figure 14.84
Result of applying Colored Pencil filter.

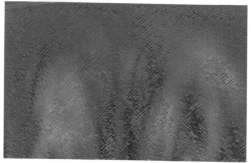

Figure 14.85
Adding a little dimension by applying the Emboss filter.

Car Wash Foam

Let's try to create that foam they spray all over your car when you send it through a car wash. First, you want to start with a screenful of black and white noise. To do this, create a new layer and fill it with white by pressing D, then Option-Delete. Next, choose **Filter>Noise>Add Noise**, set the Amount to 850, the Distribution to Uniform, and turn on the Monochromatic checkbox.

Now let's distort that noise to get something a little more useful. Choose **Filter>Distort>Spherize**, set the Amount to 100% and the Mode to Normal. Next, choose **Filter>Pixelate>Pointillize** and use a Cell Size of three. Now, choose **Filter>Distort>Polar Coordinates** and use the Polar to Rectangular Setting (see Figure 14.86).

Finally, to turn this image into foam, choose **Filter>Sketch> Plaster,** set the Image Balance to 38, the Smoothness to 1 and the Light Position to Top (see Figure 14.87). Then choose **Image>Adjust>Invert.** If you want to add a little color, choose **Image>Adjust>Hue/Saturation** and turn on the Colorize checkbox. I usually move the Hue slider around until I find a nice cyan-ish blue, then lower the Saturation setting until there is just a hint of color visible (see Figure 14.88).

Applying Dimension to a Photo

After creating an interesting background texture, you might want to use it to add some dimension to your photograph. There are many ways to add dimension to an image. Let's explore just a few so you get a general feeling for your options.

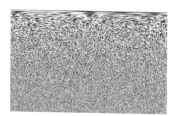

Figure 14.86
Result of applying Spherize, Pointillize and Polar Coordinates filters.

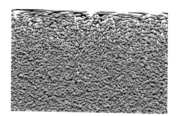

Figure 14.87
Result of applying Plaster filter.

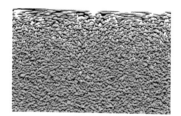

Figure 14.88
Result of colorizing the image.

Figure 14.89
Apply a texture using the Hard Light blending mode. (Original image © 1998 PhotoDisc)

Figure 14.90
After using the Eraser tool to remove some of the texture.

Figure 14.91
Texture to be applied to the photograph.

Blending Modes

You can apply any of the grayscale textures described at the beginning of the Background section by using three blending modes. Place the texture you would like to apply on a layer above the image. Change the blending mode of the texture layer to Overlay, Soft Light, or Hard Light (see Figure 14.89). If the effect is too strong, lower the Opacity setting of that layer. If you would like to intensify the effect, just duplicate the texture layer. You can also remove the texture from certain areas of the image by applying the Eraser tool to the texture layer (see Figure 14.90).

Lighting Effects

Using the Lighting Effects filter is a little more sophisticated than the last technique we covered. And it also takes more time because you have to experiment with all the settings that come along with this filter. But it's worth it.

To get started, open the Channels palette and create a new channel by clicking on the New Channel icon (the one that looks like a sheet of paper). Now you need to create a texture in the Channel you just created. You can use any method you'd like, but just for kicks, I'll create one we haven't made before. Reset your foreground and background colors by typing D, then choose **Filter>Render>Clouds**. Now choose **Filter>Stylize>Find Edges**, then choose **Image>Adjust>Levels** and pull in the upper right and left sliders until they touch the histogram. This should add contrast to the image. To finish the texture off, choose **Filter>Artistic>Colored Pencils**, set the Pencil Width to 18, set the Stroke Pressure to 4, and the Paper Brightness to 25 (see Figure 14.91).

Now, to apply the texture to the photo, click on the topmost (Composite) channel and then open the Layers palette. Click the name of the layer to which you would like to add texture, and choose **Filter>Render>Lighting Effects**. At the bottom of the dialog box that appears, you should find a pop-up menu called Texture Channel. You'll need to set this menu to the name of the channel you created earlier (it should be the bottom choice in the menu). Then adjust the Height slider to determine how strong the texture will appear (see Figure 14.92).

If you would like to remove the texture from areas of the image, open the History palette and click just to the left of the step that is directly above the Lighting Effects step (see Figure 14.93). Then use the History Brush to remove the texture from areas of the image (see Figure 14.94). I usually use a really soft-edged brush so the texture smoothly blends into the image.

Figure 14.92
Result of applying the Lighting Effects filter by using a texture channel.
(Original image © 1998 PhotoDisc)

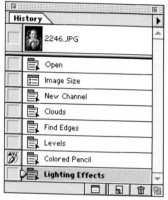

Figure 14.93
Set the History palette to the second to the last step.

Figure 14.94
Apply the History brush to remove the texture from areas of the image.

Closing Thoughts

As usual, we've just scratched the surface of what you can create in Photoshop. That's what's so great about the program. Just think about it. There is only so much you can do to text in other programs, but in Photoshop it is endless. With almost 100 filters, the sky is the limit.

Ask Adobe

Q: How can I avoid the jaggies when creating type effects?

A: Use anti-aliased type and use a resolution appropriate for your output medium. Because type involves complex edges, you may need to go with a higher resolution than you would for purely photographic material. You should also consider setting the type in a program such as Illustrator or PageMaker if you don't need the special effects provided by Photoshop. This will allow you to create the image at a resolution appropriate to the raster material without worrying about having enough resolution to preserve the complex edges of the typography.

Q: When should I render a Type layer, and why?

A: Rendering it would make it more difficult to re-edit, so you could choose to render before handing the file off to someone if you didn't want them editing the type. (Though you might want to just give them a flattened copy in that case.) The file contains a fully rendered version already, however, so you don't have to worry about font substitution when transferring files in which the text doesn't actually get edited. Generally, you render a Type layer when you become interested in doing things that go beyond the bounds of re-editable type.

Q: Why are filters unavailable for Type layers?

A: Because if you ran a filter on a Type layer and then re-edited the layer, the filtering effects would necessarily be lost because the layer contents would be recreated from the type data.

Ben's Techno-Babble Decoder Ring

Point—A unit of measurement used in the publishing industry that is 1/72 of an inch (there are 12 points to a pica, and 6 picas per inch). Most programs measure text in point sizes because it is much more friendly than using fractions of an inch. But there is very little consistency in the size of text—12 point Times is taller than 12 point Helvetica, so you can think of the point size as a general (not exact) measure of the size of your text.

Baseline—The invisible line that a line of text sits on. Letters that drop below the baseline (such as lower case j, g, q, and y) are known as descenders.

Leading—The line spacing of a paragraph of text measured from one baseline to the next. Named after the strips of lead that were used to increase line spacing in hot metal typography. In order to make sure the lines of text don't overlap, you'll usually want to use a leading setting larger than the point size of the text.

Kerning—The art (lost art, really) of removing space between letters to create consistent letter spacing. In Photoshop, the kerning increases (positive setting) or decreases (negative setting) the space between two letters.

Tracking—The act of increasing or reducing the space between all the letters in a range of text. Often used with upper case text to increase readability.

Courtesy of David Bishop

I worked in tandem between Photoshop and Illustrator when creating this image. Everything except the Muybridge horse and the TV tube (taken from a photo clip-art CD) was generated on the computer. I used Photoshop's layers feature to its fullest, shifting the background layers around and adjusting attributes to achieve the right composition. I find the Layer Mask feature extremely useful because it allows me to hide artwork without deleting it. Using the Layer attributes feature, I was able to preview the multi-layered TV in various modes, often discovering a cool effect unexpectedly. All the color was orginated in the computer by manipulating the individual CMYK channels to achieve an intense glowing effect.

–Brian Peterson

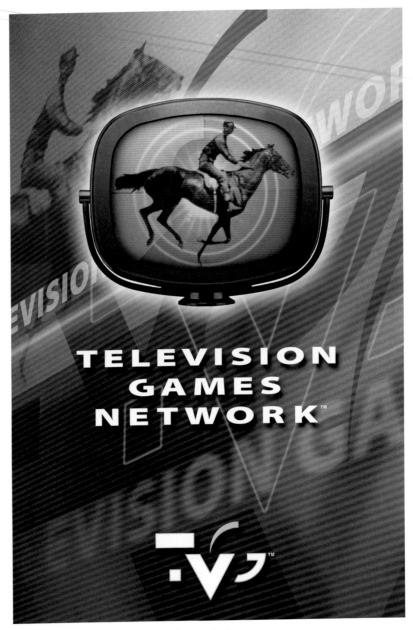

Courtesy of Brian Peterson, World West Communications

Where Do We Go From Here?

I found it difficult to sit down and write the conclusion to this book. Probably because whenever I think of Photoshop it's never in finite terms. Even now, after years of unwavering involvement with the program, I still get a thrill whenever I sit down to start a new creation. It's because I know that there really is no end to where I can take it. And in that sense, there is no conclusion to the subject. So instead, I'll leave you with a couple of thoughts that you can reflect on as you set off on your own flight into the upper atmosphere of Photoshop.

First off, there's no question that as soon as this book is printed, I'll start coming up with new techniques. It's the natural progression of any new release. There are hundreds of thousands of people out there trying out new things and doing their own experimentation (including yours truly). In the coming months, I'll start presenting seminars with Photoshop 5 and whenever that happens I always get challenged to solve a multitude of problems and come up with great new techniques. Whenever that happens, and I get something that I think is really juicy, I'll post it to my website (**www.digitalmastery.com**), so you can get it too. That way the book doesn't have to stop here. And beyond that, I'd really like to hear from you. Any reaction you have to the book would be most welcome, as well as your own personal feedback and insights into Photoshop.

And finally, if anyone ever tells you that this program is too difficult, or you ever have any doubts about your abilities to learn Photoshop, throw them in the garbage instantly (the doubts *and* the negative person!) I can attest to you that I am the original poster child for the "Self-Taught Photoshopper." When I first played with Photoshop, there were no books, seminars, or CD-ROM's to show you what to do. The point is, *anyone* can learn Photoshop. All you need is a few ounces of patience, a little bit of faith, and a true desire to learn this amazing program. And never forget the words of the great Gordon MacKenzie, "Orville Wright did not have a pilot's license."

Index

Licensing Agreement

By opening this package, you are agreeing to be bound by the following:

This software product is copyrighted, and all rights are reserved by the publisher and author. You are licensed to use this software on a single computer. You may copy and/or modify the software as needed to facilitate your use of it on a single computer. Making copies of the software for any other purpose is a violation of the United States copyright laws.

This software is sold *as is* without warranty of any kind, either expressed or implied, including but not limited to the implied warranties of merchantability and fitness for a particular purpose. Neither the publisher nor its dealers or distributors assumes any liability for any alleged or actual damages arising from the use of this program. (Some states do not allow for the exclusion of implied warranties, so the exclusion may not apply to you.)